William Humphrey

The religious state : A digest of the doctrine of Suarez

Contained in his treatise. Vol. 3

William Humphrey

**The religious state : A digest of the doctrine of Suarez**
*Contained in his treatise. Vol. 3*

ISBN/EAN: 9783337132170

Printed in Europe, USA, Canada, Australia, Japan

Cover: Foto ©Lupo / pixelio.de

More available books at **www.hansebooks.com**

# THE RELIGIOUS STATE.

## A DIGEST

OF

## THE DOCTRINE OF SUAREZ,

CONTAINED IN HIS TREATISE

## "DE STATÛ RELIGIONIS."

BY

### WILLIAM HUMPHREY,
PRIEST OF THE SOCIETY OF JESUS.

VOL. III.

BURNS AND OATES.

LONDON:
GRANVILLE MANSIONS,
ORCHARD STREET, W.

NEW YORK:
CATHOLIC PUBLICATION
SOCIETY CO.
BARCLAY STREET.

# CONTENTS OF VOL. III.

---

## CHAPTER XVI.—(*continued.*)

### THE SOCIETY OF JESUS.

PAGE

VII. In what degree of perfection is the Society constituted?  .  1

VIII. It is prudently ordained in the Society that there should not exist in it any ordinary exercise of Chant or Choir  .  6

IX. Does the Society profess a strict or a lax Rule? .  .  .  11

## CHAPTER XVII.

### ON ENTRANCE INTO THE SOCIETY; AND THE PROBATION WHICH BOTH PRECEDES AND FOLLOWS ENTRANCE.

I. Have certain impediments been rightly instituted which substantially hinder entrance into the Society? and what are these?  .  .  .  .  .  .  .  .  .  .  .  20

II. The impediment from defect of origin; and how far it obtains in the Society .  .  .  .  .  .  .  .  .  31

III. What probation should precede admission? and what conditions are to be observed in order that a person should be rightly received into the Society? .  .  .  .  .  32

IV. Is an entire period of two years rightly fixed for the noviceship in the Society? and for what reason?.  .  .  .  40

V. The observances, the experiments, and the place in which the Novices of the Society should be exercised during the time of their noviceship  .  .  .  .  .  .  .  45

## CHAPTER XVIII.

*THE ADMISSION OF SCHOLASTICS INTO THE SOCIETY BY MEANS OF SIMPLE VOWS; AND THE DISMISSAL OF SCHOLASTICS FROM THE SOCIETY.*

|  | PAGE |
|---|---|
| I. The reasons for this peculiarity of the Society | 58 |
| II. Does the admission of Scholastics into the Society constitute them true religious? | 65 |
| III. Is it to be called *Profession*? | 66 |
| IV. What conditions are necessary on the part of the subject, in order that the vows of Scholastics may be validly made? | 67 |
| V. What conditions are necessary on the part of the Society for the same end? | 68 |
| VI. Can there be *tacit* profession or incorporation of the Scholastics of the Society? | 69 |
| VII. In what way can their vows be dissolved? | 70 |

## CHAPTER XIX.

*THE VOWS OF CHASTITY, POVERTY, AND OBEDIENCE, AS MADE IN THE SOCIETY.*

|  | |
|---|---|
| I. Of what nature is the vow of chastity made by Scholastics of the Society? and does it annul subsequent matrimony? | 75 |
| II. Do simple vows in the Society dissolve matrimony which has been contracted, but not consummated? | 77 |
| III. By what means does the Society aid its subjects to the observance of their vow of chastity? | 77 |
| IV. The vow of poverty of the Scholastics of the Society does not render them *incapable* of dominion; and capability of dominion is nevertheless not incompatible with their religious state | 79 |
| V. To whom can or ought the Scholastics of the Society, according to the Rule, to distribute their goods? | 82 |
| VI. This distribution, as regards their vow of poverty | 85 |
| VII. To what practice or exercise of poverty are individual religious of the Society bound, *in virtue of the Rule*? | 88 |
| VIII. To what are they bound *in virtue of their vows*? | 97 |
| IX. The poverty which is proper to Professed Houses of the Society | 99 |

## CONTENTS.

|   |   | PAGE |
|---|---|---|
| X. | To what community poverty are the Colleges of the Society and the Houses of Probation bound? | 101 |
| XI. | Can the religious of the Society be bound in virtue of their vow of obedience in every matter whatsoever which is good in itself? | 104 |
| XII. | The counsel of obedience in the Society, as regards perfection of execution. | 108 |
| XIII. | The same counsel as regards the will. | 109 |
| XIV. | The same counsel as regards the understanding. | 118 |
| XV. | Is the promise to enter the Society, which is made by the approved Scholastics when they make the three substantial vows, a true vow befitting their state? | 130 |
| XVI. | What are the effects of this promise? | 131 |

## CHAPTER XX.

THE SCHOLASTICS OF THE SOCIETY, AND THEIR STUDIES; AND THE PUBLIC SCHOOLS OF THE SOCIETY FOR EXTERNS.

|   |   |   |
|---|---|---|
| I. | Is a religious state in the Society rightly destined for study? | 134 |
| II. | Is the study of and skill in the Classics, in languages, and in liberal arts becoming to religious of the Society? | 140 |
| III. | The method of study in the Society | 144 |
| IV. | Does it become religious of the Society to have public schools and universities, and to teach in them? | 154 |
| V. | Has the Society fittingly undertaken the education of boys? | 161 |
| VI. | The means employed by the Society in the education of Externs | 169 |

## CHAPTER XXI.

THE PROFESSION OF FOUR VOWS, WHICH IS MADE IN THE SOCIETY; THE PROBATION WHICH PRECEDES IT, AND THE SIMPLE VOWS WHICH FOLLOW IT.

|   |   |   |
|---|---|---|
| I. | Is profession rightly deferred in the Society for a long time? | 173 |
| II. | For what reason is a third year of probation required of Scholastics of the Society before profession? | 181 |

|   |   |
|---|---|
| III. Does the special form of profession in the Society induce a special obligation with regard to the teaching of children? | 187 |
| IV. Is the vow of obedience to the Supreme Pontiff, which is made by the Professed in the Society, a solemn vow, and distinct from the three substantial vows? | 192 |
| V. Is profession made in a fitting manner in the Society? | 206 |
| VI. The simple vows which follow profession; and, first, the vow not to assent to relaxation of poverty | 207 |
| VII. The vow which is made by the Professed of the Society not to seek dignities | 213 |
| VIII. Is a vow not to accept the Episcopate without a precept from the Superior fittingly made in the Society? | 217 |
| IX. The vow which the Professed of the Society make to listen to the counsels of the General, if they should happen to be raised to the Episcopate | 224 |
| X. Their vow to manifest to the Superior those who procure dignities | 229 |
| XI. Why are these vows simple and not solemn? | 230 |

## CHAPTER XXII.

*THE PROFESSED OF THREE VOWS; AND THE FORMED COADJUTORS OF THE SOCIETY.*

|   |   |
|---|---|
| The Spiritual Coadjutors of the Society | 237 |
| The Temporal Coadjutors of the Society | 244 |
| How many grades of persons are there in the Society? and how are they distinguished? | 250 |

## CHAPTER XXIII.

*THE MEANS WHICH THE SOCIETY EMPLOYS FOR THE SPIRITUAL PROGRESS AND PERFECTION OF ITS MEMBERS.*

|   |   |
|---|---|
| I. Ought the religious of the Society, in virtue of their Institute, to give themselves to mental exercises? and to what extent? | 253 |
| II. Are they bound, in virtue of their Institute, to any vocal prayers? | 256 |
| III. Are they specially bound to celebrate or communicate frequently? | 261 |

| | PAGE |
|---|---|
| IV. Frequency of confession, and general confession | 265 |
| V. The reservation of sins in the Society | 266 |
| VI. In what way does the Society aim at perfection of charity? | 271 |
| VII. The *negative* means by which fraternal charity and concord is preserved in the Society | 271 |
| VIII. The *positive* means by which it is conciliated | 277 |
| IX. By what means are the religious of the Society aided towards the acquisition of solid virtues? | 281 |

## CHAPTER XXIV.

### THE MEANS, OR MINISTRIES WHICH THE SOCIETY EMPLOYS FOR THE SALVATION OF EXTERNS.

| | |
|---|---|
| I. What can and ought the religious of the Society to do with regard to the ministry of preaching the Word of God? and what has been granted to them with regard to this ministry by the Apostolic See? | 286 |
| II. What can and ought they to do in the administration of the Sacrament of Penance? | 299 |
| III. What can and ought they to do in the administration of the Sacrament of the Eucharist? | 304 |
| IV. What can they do as regards the administration of the other Sacraments? | 306 |
| V. The Spiritual Exercises which the Society employs in order to the assistance of its neighbours; what are they? and what is their doctrine? | 307 |
| VI. The art or method of the Exercises | 310 |
| VII. The use of the Exercises, both by Ours and by Externs | 315 |
| VIII. Ought the religious of the Society to aid their neighbours by means of familiar conversation with them? | 317 |
| IX. Ought the Society to have a special care in the aid of those of its neighbours who are in danger of death? | 320 |

## CHAPTER XXV.

### THE GOVERNMENT OF THE SOCIETY.

| | |
|---|---|
| I. Is the Society fitly governed by way of monarchy? | 321 |
| II. Is it expedient that the appointment of the General should be for life? | 326 |

|  | PAGE |
|---|---|
| III. Are the other Prelates fitly instituted in the Society? | 329 |
| IV. The power of jurisdiction which exists in the Society | 340 |
| V. This power of jurisdiction which exists in inferior Prelates of the Society | 343 |
| VI. Do the Prelates of the Society rightly exact from their subjects a manifestation of their consciences in order to their individual government? | 345 |
| VII. Is fraternal denunciation rightly made in accordance with the Rule and particular government of the Society? | 352 |
| VIII. The general doctrine of denunciation; and its application to the practice of the Society | 356 |
| IX. The three modes of procedure in external judgment against the offences of subjects; and, first, Visitation, or General Enquiry | 361 |
| X. The mode of proceeding by way of Special Enquiry; by way of Judicial Denunciation; and by way of Accusation | 365 |
| XI. What form of judgment is observed in the Society? | 369 |
| XII. Is the Rule of the Society well adapted and sufficient for the fitting government and religious direction of the Order? | 375 |

## CHAPTER XXVI.

### SEVERANCE FROM THE SOCIETY.

|  |  |
|---|---|
| I. Can a Professed Father be expelled from the Society? and for what causes? | 385 |
| II. Can he be transferred to another Order? and in what way? | 385 |
| III. To what is a Professed Father of the Society bound who has been expelled from it, or who has left it in any other way? | 387 |

# THE RELIGIOUS STATE.

## CHAPTER XVI.—(*continued.*)

### THE SOCIETY OF *JESUS*.

#### VII.—IN WHAT DEGREE OF PERFECTION IS THE SOCIETY CONSTITUTED?

EVERY religious Order is not engaged in *all* the works of counsel; but some are engaged in higher works than others; and each is engaged in accordance with its own proximate end at which it aims. In order therefore to a perfect knowledge of the Society, we must enquire, so far as this may be done without invidiousness and arrogance, to what degree in the order of perfection the Society attains. Some have accused it of great imperfection, both as regards the contemplative and as regards the active life. As regards the contemplative life, because it does not fulfil a chief function of this life, namely, that of psalmody and chanting the divine praise. Psalmody was so regarded by the Founders of the more ancient Orders; and Mendicants, who in virtue of their Institute are supported by the alms of the faithful, seem bound by a special title publicly to chant the Divine Office. A body which does not do this has been said hardly to merit the name of religious, since it is shorn of one of the chief splendours of religion. With regard also to the active life, it has been urged as an imperfection in the Society, that it does not imitate the austerities of the old Orders, which were regarded in them as so necessary to perfection; and that it professes scarcely anything special beyond that which all by common custom, or by the precept of the Church, are bound to observe.

Nevertheless, we must maintain that the Society is in virtue of its Institute most perfect; and that it is constituted in the highest order of religious states, and that in that order it does not occupy the lowest place.

St. Thomas teaches that religious bodies which profess the *purely contemplative* life are of their kind more perfect than those which profess the *purely active* life; but that religious bodies which in virtue of their institutes *embrace both lives*, are more perfect than those which profess either the purely contemplative life, or the merely active life. He says also that those hold the highest place among religious bodies, which are ordained for teaching and preaching. In this sense therefore we affirm that the Society is constituted in the highest order of religious perfection.

Again, the Society is a religious body of priests, and a religious body of clerics is, of its kind, more perfect than a religious body of monks. This is signified by St. Jerome when he says—"So live in the monastery, that you may deserve to be a cleric."

Further, since the highest in any genus gives measure to all others who are comprehended within that genus, and since, in the state of perfection, bishops hold the highest place, a religious body which more nearly approaches the episcopal state will be, of its kind, in a higher state of perfection than are bodies which do not, or which less nearly approach that state. Bishops are said to be in the state of perfection chiefly because they are in the state of *those who communicate* perfection ; and because to this they are bound by their office, even to the giving of their lives, if need be, for the sheep, and because in this function they derive stability from the obligation of their state. In all this the Society largely shares. In virtue of its end it is ordained not only to the acquiring but also to the *exercising* and communicating of perfection ; and in virtue of its vows (and this is proper to the Society), it is bound to do so, notwithstanding any difficulty, journeying throughout the entire world, begging if need be, and facing all perils, even to bloodshed ; and in this function its stability is sealed by the obligation of a vow. In this way therefore it approaches closely to the state of episcopal perfection. It differs from that state inasmuch as its office in perfecting its neighbours is not principal, but ministerial; and again because it does not extend to the ministering of that sacrament which completes the christian state, namely, Confirmation, or that other sacrament which creates ministers of perfection to others, namely, the Sacrament of Order. In these ways all religious bodies are inferior to the bishops, to whom they are coadjutors. But with regard to the Society it is particularly to be noted that it was specially instituted for the service of the Apostolic See, as appears from the

Bulls of the Pontiffs; and Clement VIII. deigned to call it "the right arm of the Apostolic See;" and from that See very many graces and faculties have flowed to the Society for the exercise of its ministry in the salvation of souls, and in order that it should be furnished with due power for its work of the perfection of its neighbours.

Further, in the highest order of religious states the Society holds not the lowest place. This follows from its end which, without doubt and by the confession of all, is the highest, being the same as that of the Apostolic Institute and closely approaching the end of the Advent of Christ into the world. Although many religious bodies may in a manner aim at the same end, yet the Society in a perfect manner shews itself intent upon this end; for it seeks it by actions which are the most perfect of their kind, and by all manner of actions; and St. Thomas teaches that, of religious bodies which aim at the same end, that body is the most perfect which attains its end by the most perfect action and, all else being equal, by the greatest number of perfect actions.

The perfection of the Society as a religious state follows also from the perfection of the three vows, in which the substance of religion consists, and especially from the vow of obedience which is the most excellent of the three; as well as from the other means which it employs in order to its end, for these are very many, very perfect, and exceedingly well proportioned to the end at which it aims.

Its perfection as a state is manifest, moreover, from

the perfection of charity which it professes towards its neighbours, whether friends or enemies, believers or unbelievers, labouring for their welfare without stipend[*] or compensation, whether for sacrifices or education, counsel or doctrine. With this is connected the perfection of its charity towards God, for one of the chief signs of love of God is love of one's neighbour, and since, in virtue of its Institute, it is bound not to seek in the salvation of souls any temporal emolument or advantage or honours or dignities, what remains save to seek the divine glory for its own sake, as in the Constitutions Ours are often admonished.

And finally, there is the singular grace of its vocation. This grace of a special vocation God bestows on all religious bodies according to the measure of their office and obligation; and it is also increased according to the dispositions of individual religious, in proportion as they face greater difficulties for the love of God, and as they the more thoroughly deny themselves. In both ways does a singular excellence belong to the Society; for on the part of the Holy Ghost it has been instituted as a means or instrument in order to the more excellent effects of the divine grace, such as the propagation of the Church, the defence of the faith, and the conversion and perfection of souls; while, on the part of those who are called to the Society, there is demanded of them a singular self-abnegation, so that they can have neither place nor office nor anything else certain and secure, but must remain always exposed to every chance of change or difficulty. Add to this the singular provi-

[*] See vol. ii. p. 382, note.

dence of the Society, in virtue of its Institute, over its subjects, for the furtherance of their spiritual good, for the avoidance of evil, and for the removal of all spiritual hindrances.

VIII.—IT IS PRUDENTLY ORDAINED IN THE SOCIETY THAT THERE SHOULD NOT EXIST IN IT ANY ORDINARY EXERCISE OF CHANT OR CHOIR.

It does not belong to the perfection of a religious body that it should embrace and profess *all* the counsels *collectively,* or *every counsel in particular;* and this for an evident reason, because it is impossible that all the counsels should be put in execution at once. Some counsels are incompatible with others, such as preaching and serving the sick at the same time, or as continuous duties; and the very multitude of the counsels would be too much for human nature, for the bodily powers would fail and fervour of spirit would be extinguished, and so by reason of an indiscreet burden virtue would oftentimes not be persevered in. The Apostles themselves said to their disciples—" It is not meet that we should leave the Word of God and serve tables."

When comparison is made between religious states, and one state is seen to lack some religious observance and the exercise of some work which falls under counsel, it is not at once to be reckoned imperfect or absolutely inferior to other religious states. Two things have to be weighed; first, the question whether such a work is adapted to the end of that Order, or whether looking to this end it may not be more expedient to exclude that work? and secondly, the further question whether the absence of this good work is counterbalanced by the doing of a better work, with which the other is morally incompatible.

It has been prudently ordained in the Society that there should not be any ordinary exercise of choir and ecclesiastical chant and psalmody; for this, although in itself most excellent, would not advance the end of the Society, nor would it be a means in proportion with that end. The reasons of St. Ignatius for not imposing on the Society the burden of choir were all taken from the point of view of the end of seeking the greater glory of God in the salvation of souls, and seeking this by those means which should most contribute thereto. He considered, in the first place, that the observance of choir by the Society was not at that time necessary in the Church in order to this end. He well understood that the holy work of publicly praising God by chanting the divine office was good in itself, both for the praise of God, and in order to the holy contemplation of those who are engaged in it, and also useful to others by exciting their devotion, and attracting them to the divine worship; but he considered that this was already provided in the Church in sufficient abundance. Hence it is left to the prudence of the Society, whenever it shall be judged expedient for the greater fruit of souls, to take up some portion of this holy exercise, as for instance, for the purpose of attracting the faithful to come more frequently to hear sermons and to confession.

St. Ignatius also considered that the works to which

the Society gives itself for the salvation of souls are so numerous and so important that, without great interference with these, it could not be occupied in chanting the divine office.

The Houses of Probation, in the first place, are not suited for the performance of this exercise as a duty, for, if the older and graver members should not engage in it, it could not be performed with dignity and due splendour. Again, in every Order the novices should be instructed and exercised in those acts and ministries in which they are afterwards to be as a rule engaged. The Society in the probation of its novices is so intent upon their spiritual instruction, and exercise in daily meditation and contemplation, and training in works and actions in which humility, self-denial and charity towards their neighbours is practised, that it could not conveniently be distracted from this by public offices. Add to this that a considerable portion of the noviceship is taken up by pilgrimages, service in the hospitals and other trials outside the House and at a distance from choir.

In the Houses of Study the case is still more evident. In the Colleges specially devoted to studies, even in those Orders which most sedulously profess this ministry of choir, both masters and scholars are relieved from this duty. Studies, and especially studies so grave and manifold as are those which the Society professes, if they are to be made seriously and with superlative fruit, as the Society demands, require the whole man and the whole of his time.

In the Houses also of the Professed the occupations

of the Fathers for the benefit of their neighbours are most important, and of such a nature as will not permit them to interrupt their studies in theology, in divine things, and in cases of conscience. There is besides the necessity of time for their own private duties of consideration, meditation and contemplation, both long and frequent so far as their occupations will permit, in order that they may fulfil their functions with fruit to souls, and to the increase of their own perfection, and avoidance of the perils which mingle with their ministries; and this is much more useful than it would be for them to be engaged in choir and chant. Since both occupations could not be attempted without too great a burden and the chance of both or either being done imperfectly, St. Ignatius rightly and prudently judged that the Society should be relieved from this duty, and set free for those occupations of great moment which are more proper to its Institute and vocation; and his judgment was confirmed by the approbation of the Pontiffs.

But St. Ignatius was not the first whom the Holy Ghost directed towards this idea. Pope Gregory declared in a public allocution that in the Holy Roman Church a very reprehensible custom had sprung up, that certain deacons were devoted to singing whom it became to give themselves to the office of preaching and the administration of alms; and he ordained that henceforth their place in singing should be taken by sub-deacons or minor clerics. St. Thomas also teaches that it is a more noble manner of exciting men to devotion to do so by teaching and preaching than by chant, and therefore that deacons and prelates, to whom it belongs to excite the souls of men towards God by teaching and preaching, should not give themselves to chant, in order that they may not be withdrawn from greater things. The ministry of preaching, under which all ministries are comprehended which directly procure the salvation of souls, is to be preferred to that of psalmody or ecclesiastical chant, when they cannot be exercised together both perfectly and regularly. Moreover, there is this difference between them, that preaching is an action which is proper to priests or deacons, while the chant may be performed by any inferior clerics, or by laymen, if necessary, and especially if the latter are devoted to the divine service. Hence the religious Orders of monks, which in themselves are not Orders of priests but of laymen, profess the ministry of the choir, which may be excellently fulfilled by them, and which is adapted to their end, namely, to contemplation. But this is not the case with regard to all Orders of priests; for it is not the only duty of a priest to give himself to the divine office, and it is chiefly his duty to procure the salvation of men.

Finally, Choir, or the recitation of the Canonical Office in community, is certainly not of the substance of religion, or necessary either to acquire or to preserve the perfection of charity; or even as a means in order to the general end of the contemplative life, for this life was professed in its perfection by the hermits, who led a solitary life. St. Thomas says that an Order which professes extreme poverty ought not at once to glory in itself as if it were absolutely more perfect than other

Orders; since it may at most be only relatively more perfect, for by other Orders it may be excelled in other matters, as for instance, in obedience; and that which excels in things better is in itself and absolutely better.

## IX.—Does the Society profess a strict or a lax Rule?

Three things are to be distinguished, for they are very distinct from each other,—Austerity, Penance and a Strict Rule.

*Austerity* signifies a special roughness in the external, ordinary and common treatment of the body; as, for instance, with regard to food, by abstinence from flesh or even other meats, or by diminution of quantity, or more frequent fasting; with regard to clothing, by disuse of linen, or coarseness of habit, or by going barefooted; with regard to repose, by hardness of bed or roughness of covering, or by sleeping on the ground.

*Penance* is more extensive than Austerity, for it includes secret and hidden actions, such as private flagellations, use of hair shirts, extraordinary watchings, great labours undertaken for pious causes and the like.

*Rigour* or *Strictness of Rule* does not consist in these things merely, or even principally in them, but is more subtilely and more spiritually to be weighed. Although a strict rule does not omit sufficient austerity and penance, it consists principally in a rigorous observance of the three vows, and in all observances which may in themselves be reduced to these, as means which are of themselves necessary in order to a perfect observance of the vows, or as worthy fruits of them. For instance, in the observance of chastity, a Rule is strict which not only represses every evil act or motion, but also vigilantly provides for mortification of all the senses, and forbids and prevents not only all lascivious words, but all words which are vain or which may even remotely offend against purity. So also a Rule is strict in the matter of poverty, when the one and only reason for using temporal goods is necessity, and when this use of them is common to all alike, and is in all things dependent on the judgment and will of superiors. The greatest rigour and strictness of Rule is that which is possible in the case of obedience; for since obedience is more excellent than the matter of the other vows so also is it more difficult, and demands greater self-abnegation and abjuration of all private affections; for, as St. Gregory says—abnegation of what one *has* is little, but abnegation of what one *is*, is a great deal.

The Society does not profess any fixed mode of austerity or penance, as of regular observance and proposed to all; as is declared in its Constitutions. Its mode of life in external things is common, and it has no ordinary penances or bodily afflictions which are of obligation. In the Bull of Confirmation of Julius III. the narrative of the Institute sets forth that as regards food and clothing and other external matters the members of the Society follow the common and approved practice of respectable priests, and that whatsoever may be subtracted, from desire of spiritual profit, is offered of devotion, as a reasonable homage of the body to God, and not as of obligation. This the Pontiff approves as pious and holy, and as excellently in accordance with the end of the Institute, for he adds that in the said Society and in its laudable Institutes there is nothing found which is not pious and holy, and that all things therein contained tend to the salvation of the souls of its members and of the souls of the faithful, and to the exaltation of the faith.

The members of the Society, however, in virtue of its Rule, ought to make use of penances and afflictions of the body, in the manner prescribed by its Constitutions. St. Ignatius indeed abstains from the use of the word *ought*, lest he should seem to induce an obligation in conscience; but if this word is understood as indicating not obligation under fault, but only a direction of the Rule to that which is more perfect, and is counselled by the Rule, it may be truly said that the members of the Society *ought* in virtue of the Rule to make use of penances and bodily afflictions. They ought, so far as they are concerned, to desire and ask for these, and according to the judgment of their superiors faithfully to execute them. If any one should be negligent in this matter, the superior ought, in accordance with his office, whereby he is bound to aid his subjects to their greater spiritual profit and not only to punish their defects, to enjoin on them such penances; and it is manifest that subjects ought to perform them, since they are bound, in virtue of their state, to aim at perfection. In this sense the Rule has been understood by the whole Society, as the idea of greater perfection demands; and this understanding of the Rule has been confirmed by perpetual custom, which is the best interpreter of a law. St. Ignatius seems solicitous in the Rule to provide remedies rather against *excess* in this matter than against shortcoming; and this because he supposes a religious solicitude both in superiors and in subjects, as spiritual men and given to prayer, to exercise themselves in works of penance so far as these are compatible with the other labours of the Society.

Were it otherwise, a great instrument of perfection would be wanting to the Society, for although sanctity does not consist in afflictions of the body, yet these are in no way to be neglected, since they are necessary for purity of heart, by purification from past and prevention of future sins, for humility, for imitation of Christ and for many other spiritual fruits.

St. Ignatius would not prescribe one rule or mode of penance for all, because of the great variety of persons and circumstances in the Society; and he therefore left it to be measured in the case of each by the prudent judgment of superiors. That his view was most holy as well as prudent, is evidenced by its accordance both with reason and with the counsels of the ancient fathers and founders of Orders, such as St. Basil, St. Augustine and St. Benedict. St. Chrysostom speaks of the manner of life of a certain holy young man in terms which exactly express the mind of St. Ignatius. He says —" And what is still more admirable, he seemed in external observance to differ in nothing from others, for he was not made noticeable by rustic or uncultured manners, by unkempt hair, or by being meanly clad, but all was ordinary in habit, in speech, in appearance and in all other things. Hence he could more easily get greater numbers of his comrades into his nets, and he had a wonderful substructure of wisdom. Had one seen him at home, he would have thought him one of those who dwell in mountains and in deserts, for his house was so ordered and furnished that it left nothing of a monastery to be desired, and he had nothing more than what was necessary." Equally to the mind and spirit of St. Ignatius are the words of St. Basil—If we neglect by immoderate want, that for the sake of which we choose abstinence from food, we act contrary to our purpose; for, the instrument being broken and shattered, we can neither cleave to God by our endeavours in prayer and reading, nor perform the offices of humanity for the welfare of our brethren. Care of the body is therefore necessarily to be taken, not for its own sake, but in order that we may use its services for the study of the true wisdom. St. Thomas teaches that if one is bound to any work, whether it is liberal, such as lecturing, preaching, or chanting, or whether it is mechanical, such as building, digging, or the like, an abstinence which should hinder one's capability for such works would not be an act of virtue.

Since therefore, in this matter, one and the same measure would not be equally suitable for all persons, the Society rightly would not ordain one and the same rule for all its subjects, but committed the measure to the Living Rule, namely, to the superior. St. Ignatius did not hereby disparage the custom of other religious Orders, in which austerities are prescribed by general rules; for in these Orders this may holily and prudently be done, for although those rules cannot equally be observed by all, yet they may be observed by the greater number, and so those who are dispensed may as a rule be in the minority. In the Society this could not be so, and if it had been absolutely necessary that one rule should be prescribed for all, it would have been *too moderate*, and therefore the matter was left as we have seen.

The special reason which moved St. Ignatius in this matter, was the *end of the Institute*, which is the salvation of souls. This end is so aimed at by the Society that the whole weight of religion is, as far as may be, thrown upon it; and therefore the manner of life in the Society, and even its mode of seeking personal perfection, is in every particular adapted to this special end.

In this St. Ignatius willed his companions to imitate Christ their Leader, Who conversed familiarly with men, and in external things, especially as regards meat and drink, led the common life of other men, in order that He might accomplish the end for which principally He was made mortal flesh, that is to say, that He might draw all men to Himself and gain all. So also His Apostle—"I became all things to all men, that I might save all" (1 Cor. ix. 22).

Even the religious Orders of monks who, and especially since the times of St. Francis and St. Dominic, have taken their share in the assistance of the bishops, in their ministries to souls, have moderated the rigour of the ancient monks who observed entire separation as regards habitation; and they now erect their monasteries in cities and dwell amongst their fellow-men. In proportion as the Society lays herself out still more for this office so does she hold intercourse with men, not only dwelling in cities and amicably receiving those who come to her, but even seeking them in the streets and public places, and journeying throughout the entire world, to gain all for Christ; and in this she imitates both Him and His Apostles. She strives also, in their spirit, after a right intention and prudence, in order that she may accomplish so great a work, not only with fruit to others, but also without loss to her own members. It is most fitting that he who converses with others in order to the gaining of their souls, should conform himself to them in His manner of life, for this helps in no small degree to conciliate them, and to dispose them so that his intercourse with them may be fruitful.

The journeyings of the Society being, as Gregory XIII. says, a grace of its vocation, its members ought not, in virtue of their Rule, to be bound to this or that kind of food, but should keep the rule of the Gospel—" Eat such things as are set before you" (St. Luke x. 8), for it is not expedient either to be always having dispensations, or to have one manner of living at home and another abroad, or to be burdensome to others with whom one must sojourn, and by whom one is boarded.

As the Society imitates Christ in His common life, so also in His life of austerity she does not shrink from following in His footsteps. In the first place, with this kind of life she conjoins a perfect poverty. In the Houses of the Professed she observes both individual and community poverty; and in the Houses of Study, she retains that kind of poverty which is best suited to the occupations of the inmates. Moreover, and this is the chief point, with regard to the poverty of individuals she observes the utmost rigour. In missions and journeys for the salvation of souls, the members of the Society should, as far as possible, live by begging. In undertaking labours for the salvation of souls she closely imitates Christ, since her members are bound to spare no labour to attain that end, and should be prepared to bear all injuries and sufferings, with entire self-abnegation, and contempt of all things temporal, and a desire of suffering with Christ.

St. Ignatius looked for several advantages to the Society from this rule, and these his successors have by the grace of God found in their experience. He desired that the penance of the Society should be not penance only, but obedience also and humility. These virtues are exercised in no small degree when a religious lays bare to his superior whatsoever he does and desires, and conforms himself to his judgment and will by way either of moderation or of increase of penance. Secondly, the saint considered that corporal and spiritual welfare is better provided for, by reference to a living rather than to an inanimate Rule. Thirdly, he reckoned that its result would be a greater practice of penance than if penance were prescribed by any definite rule, laid down in accordance with the end of the Society and considering the very great variety of its members, since that would of necessity have been exceedingly moderate.

From all this it follows that the Society serves God under a Rule which is *very strict and rigorous;* for a Rule is not to be reckoned strict or lax inasmuch merely as its corporal afflictions are greater or less, but its strictness is to be measured chiefly by its rigour and observance in all works of virtue and counsel. There is greater strictness where there is greater observance in those things which are of greater moment and perfection. The Society would not be perfect or prudently instituted, if its life were one of penance and austerity at variance with its end.

Finally, the individual members of the Society will be imperfect if, so far as lies in them, they do not use bodily afflictions in accordance with their circumstances; and it will not be sufficient excuse that they are occupied in other labours, such as study or works of piety, or that they exercise themselves in other self-abnegations and interior mortifications, and have care and vigilance in the custody of their senses; for each is bound by the Rule to some fitting external penance at the will or by the command of the superior; and the superior will himself contravene the Rule if he does not watch over his subjects in this matter.

# CHAPTER XVII.

*ON ENTRANCE INTO THE SOCIETY; AND THE PROBATION WHICH BOTH PRECEDES AND FOLLOWS ENTRANCE.*

I.—HAVE CERTAIN IMPEDIMENTS BEEN RIGHTLY INSTITUTED WHICH SUBSTANTIALLY HINDER ENTRANCE INTO THE SOCIETY? AND WHAT ARE THESE?

AMONG the ordinances or rules of the Society those come first which regulate the manner of receiving the members who are to be aggregated to it. They are chiefly contained in a little work or treatise which is called the *General Examen*, because it is in accordance with it that those who are to be received into the Society are examined. The Examen is also to be set before them, in order that they likewise may deliberate with greater light on the subject of their entrance.

Five impediments are there laid down. The first is—to have left the bosom of the Church by denying the faith, or by running into errors contrary to faith so as to be condemned for some heretical proposition, or declared by public sentence suspected of heresy, or to be infamous by excommunication as a schismatic who has spurned the authority of the Church.

There are in this impediment four degrees, namely, apostasy from the faith, error with regard to some heretical proposition, suspicion of heresy, and schism with spurning of the authority and providence of the Church. In the second degree, it is manifestly demanded that a sentence should have intervened by which the person has been condemned for such error. In the Constitutions, however, it is laid down as sufficient that the error should have been public, and that there should be reason to fear the matter coming before the Courts, and the case is therefore left to the judgment of the General. It is not said that the person *cannot* be received, but that he *ought not;* and therefore public knowledge alone without a sentence does not constitute an impediment which invalidates, but only one which hinders entrance. Again, it is not required that one should be heretical and truly contumacious, but it is enough that he should have propounded errors contrary to catholic doctrine; and therefore it is rightly demanded that he should have been condemned by sentence of error by reason of a heretical proposition, because, until he is so condemned, his heresy is not proved, and, as a rule, there will not have been contracted an infamy so grievous that by reason of it he should be altogether excluded. The question of his admission is therefore prudently left to the judgment of the Supreme Prelate.

It is the same with regard to the third case, in which neither certain heresy nor clear proposition of error is supposed, but only suspicion of heresy; and therefore it is expressly required that the person should have been declared by public sentence suspected of heresy. It is added however, in the declaration of the Examen, that he who is suspected of any erroneous opinion in a matter pertaining to faith, is not to be admitted so long as the suspicion remains; and thus a difference is insinuated between him who has been declared by sentence suspected, and him who is suspected in some other way. In the first case the impediment is perpetual and, so to speak, incurable, however much the person might amend, and the suspicion be removed; while in the second case, although the suspicion hinders entrance so long as it remains, if it is taken away the impediment disappears with it. The suspicion might be removed in two ways. The first is, when it is publicly and sufficiently apparent that the suspicion was false, and that the person never really held an erroneous opinion with regard to a doctrine of faith. This is the best removal of suspicion, and undoubtedly in this case suffices. The second is when there is no longer suspicion in the present that the person now holds such an erroneous opinion, although there remains a suspicion with regard to his having held it in the past. This does not wholly purge the person from the infamy which remains from his preceding fault even after amendment, yet nevertheless the impediment is thereby removed, although there is need for much prudence in determining whether it is expedient that the person should be received. The words of the declaration appear to be rather directive and declarative of circumspection and the obligation of the superior to whom the reception belongs, than constitutive of a new invalidating impediment.

In the fourth degree or mode of this first impediment, infamy is necessary, but it need not be founded in a public and juridical sentence, for it may be incurred by means of excommunication *ipso facto* as a schismatic.

The proper and precise reason of this impediment, as regards these three heads, is to be found in the infamy which has resulted; for other inconveniences might be averted, or would merely suggest a question for prudence. Infamy springing from such sources would be a great impediment to the efficiency of the Society, not only for general reasons, but also specially because the Society has been instituted for the defence of the faith, and professes a special obedience to the Apostolic See; and he is therefore rightly considered to be unadapted for it who has been condemned for errors contrary to the faith, or for suspicion of heresy, or who has become infamous on the ground of public schism.

The second substantial impediment to entrance into the Society is to have perpetrated homicide, or to have become publicly infamous for enormous crimes.

The impediment of homicide is more probably to be restricted to homicide which is sinful; but sinful homicide, considered as an impediment to entrance into the Society, comprehends not only homicide which is voluntary, but also homicide which although casual is sinful, and homicide which is hidden, and instigation to homicide actually perpetrated by another. In other crimes the ground of the impediment is the infamy thence arising, but in the impediment of homicide it is the crime itself; and in practice when one who is examined, confesses that he has perpetrated homicide, there is no farther interrogation with regard to infamy or publicity to be made, but he is held as disabled for entrance into the Society.

There is a difference between this impediment and that of apostasy by denial of the faith, since the homicide need neither be public nor capable of proof, while the apostasy, although it need not be public in the sense of notorious, must at least be capable of proof. There must also be a concurrence of internal with external heresy; for if one were merely externally to deny the faith from a motive of fear, or human love, while internally he retained the faith, he would not incur the impediment, for he did not absolutely deny the faith, but pretended to deny it. Further, such a person must have been for some time of the number of the faithful, as an adult and sufficiently instructed in the Catholic Church; for if he was educated from infancy among heretics even if he had been baptized, and when he came to adult age had imbibed their errors, he could not be said properly and strictly to have departed from the bosom of the Church by denying the faith. So also when the heresy is only generally that of a province or nation, as in the case of the Greeks who are held to be schismatics, the infamy attaches to the nation rather than to the person, and so does not hinder entrance into the Society. With regard to the impediment of public infamy by reason of enormous crimes, it is committed by the Constitutions to the General to judge what sins are to be reckoned enormous; and this infamy forms an impediment in that place only where it has arisen, and not in remote regions, if the person has sufficiently amended, and if there is no moral risk of the rumour reaching those regions.

The third substantial impediment to entrance into the Society is to have received the habit of any religious Order of Friars or Clerics, to have lived some time with them under obedience, whether with or without profession; or to have been a hermit with a monastic habit.

To have worn the habit of a religious Order, even for one day, if it was assumed with intention to embrace the religious state, or to enter on its noviceship, is sufficient to create this impediment.

By friars all monks are to be understood, but not the Knights of military Orders.

With regard to those who have been actually professed in other Orders, St. Thomas teaches that departure from one Order to another is not in itself laudable, and is justified only by reasons of great necessity or special advantage; and because the exception is rare and extraordinary, it is not taken into account by the Society in this law, which is therefore made absolutely. If, in any particular case, it should be judged expedient, both for the Society and for the person desiring entrance, to admit him, recourse can be had to the Supreme Pontiff for dispensation.

There is a greater difficulty at first sight with regard to the grounds for the impediment in the case of those who have worn the habit of novices in another Order for some brief space of time. This impediment seems hard and novel, since it does not exist in any other

Order, and since the time of noviceship is granted expressly for the sake of probation, and since therefore not to persevere up to profession does not indicate inconstancy or levity of mind. A person might by means of his probation in another religious Order be led to judge prudently that he was not adapted for that Order, and that he was called by God to the Society, and why should he be excluded? The difficulty seems even greater in the case of a hermit with a monastic habit, since his life is not a *state*, and is merely a private mode of life.

The first reason for the creation of this impediment is, as St. Ignatius himself observes, because a good christian should be firm in his first vocation, especially since it is so holy, he having left the world and dedicated himself wholly to the greater service and glory of his Creator and Lord. Although therefore to change his Order before profession is a less inconstancy, it does nevertheless for the most part betray some inconstancy and changeableness of mind.

The second and chief reason is because St. Ignatius would have all who are in the Society to be "of one colour and likeness," for the promotion of union and mutual love, and rest and peace; and although a person who has made trial of and left another Order, has not made profession in it, there may nevertheless always remain in him some traces of his sojourn in that Order, or some conceptions or views which differ from those which belong to the Institute of the Society; and so there is always to be dreaded some divergence which might imperil peace, especially since the Society professes a manner of life which differs in many points from that which is led in other religious Orders. Hence, if a person who has once entered the Society leaves it, his life in it does not disable him for reception if he should again wish to enter the Society; for although he has shewn inconstancy, the second reason for this impediment is absent, and therefore that reason appears to be the principal one for disabling a religious of another Order for entrance into the Society.

A third reason is greater edification, and this may be twofold, namely, in the first place, as regards other Orders, who ought to be gratified that those who leave them may not be received into the Society; and, secondly, as regards the rest of the faithful, who always consider it as a sort of stigma to have left an Order which has once been entered. Since the Society exists wholly in order to the gaining of the faithful, and the procuring of the salvation of souls, it studies to avoid in every way whatever might diminish the esteem or benevolence of its neighbours. Hence this perhaps has weighed with the Society, that he who has not shewn himself constant, and able to persevere in an Order which was instituted principally for his own individual perfection, does not seem adapted for an Order which gives itself to promoting the perfection not only of its members but of its neighbours.

The fourth substantial impediment to entrance into the Society, is the bond of consummated matrimony, or that of lawful servitude.

The first part of this impediment is founded in natural reason, for a husband, after consummated matrimony, is no longer master of his own body, and so cannot freely bestow it on another, even if that other should be a religious Order. This impediment is also founded in Common Law, and obtains in other Orders, as appears from the Rule of the Friars Minor, and the Constitutions of the Order of Preachers, and St. Basil also makes mention of it in his rules. According to the Common Law, however, the impediment ceases when leave for entrance is granted by the wife, and when those other circumstances are observed which according to sound doctrine and the practice of the Church are wont to be observed; and these are that the wife should enter a monastery if she is young, or that she should make a vow of continence. But here is to be observed a difference between what is ordained in the Society, and what is ordained at Common Law. According to the latter, if a husband enters with consent of his wife, but without the other circumstances required by the law being observed, his entrance and profession are substantially valid, although his practice of the religious life may be hindered, if his wife should recall him. In the Society, on the other hand, the reception of a husband will, in virtue of this impediment, be null and void, even if made with consent of his wife, if the other circumstances required by the law have not been observed. Further, although when consent has been given and the necessary circumstances have been duly observed, the impediment ceases as it is an essential impediment; it nevertheless always remains an impediment, so that the husband ought not to be received without the leave of the General, and a Provincial has no power to dispense.

Matrimony, contracted but not consummated, does not disable for reception into the Society. No person so bound ought, however, to be received into the Society without the consent of his wife, and due conversion of her state as required by the Common Law in the case of consummated matrimony; unless perhaps by dispensation of the General, and with the intention of admitting him after his two years of probation to *solemn* profession if he should be approved, or of at once dismissing him, if he should not be approved.

With regard to the impediment of servitude or slavery, although by Common Law it does not invalidate profession, but only induces an obligation to satisfy the master, or to restore the slave, who nevertheless remains a religious, yet in the Society his reception is, in virtue of this substantial impediment, null and void. This is the case however only so long as the state of slavery continues; for it is not—*to have been* but *to be* a slave, as it is not—*to have been* but *to be* married, which constitutes an impediment. If therefore the slave is manumitted by his master, or if he in any other way truly redeems himself from his bondage, the impediment is thereby removed; and it will belong to the prudence of superiors to consider whether it is expedient to receive him, since a certain dishonour or degradation always attaches to such a person and, having regard to the end of the Society, this might render him less well fitted for its functions, although if he were admitted for temporal ministrations only, there would not be the same ground of objection.

The fifth and last substantial impediment to entrance into the Society is any infirmity whereby the judgment is wont to be obscured or rendered less sound, or any notable disposition towards such infirmity. The reason is manifest, for to receive such a person would be no small damage to the Society, since he would be unfitted for its ministries.

Every one of the foresaid five impediments renders a person incapable of reception, and consequently incapable of every other more intimate admission into the Society; and reception and admission with any such impediment is null and void, and induces no obligation. It was without doubt the mind of St. Ignatius to deprive the Society of all power in this matter, and so to disable all persons labouring under such impediments; and neither the General nor the Society itself, and consequently no one except the Supreme Pontiff can dispense from any one of them. Without voluntary acceptance on the part of an Order, all reception into it is null, since it is a mutual contract, and so must be voluntary on both sides, and it would not be voluntary on the part of the Society if the person who sought admission were to conceal any one of those substantial impediments. So entirely null is profession or vows made with a concealed substantial impediment, that no obligation arises, even on the part of the individual deceiving, either to observe his vows if he is expelled from the Society, or to remain in the Society and accept dispensation from the impediment, even if the Society should be willing to retain him, and to ask for dispensation. Such an one did not make the three vows simply and absolutely, but made those vows as annexed to the religious state in the Society, and to the tradition or delivery of himself which he made to the Society; and this state and tradition being null, the nullity of the vows necessarily follows. There was on the part of the subject no other obligatory action besides the tradition, and that was not voluntarily and therefore not validly accepted by the Society; and hence there remains no obligation to perseverance, which would be in reality a new donation of himself after he had been rendered capable by means of dispensation.

II.— THE IMPEDIMENT FROM DEFECT OF ORIGIN; AND HOW FAR IT OBTAINS IN THE SOCIETY.

The Fifth General Congregation added an impediment of defect of origin, namely, lineal descent from the race of the Jews or Saracens. This impediment, although primary, and to be taken into much account in admitting, especially to profession, is nevertheless not an essential impediment like the preceding impediments. It is ordained not from hatred to any nation, or solely from regard to human nobility and ignobility, but for reasons which relate to the common good of the Church, and the preservation of the faith. Such impediments, of which there are not a few in the statutes of Cathedral Churches, Colleges and other Orders, are sufficiently justified by the fact that they have been created by so many men who were illustrious both for learning and sanctity, and, what is most to the point, that they have been approved by several of the Supreme Pontiffs.

Moreover, reception into an Order, as it relates to this or to that person or class of persons, is not due, but is voluntary on the part of the Order, which has power therefore to lay down certain conditions which preclude admission.

III. — WHAT PROBATION SHOULD PRECEDE ADMISSION? AND WHAT CONDITIONS ARE TO BE OBSERVED IN ORDER THAT A PERSON SHOULD BE RIGHTLY RECEIVED INTO THE SOCIETY?

In order that the reception of a subject into the Society should be duly accomplished, there must, in the first place, be diligence and care to discover whether he has the gifts both of nature and of grace which the Institute of the Society requires, in accordance with the grade therein which he is to occupy; and consequently, whether he has any defects which exclude such gifts, or notably diminish them. This is agreeable to reason, since nothing is more due to a religious Order, or more necessary for its preservation, than that those who are to be received into it, should be adapted and fitted for the attainment of its end. St. Buonaventure declares that to receive all persons indiscriminately is not expedient either for an Order, or for the Church of Christ; and Nicholas III. gravely exhorted the prelates of the Friars Minor, that they should not admit all applicants indifferently to the Order, but those only who by reason of learning, fitness and other circumstances might be useful to the Order and to themselves by the merit of their lives, and who should profit others by their example. St. Ignatius also says that it very much relates to the divine service to make fitting choice of those who are admitted, and to use diligence to discover their gifts and vocation, and that no one should be received unless he is endowed with those gifts of God which this Institute demands in order to His glory. "We are," says he, "greatly persuaded in the Lord, that, in order that the Divine and Supreme Majesty should deign to use the ministry of this least Society, it greatly contributes that those who are admitted thereinto should not only be long proved before they are aggregated to its body, but also that they should be very well known before they are admitted to probation." He would not have men received into the Society, solely in order to its increase or propagation, since its good consists not in the multitude of its members, but in their probity and aptitude for its ministries. A multitude collected without discrimination, which St. Ignatius calls a mob, cannot be governed rightly and with fruit to the whole body; and St. Buonaventure numbers among the causes of the falling away of an Order from its first fervour, and as a chief cause, the multitude of its members, if they have not been selected with great prudence.

When a person who desires to enter the Society,—and this applies also to any other Order,—is sufficiently known as regards all the necessary conditions and qualities, all that remains is to observe the line of rectitude, so that, apart from any private affection, and looking only to the greater good, first of the Society and then of the individual, reception should be either granted or refused. Here a grievous sin may be committed, either against justice as regards the Society, or against charity as regards the individual, if, by reason of any depraved affection or notable negligence, a fit person is rejected or an unworthy one is admitted. If the condition and capacity of the person is not known, it would be most imprudent straightway to admit him without sufficient inquiry and examination. Either he is admitted to be retained, whatever he may be, and this is to the great prejudice of religion, and of the Society especially, by reason of its end and the very weighty matters to which it gives itself, and the damage done by a useless member redounds also to the great detriment of the Church; or he is received to be at once rejected if he should afterwards be found unfit, and this is injurious to him. He would also be burdensome to the Society, both by reason of the useless labour and the money expended on him, and because rash reception and frequent dismissal must beget scandal.

Two things are therefore most fittingly prescribed in the Society before reception of a member. One is examination, and the other is a probation which is called his "first probation," because it should precede the other probation, and be followed by further probations before his profession. The examination which is prescribed in the Society is transacted immediately with the individual himself; for he it is who ought to be interrogated, and who is compelled to manifest himself by means of various interrogatories, all of which tend towards the ascertaining of his capabilities, his natural and habitual dispositions, and his actual vocation or conversion; for on these three points his worthiness or fitness for the Institute chiefly depends.

The applicant is bound in conscience sincerely to lay bare the truth, for, since he desires to enter into a covenant with the Society, and therefore voluntarily subjects himself to examination, he is justly interrogated; he is consequently bound to tell the truth, and there cannot be, as it were, a just conflict between the parties. If he were by means of falsehood to deceive the Society in matters of grave moment, and such as would render him wholly useless in the Society, his reception would be null and void; not because there existed in him impediments which disabled him, but because the Society, being deceived in a substantial matter, would not be a consenting party to his reception, its ignorance causing its action to be involuntary. This examination is also very useful for other reasons, because in the course of it the person becomes known, and a judgment may be formed of him from his manner of answering; and the examiner may not always be content with simple interrogation, but may insist on further inquiry, and sometimes also put to proof the truth of the answers.

Even when nothing results from the examination which can in any way hinder reception, and the person appears therefrom to be a fit subject, the Society is not content but desires further to prove him, and especially as regards vocation and constancy, capacity for spiritual exercises, and for progress in letters, or for corporal labours, if he is to be exercised in these. It is ordained therefore that those who are to be received should remain as guests for twelve or fifteen days in some separate place, in order that they may there be proved before they are received.

The first act of probation during this time is for the applicant to see and consider the apostolic diplomas of the Institute of the Society, and the Constitutions and Rules which every one must observe. This is ordained in order that he who enters should have greater light and knowledge of the state which he embraces; and also in order that the Society may more and more prove his constancy, when he perseveres in his love and desire of the Institute notwithstanding his consideration of the perfection and difficulty which it presents.

The second act of probation and, at the same time, of preparation, is to exercise him in the spiritual actions of meditation and penance, and he will make a general confession and receive the Sacrament of the Eucharist. The end of this is to prove his capacity and inclination for spiritual exercises, and bodily austerity, and also at the same time to dispose him for the reception of greater grace and divine aid, so that he may with greater fervour and purity of soul enter upon the state of perfection.

The third act of probation, if he who is to be received is intended for the grade of a scholastic, is to prove him in those things which may manifest his talent and learning; or, if he is intended for temporal ministries, his bodily powers. In the latter case he will ordinarily be proved for a longer time at the discretion of the superior, and in accordance with the character of the individual.

In the Temporal Coadjutors, besides other requisites

which ought to be common to all, it is specially demanded that they should be content with the lot of Martha in the Society, and that they should be of an age and strength of body fitted for the labours which occur in the Society, and that they should not be men of difficult temper.

In others who are admitted for spiritual ministries, intellectual capacity, good judgment and sufficient tenacity of memory is required; and, as regards the will, that they should be studious of every kind of virtue and perfection, quiet, constant and strenuous in all that pertains to the divine service; and, what is special to the Society, that they should have a zeal for the salvation of souls, and for that reason be affected towards its Institute. Finally, as regards the body, there should, in the first place, be suitable age, and this, as concerns first entrance, should exceed fourteen years at least. There is required also good health, and sufficient strength to endure the labours of the Institute, and a respectable external appearance adapted for edification; while there is much to be desired that graciousness of speech which is so necessary in dealing with others. As regards other external gifts of fortune, such as nobility and the like, they will not of themselves suffice, nor are they necessary; but, if possessed along with other gifts, they are by no means to be lightly esteemed.

There are, besides the foregoing, certain other impediments which are called *secondary* impediments, because they do not wholly exclude, but only render a person less well fitted for the Society; and it is possible that so many of these might be found multiplied in the person of one applicant, as to render his admission in no wise expedient.

Of these secondary impediments some belong to the understanding, such as slowness of understanding, or defect of memory or of judgment. These are impediments when they are notable, so that the person does not attain even to mediocrity.

As regards the judgment, obduracy in one's own opinion may also be a great impediment, since it is wont to breed great disturbance in every congregation.

As regards the will, a nature which presents difficulties to progress in virtue, by reason of vehement affections which seem scarcely capable of being subdued, and habits of sin which have become so confirmed by long practice that no great hope of amendment can be indulged, are impediments. Also indiscreet devotions which are wont to be the cause of illusions and errors, when such devotions have grown into an inveterate custom which cannot without great difficulty be uprooted. Defect of actual due disposition is an impediment, as when for instance the intention is not sufficiently upright, or not sufficiently firm and constant as regards change of state, and affection towards the Society. It does not suffice to have a firm purpose or fervent affection towards religion in general, if towards the Society in particular the mind is remiss, or has but little firmness.

The impediments which concern the body are such defects as are contrary to the perfections above mentioned, such as debility, disease, notable deformity, and defect of integrity of body, and of legitimate age. The last may occur by one's being either too young or too old, under fifteen or over fifty as it is reckoned in the Rules of Provincials. Excess of age is never an invalidating impediment, if the judgment remains entire; and as regards first entrance, it is certain that no fixed age is, so to speak, substantial. It is essential only for second entrance, that is, for incorporation by means of the three substantial vows.

As regards external goods, debt and civil obligations are impediments.

Among the interrogatories in the Examen one occurs as to whether any of the applicant's progenitors were declared or known to be guilty of any error contrary to the Christian religion, and if so, in what way.

In order that reception into the Society may, as regards the receiver, be lawfully transacted—supposing the power to receive, which exists primarily in the General, and through him in the Provincials,—no other rule can be assigned except that of prudence. All the conditions which have been explained are not always to be demanded of the individuals who present themselves, nor does every one of the foresaid defects always hinder a person from being lawfully received; otherwise it would be most difficult to admit any one lawfully, since it is rare to find men who are endowed with all those gifts of nature and grace together, and in whom there are none of those defects. An excellent rule of prudence is indicated in the Declarations, namely, that when there occurs any one of the foresaid impediments, or a defect in any of the above-mentioned gifts of soul or body, it should be considered whether there is such an abundance of other gifts as, according to right reason, to counterbalance and compensate this; for so, weighing all things, the person might be accounted fit and worthy to be admitted. This compensation has place only when the defect is not in vocation as regards intention and firmness, or in aptitude and docility as concerns virtue. Defects in these cannot be counterbalanced, but must first be corrected by the aid of divine grace along with the co-operation of the individual's free will, by the formation of a habit, or by perseverance.

IV.—Is an entire period of two years rightly fixed for the Noviceship in the Society? and for what reason?

An entire period of two years is required for probation in the Society; and this period may be extended, if at the end of it the Society is not yet fully satisfied, so as to make a satisfactory judgment with regard to either dismissal or admission.

This is one of the objections which are commonly made against the Society, on the ground of novelty, since the most ancient Orders were content with one year of noviceship, as appears from the Rule of St. Benedict and from the Rules of other religious Orders. It appears also, at first sight, to be singular, since one year of noviceship is received by the common consent of all religious Orders, and was approved not only by the earlier law, but by the more modern law of the Council of Trent. The objection seems also to have more force when it is considered that even this lengthened probation is not considered by the Society sufficient for profession, and that further probations are demanded.

But, in the first place, this extension of time is not a novelty, but is derived from antiquity. No fixed period of probation was prescribed by St. Basil, who left it indefinite, and said that the novice was to be proved for as long a time as should seem sufficient; the old monks of Egypt were proved by three years of noviceship; and Justinian required a term of two years before profession. Even if it is argued that this was necessary at that time, by reason of the greater rigour of the Orders or monks of those days, and that after this became moderated the period of probation came to be shortened, and that the longer period was ordained only for certain cases or persons and for special reasons, the principle nevertheless remains that, where there occurs a special cause, probation beyond a year can be exacted by a religious Institute. Now, in the Society, looking to her end and her ministries, a special reason does occur, and a much greater necessity exists for a longer probation than is found in other religious Orders. The Society professes and embraces both the contemplative and the active life in a perfect degree, and therefore holds it necessary to instruct and ground and try her novices sufficiently in both lives, and therefore she requires for this a longer time than one year. She requires at least one year for each of those parts of her life; and, as that life is twofold, she rightly demands that the period of probation should be doubled.

Considering, moreover, in particular all the actions and ministries by which she proves her novices, it will be seen how a term of less than two years would not suffice. Further, the Society, since she deems it necessary, by reason of her end, for her members immediately after their probation to give themselves intently up to study, or to be occupied in external actions, according to their individual condition and capacity, it is necessary that the novices should strike deeper root in the exercise of virtues, and be more fully instructed in the exercise of prayer, and as far as possible be habituated thereto and experienced therein. This could not be done in the space of one year, during which spiritual exercises scarcely begin to be relished, and therefore there is rightly added another year, during which the principles which have been laid down may mature. This has been found necessary by experience, and for this reason it has also been prudently ordained that, after the two years' probation and the taking of their vows by the scholastics, the juniors should be kept for other two years at least under considerable custody and discipline.

Finally, a reason for a lengthened period of probation may be derived from an objection which has been made against the Society, that she professes not an austere, but a moderate life in externals. Although this does not diminish her perfection, looking at it in the light of her end, yet, all else being equal, that perfection will be greater in proportion as this absence of external austerity is counterbalanced by another kind of austerity. This is effected by means of the manifold probation of the Society which is, so to speak, among other austerities, her own proper austerity, and is exercised in great part by the length of time given to noviceship.

This institution of two years' noviceship is further confirmed by the authority of the Church, which has specially established it in the Society, both by the Bulls of Paul III. and Julius III., and especially by the Council of Trent. The Council, when specially treating of the year of probation, and ordaining generally that, on its completion, novices should be either admitted to profession or dismissed, specially excepts the Society. This exception shews that her practice is not a reprehensible singularity, but a pious and holy speciality.

Since the Society has no particular habit, there is no question of a reception of or change of habit as necessary for the beginning of the period of probation, and it suffices that he who has power to admit should have here and now the will to receive the applicant to the probation of the Society and that by means of any words or external signs whatsoever he should sufficiently declare this his will; he who is received also consenting and externally accepting it, so that he should then begin to live under the obedience and government of the Society. It is left to the judgment of the Superior whether this probation of the applicant is to be made in the same garments which he wore in the world, or in others. It may sometimes contribute to greater humility and mortification to perform the more menial ministries of religion in his own garments, and to appear to others to be a servant rather than a religious, and so also to seem to tread under foot, as it were, in religion the adornments of the world. It was for these reasons perhaps that this was the practice of the ancient monks; as well as to leave the novices more free, if they should desire to leave the Order, since they had not yet put on its habit.

If a prelate of the Society were to admit a novice to profession, or to any degree of incorporation, after one entire year of probation, and before the completion of the two years, the admission and vows of the religious would be valid, even if the prelate in so doing should have acted wrongly; and it is certain that the General could for a just cause dispense in order to such admission. It does not follow that the Society, in adding another year of probation, added it under the same law and necessity as the one year of noviceship which is required by Common Law; and the law of the Society on this point is older than the law of the Council of Trent, before which not even one year of probation was so necessary that it could not be renounced by consent of parties, except in the case of the Mendicant Orders, among which the Society was not then numbered.

Such dispensation is however most rare in the Society.

Dispensation is sometimes granted for the novices before the completion of the two years to give themselves to study, especially after the first year; and this power is committed to the Provincials by concession of the General.

In such case, however, there is no dispensation as regards the period of probation, since there is no admission to vows; nay, such novices are not wholly exempted from the exercises of the novices, for they have a separate habitation, and are specially instructed and exercised under their own master, and, what is the chief point, they understand that they always remain free to depart if they should desire to do so.

Vows made of devotion before completion of the two years of probation, whatever they may be as private vows, are not vows of the Society, or such as to constitute a true religious. They are not made publicly, nor are they admitted by the Society, and therefore they in no way bind the Society, which can as freely dismiss the novice as if he had made no vow. If so dismissed, his vows will cease, unless his express intention in making them was otherwise, which it might be especially as regards his vow of chastity. Since young men may easily be led by indiscreet fervour to make such vows, they are not only not admitted or counselled by the Society, but they are not even permitted to be made save after great consideration and consultation, and with observance of due form and subordination to the Superior.

V. — THE OBSERVANCES, THE EXPERIMENTS, AND THE PLACE IN WHICH THE NOVICES OF THE SOCIETY SHOULD BE EXERCISED DURING THE TIME OF THEIR NOVICESHIP.

The period of probation is ordained for two ends; first, for trial and knowledge of the subject, and secondly, for delivering the rudiments, or laying the foundations of virtue which are necessary in this Institute. The first end has also two parts, namely, that the Society should have sufficient knowledge of the nature and genius of the novice, and that the novice himself should have a greater knowledge of the Institute, so that he should with greater deliberation make his choice to persevere in it.

One of the principal observances of the noviceship is that the novice should, every six months, read that part of the Institute which should impart to him a necessary and sufficient knowledge of it, namely, the diplomas of the Pontiffs, the General and Common Rules, and the Constitutions, or at least the Compendium of the Constitutions. This progress in knowledge of the Institute, although it is in itself and primarily for the benefit of the novice, redounds also to the Society's knowledge and experience of its subject; for, in his persevering in spite of his increased knowledge, he affords a greater proof of his constancy. This, although very important, and in accordance with the practice of the ancient Fathers, is nevertheless not of the *substance* of the noviceship, so that the validity of future probations or admission into any grade of the Society should depend upon it. St. Benedict says in his Rule, that the hard and difficult matters of religion are to be set before the novice before he is admitted, and that after two months the Rule is to be read to him, and again after six months, and once more after four months, that is, at the end of his year of noviceship; and that he is to be admonished to consider it as a law from which he is still free to deliver himself, but to which he will afterwards by his profession subject himself, and so deprive himself of freedom from that law.

This reiterated consideration of the Institute is ordained not only in order to *deliberation* with regard to perseverance, but also in order that the novice may dispose and prepare himself and, as far as possible, clearly and distinctly foresee the difficulties and burdens which he may afterwards encounter. By so doing these will be lightened, and he will also more efficaciously demand of God the grace to embrace them with greater affection in the present, and to overcome them with greater fortitude in the future.

Secondly, the novice is to be examined every six months by the Master of Novices, in order that the Society may have a more full and certain knowledge of him, and especially in order that it may know whether any change worthy of consideration has taken place in him, and with what fruit he has up to that time borne the exercises and experiments of the noviceship, and with what manner of purpose he is prepared to proceed, and perpetually to persevere in the Society. After this examination, he will also every six months make a general confession beginning from the last, to any priest who may be designated by the superior, and also give an entire account of his conscience, so that in all things he may be the better instructed and directed. This also, like the foregoing, although most excellently adapted for the end which is aimed at, and requisite for the observance of due order and method in the probation, is nevertheless not of the *substance* of noviceship.

Thirdly, besides these observances, by means of which the novices are aided to deliberation with greater knowledge and freedom as regards their perseverance in the

Society, other exercises are appointed for them by means of which they are gradually and in accordance with their capacities instructed and disposed towards virtue and the spiritual ministries which are necessary in the Society; and by means of these greater trial is daily made of them.

These experiments or trials are reduced to six heads. The first is that they should be engaged for a month, more or less, in spiritual exercises; that is, in recognition of and sorrow for their sins, in meditation and contemplation of the mysteries of the life of Jesus Christ, and generally in mental or vocal prayer. This is of itself most necessary in order both to the purification of their past lives, and to a good beginning of another and spiritual life. Although there is a daily exercise of prayer, it is nevertheless of great assistance that some entire days should be given up to prayer, free from every other action, and apart from all intercourse with others, in order that the whole mind should be more recollected, and that a greater facility and a habit should be acquired in this difficult exercise. This is also of great service in proving the constancy and patience of the novice, and in discovering his nature and aptitude for spiritual occupations.

A second experiment is serving in one or more hospitals for another month, as may be enjoined. The reason given is that the novice may the more abase and humble himself, and so demonstrate, as by way of argument, that he is taking an entire departure from this world, and from its pomps and vanity. Although this work in itself pertains to mercy, or to charity towards one's neighbour, yet it is here considered chiefly as it is an indication of humility and self-abjection. Cassian relates that this practice was observed with regard to their novices by the ancient monks.

A third experiment, for the same end, is a pilgrimage for a month, made without money, and by begging on the highway for the love of Christ. This is done, says St. Ignatius, in order that the novices may become accustomed to inconveniences in eating and sleeping, and in order that, laying aside all reliance on money and other created things, they may place their reliance wholly and with true faith and ardent love in their Creator.

It might appear at first sight that this third experiment was less well adapted for novices in religion than for more advanced religious; inasmuch as their virtue is less well rooted, and that therefore they require greater custody and enclosure; and that, in evidence of this, this method of probation is not practised in any other religious Order, by reason of the many spiritual perils which beset pilgrimages. St. Jerome also for this reason, and from the example of the ancient monks, proves that it is not necessary for a monk to visit the Holy Places by way of pilgrimage. But the same St. Jerome himself distinguishes between an institute of clerics and an institute of monks, and declares that he speaks not of the former, but of the latter; and since the Society is an Order of Clerics who are destined to undertake any pilgrimage by obedience for the salvation of souls, this trial of the novices is prudently adapted as a means towards the end at which the Society aims.

St. Jerome moreover does not say that a pilgrimage is unbecoming a religious man, but only that it is not necessary in order to sanctity, and that it is not much to be sought after by those who profess a monastic and solitary life. It is certain that pilgrimage is in itself a very religious work, as the Council of Trent declares, and one which was in use among the holy fathers. It is not to be reckoned as disproportioned to the state of novices, for it belongs to the prudence of superiors to consider the condition, strength and age of individuals, and to assign such companions that the pilgrimage may be made without peril, and with the spiritual fruit which is aimed at by the Society.

A fourth experiment is for the novice to be exercised in various abject and humble offices, such as those which belong to the kitchen and refectory, the care of the sick and other similar domestic offices. For this no definite time is fixed. During the whole of the two years this example of humility and charity is to be afforded with all diligence and solicitude. An entire month, however, is to be given up, apart from other exercises, to some humble office. This kind of experiment, as it is most necessary, is also most ancient, and it has been practised in nearly all religious Orders. St. Basil says that for him especially who from some splendid manner of life hastens to imitate the example of the most modest humility of our Lord Jesus Christ, certain offices should be prescribed of the kind which in civil life are accounted sordid; and that it is to be observed whether with all alacrity of soul he shews himself in these a labourer for God who is incapable of shame or confusion. This kind of probation is, moreover, for a special reason necessary in the Society, on account of its end. Since spiritual ministries or the study of letters are to be entered upon with great diligence after the noviceship, a solid foundation of humility is necessary; and, in his Bull, Julius III. says that this Institute demands men who are wholly humble. Again, not only spiritual ministries but also corporal works of mercy have to be performed in the Society towards its neighbours, and in order that they may be spiritually profited, it is often necessary to serve them corporally, and in this to give an example of charity and humility; and therefore it is important that the novices of the Society should from the first be well exercised in those more humble ministries.

The fifth experiment is that the novices should be exercised, each according to his capacity and as the circumstances of time and place permit, in teaching christian doctrine to children and the ruder classes.

This is, in the sixth experiment, extended to the ministries of preaching and hearing confessions, after the novices have given during their probation an example of edification.

This last experiment belongs rather to the third year of probation which is made at the end of the studies, and before profession; for, as a rule, novices are not in that state in which they can be exercised in those ministries of preaching and hearing confessions, and during their noviceship they are not in the Society to be promoted to the orders which are necessary for those ministries, for as a rule they ought not to be promoted to sacred orders during the course of their studies, and until these are finished.

Nevertheless, if priests should be admitted as novices, and if they have sufficient gifts for the exercise of those functions, they are to be farther proved by means of this sixth experiment, with special approbation of the superior. Nearly all novices are in some way capable of the fifth experiment, either by themselves teaching christian doctrine, or by being the companions of others, and helping them as far as they can; and in this also there is often occasion for the exercise of humility and self-abjection.

Those fifth and sixth experiments are, like the third, proper to the Society; for in other religious Orders the novices are not allowed to go by themselves outside the bounds of the monastery, or to occupy themselves in actions which concern their neighbours, and this is the case not only with the monastic Orders, but even with the Mendicants who have more to do with their neighbours. Nevertheless in the Society these experiments are approved, as are the other Constitutions, and they have been practised with fruit; and they are in accordance with the end of the Society, both in order that the talent of the novice to aid and edify his neighbours may begin to be known, as far as his age and state permits, and in order that he also may begin to learn by experience and practice in what works he is to be occupied during the whole of his life, and so be the more affected towards those works as he has been educated in them from his tender years in the religious life. In this the Society follows the example of Christ our Lord Who, while educating His disciples in order that they might afterwards preach the Gospel throughout the whole world, did not keep them always in, so to speak, the noviceship and with Himself within the cloister, but sometimes sent them to preach throughout Judea.

Those six experiments are the *principal* experiments for novices in the Society, but they are not the only ones, and they may be postponed, or moderated, or exchanged for others according to circumstances of persons, times and places, by the authority of the superior. They are not, therefore, absolutely necessary, but they are in accordance with regular observance, with subordination to the due providence and direction of the superior.

The fourth and last circumstance of probation in the Society is the place where it is to be made.

In this also there is something proper and peculiar to the Society, namely, that it should have separate and special Houses, destined solely for the proving and instructing of its novices. This ordinance has been approved by the Supreme Pontiffs; and a Bull of Pius IV. exempts the Houses of Probation from the obligation of paying tithes. A reason for this observance is to be found in the general principle of the Fathers, that it is very expedient for the good education of the novices, that they should have their dwelling separate from the other religious. This was observed by the ancient Fathers, and is now observed in all Orders, in a manner accommodated to the conditions of each. That the separation should be not only within the same house, but in distinct houses, is in itself very conformable to reason; for if the reasons which the founders of Orders have adduced for making a separation be considered, they all shew that the greater the separation, within the bounds of religious unity, the better, all else being equal.

St. Basil gives seven reasons for the separation of novices. First, that by rarity of intercourse they may retain a greater reverence for their elders. Secondly, to remove occasion of elation, which might arise if they were at once to be admitted with the others to common life. Thirdly, lest, if any one of the elders either really were or appeared to be less diligent in his office or in religious observance, a proclivity to imitate him might be engendered in the minds of the novices; for this kind of scandal is more easily begotten in them since they are more weak and childish, and from their freshness and inexperience often judge that there is defect or negligence where in reality there is none. Fourthly, lest they might begin to feel elated if they were to see their elders fail in matters with regard to which they themselves did rightly. Fifthly, it provides against their indecorously desiring before the time such things as are religiously and becomingly granted to others on account of their age, and for other reasons. Sixthly, in order that the other religious should not be annoyed by the noise of the young. And finally, he concludes that the separation is necessary for the preservation of due order in religious discipline. All these advantages will be better secured if the separation is made in distinct houses, if this can conveniently be arranged. Although there may be other advantages in living in the same house, which St. Basil mentions, as, for instance, that the younger members are drawn to compunction by emulation of their elders, while those who outstrip them in piety are aided not a little in prayer by the young, yet these and similar advantages are not lost by a separation of houses; for the separation can never be so great that some of the elders do not live with the novices, and the more select and well-chosen these are the better will be the example of their lives, while, on the other hand, among the elders there will always be found some who, although they are not novices, retain the fervour and stamp of novices.

Besides these general reasons for the separation of the noviceship, it has in the Society a special advantage or even necessity, derived from the peculiar end and actions of the Society. There are in the Society two kinds of convents or domiciles for those who are already members of it. Certain Houses are set aside principally for the Scholastics and for the purpose of studies, and are called Colleges; while other Houses are given up to actions and ministries towards neighbours, namely, the Houses of the Professed. Now, in neither of these could a House of Novices of the Society be conveniently established. Professed Houses cannot possess any revenues, but must live on alms, while the Houses of Probation should possess sufficient revenues, as is ordained by the Constitutions, both for the greater tranquillity and quiet of the novices and the superiors by whom they are governed, and in order that laying aside all solicitude for temporal things they may give themselves to spiritual things alone, and also in order that all occasions of distraction may be removed. Again, there is the widest of diversities between the ministries of a Professed House and the occupations of novices; for Professed Houses must necessarily be frequented by numbers of secular persons, and there must be much communication with them, and from this novices ought to be separated. Further, Houses of Probation are not the proximate and immediate seminaries of Professed Houses, for this is what the Colleges are; and therefore since the Colleges should be separated from the Professed Houses, much more should the noviceships. If the noviceships lay under any necessity of being united with other Houses, it should be rather with the Colleges than with the Professed Houses. As a rule, however, when it can be done, it is much more advantageous that the Houses of Probation should be distinct even from the Colleges, since there is a great diversity between the exercises of students and those of novices, and they cannot be kept so separate within the same house that there should not be at least some disturbance. When a House of Probation is dedicated solely and wholly to the spiritual education of the novices, all belonging to it, its whole government, order, actions and the dwelling itself is accommodated and directed towards that one end, and the care of the superior is more concentrated, and so there is no doubt that this is the better arrangement.

This separation is not however of the *substance* of noviceship, for novices may sometimes make their probation even in Professed Houses, especially when their labours are necessary for the service of the House; and for the same reason they may sometimes be admitted into the Colleges. In such cases their probation is not interrupted, the circumstance of place not being essential.

The *substance* of probation in the Society is that only which is of the substance of noviceship in any other religious Order, and is reduced to this, that the novice should live under the obedience of the Society as a member who is not yet united to it, and who has a purpose of entering it, and of living and dying in it.

# CHAPTER XVIII.

*THE ADMISSION OF SCHOLASTICS INTO THE SOCIETY BY MEANS OF SIMPLE VOWS; AND THE DISMISSAL OF SCHOLASTICS FROM THE SOCIETY.*

I. — The reasons for this peculiarity of the Society.

It is proper and peculiar to the Society to have, between reception and solemn profession, an intermediate mode of admission, whereby he who is admitted is constituted outside the grade of a novice, and is united to the Order as a true member thereof, and becomes a true religious; and nevertheless is not constituted in that last degree of perfect union with the body of the Society which is possible to a member thereof, but remains in a manner on probation with a view to that final grade.

This mode of admission exists chiefly for the sake of the Scholastics; but it extends also to the temporal coadjutors. It has been in many ways impugned as novel, as unjust, and as insufficient to constitute a religious.

In the Society it is necessary, for its welfare and preservation, that young men should be received to be well trained in letters before being occupied in the ministries of the Society; since otherwise it would be difficult if not impossible to secure a sufficient supply of subjects who should possess at once both virtue and learning.

The Society is an Order of Clerics, and as, in ancient times and according to the observance of the primitive Church, houses were specially set apart in the various dioceses, or a place in the dwellings of the bishops was reserved for young men to be trained in virtue and letters, in order to secure a supply of good and useful priests; so in imitation of this holy custom the Society introduced a grade of Scholastics, as a necessary seminary for the training of the ministers by means of whom she was to accomplish her end. Moreover, the more the priests of the Society are, in virtue of their Institute and profession, bound to sacerdotal perfection, the more perfect is the education and training from their youth upwards of which they stand in need.

It is also most becoming and morally necessary that those Scholastics should be substantially united with the Society by a true moral union, namely, by the three substantial vows of religion, along with a promise farther to unite themselves to it, and to make profession when, and in the manner in which they shall be bidden. This appears from the Constitutions and from the Bulls of the Pontiffs which approve this grade as an integral and most necessary constituent part of the Society. It is necessary both for the spiritual good of the religious themselves, and for the end and preservation of the Society. It is necessary for the perfection of the Scholastics, that from the beginning they should be dedicated to God, and bound to follow after perfection; otherwise, and if this were deferred to the end of their studies, they would be deprived of great spiritual advantages and graces, and would also be exposed to great peril of inconstancy. Unless there were on their part an obligation to remain in the Society, the end and labours of the Society would be well nigh frustrated, since many might depart after having made their studies, if this were left to their own free will. There would also, on the other hand, be few who, having a true desire of the religious state, would be content to remain excluded from that state for so long a time. Again, the Scholastics could scarcely be properly governed, unless they had made vows of obedience and poverty, while the expedience of the vow of chastity is apparent. Finally, since such Approved Scholastics must have intimate intercourse with the other members of the Society, it would be unbecoming and monstrous if all the members were not united in the substantial union of the religious state.

We find examples of a similar state of things in antiquity. The second Council of Toulouse declared that when the minor clerics who were educated in the Episcopal Seminary reached the age of eighteen years, they were to be asked whether they would observe celibacy, and if they wished to remain they promised chastity, and so were, as it were, bound to the clerical state by that bond. It was also ordained that the clerics who had been brought up by one bishop in his College or Seminary, should not be received by another bishop into his Church. In the same way the Pontiffs have ordained that the Approved Scholastics of the Society cannot pass to any other Order, except that of

## THE ADMISSION OF SCHOLASTICS.

the Carthusians, an exception which is common also to the Professed Fathers of the Society.

The vows of Scholastics in the Society are made with the intention on their part of binding themselves perpetually to live and die in the Society, and under its obedience. The Society however does not bind itself to retain the Scholastics in perpetuity, or to accept their vows as perpetual, but only so long as it shall seem good to the General. The subject, so far as he is concerned, delivers himself absolutely to the Society; but he is admitted, not absolutely, but with an understood condition.

This kind of reception is holy and lawful on the part of both. It suffices that it has been approved by many of the Supreme Pontiffs, and that not only generally and in the same way as the Constitutions are approved, but in particular and among those things which belong to the substance of the Institute. Looking to the reasons, however, this contract or oblation is clearly lawful on the part of the religious, for in making it he does no injury to any one, nor does he act at variance with charity or any other virtue, as regards either others or even himself, since he is his own master and can dispose of his liberty as he pleases. Even if his delivery and oblation of himself may seem excessive in its liberality, yet he makes it wholly in homage to God, and in regard to God there can be no excess in liberality. Nay, this oblation, so far from being unlawful, seems to excel that other profession which is reciprocal. That oblation is less liberal for which there is a corresponding recompense. We do not mean to say that this mode of union is to be preferred to solemn profession, for between the two there is no comparison, but only to observe that it does possess this singular excellence of liberality.

This manner of reception is certainly not contrary to commutative justice, for there cannot be an injury to him who wills it with full knowledge. The religious in this case with full knowledge wills so to contract, and give himself; and to this end he has been examined during so long a period and has had distinctly set before him to what, and in what way he is to be bound, and manifold consideration and reiterated reading of the Institute and Diplomas has been enjoined upon him, and therefore what injury can possibly be done to him on the part of the Society by his reception in this manner? In human and temporal affairs similar contracts may be made with great equity of justice, and therefore why not in spiritual matters? Apart from any law prohibiting it, a man can give himself to another as his slave, and this donation made he cannot withdraw from it, or exempt himself from his servitude, while, on the other hand, his master remains free to manumit him. So long as he retains him and uses him for his own benefit, he is bound to support him, in virtue either of implied contract, or of natural law; but if he should manumit him, as the one party is freed from the obligation of serving, so is the other set free from the obligation of supporting; and in such a contract it is evident that there is no injustice. So far as there seems to be any inequality, namely, in this that the one party is bound not to withdraw, while the other is not bound to retain, there is not so much the idea of commutation as of simple donation on the part of him who voluntarily delivers himself into servitude. Moreover, even if servitude were contracted by way of commutation, there might be a concurrence of circumstances such as to cause a real equality in place of the apparent inequality; for if the servitude is for the greater advantage of the slave than of the master, why should not this greater advantage counterbalance the greater obligation of the slave? This is the case in the Society, for the delivery of himself by the religious is not only an equal, but it is a greater advantage to him personally than it is to the Society. Finally, although the Society is not bound by a special and absolute obligation perpetually to retain an Approved Scholastic, it is nevertheless bound not to dismiss him without lawful cause; and this cause, morally speaking, always depends on the will of the religious himself.

As this manner of reception is not against justice, so neither also is it against charity. The order of charity is that, observing the equality of justice, every one should consult his own proper good rather than that of another; and especially in spiritual matters; and still more when his own proper good concerns also the common good. Now, the good which is aimed at by this means is a spiritual good, namely, the perfection and purity of religion, and greater aptitude and efficiency for spiritual ministries for the benefit of souls. The good, moreover, is not private but common; not only because the Society is a community, the good of which as such is to be preferred to the private good of an individual member, but also because this common good redounds to the universal good of souls. To this it contributes not a little that the labourers of the Society should be fit and faithful ministers of the Gospel, and that the Society should be purged of every useless member, for nothing is more necessary to the preservation and increase of any religious body, and to the performance of all its actions with fruit.

When an Approved Scholastic is dismissed, he is dismissed free from his vows, and hereby his welfare is provided for. Besides the advantage of his having received his education, and tasted of piety, it is much more advantageous for him that he should be dismissed free rather than bound; for it would be a grievous burden to retain the principal load of obligation to the Society, and to lack the supports of the Society.

It cannot be argued that such a manner of life as that of an Approved Scholastic in the Society has not the moral stability which is necessary to a human state, for in order to the religious state it suffices that it should have such stability that without a grave cause and the interposition of public authority, it cannot be changed.

No doubt it follows as a consequence of this method of dismissing Scholastics, that some persons who were once dedicated to God, and admitted to His service, should return to the world and be engaged in secular affairs; but as it is not unbecoming that a thing which has once been dedicated to God should be turned to profane uses after it has lost its consecration, so neither is it unbecoming that those persons should live as seculars, after their state has been changed. This change moreover is not easily made, since it requires a grave cause, and it is not made without Apostolic authority and mature deliberation. Father Claudius Aquaviva, who was General for more than thirty years, was wont once and again to hold consultation over every case of dismissal. Although dismissal may not appear to be of rare occurrence, yet taking into consideration human frailty and the number of the members of the Society, it may be said really to be rare.

## II.—Does the admission of Scholastics into the Society constitute them true Religious?

By the reception and vows of Scholastics, they are constituted in a true and proper religious state. This is so certain that it cannot be denied without great rashness and error, nay, it rests on the infallibility of the Roman Pontiff. Gregory XIII. defined and declared that those who in the Society of Jesus have made the three substantial vows, are truly and properly religious, no less than are the professed, whether of the Society or of any other Order of Regulars, even although those vows are simple and not solemn. By the words *truly and properly* is to be understood as indicated whatever belongs to the substance and essence of the religious state.

That the Scholastics of the Society, incorporated into it by simple vows only, are truly and properly religious, did not begin to be true from the date of the Constitutions of Gregory XIII. which were, as regards this matter, declarative and not constitutive; but this was so from the beginning, namely, from the approbation of the Society, from which time such vows began to be made in the Society as in an approved religious Order, and to be received by Apostolic authority.

### III.—Is the Admission of Approved Scholastics into the Society to be called "Profession?"

If by the term "religious profession" is understood a wholly absolute tradition or delivery of oneself to a religious Order, confirmed by solemn vows, the admission and incorporation of Approved Scholastics into the Society is not profession. In this sense the grade of Scholastics is distinguished from that of the Professed, and the admission of the one is called profession, while admission of the other is not so called in the Institute of the Society, and in the Bulls and Constitutions.

If by *religious profession* is to be understood generally any firm and stable union with an approved religious Order, by means of the tradition or delivery of himself by the religious, and the substantial vows of religion, publicly admitted by lawful ecclesiastical authority, then the admission of Scholastics into the Society is a true profession.

When in the vows of the Scholastics there is not distinctly expressed a promise made to the Prelates of the Society, this is not as if the Scholastics did not bind themselves to the Society and deliver to it their rights over themselves, but only to distinguish their grade as Scholastics from that of Formed Coadjutors. The latter, although they do not make solemn vows, are constituted *in their final grade,* beyond which they are not to advance in the Society, and therefore they are united to the Society by a greater moral bond, and are constituted outside all kind of probation.

IV. — WHAT CONDITIONS ARE NECESSARY ON THE PART OF THE SUBJECT, IN ORDER THAT THE VOWS OF SCHOLASTICS MAY BE VALIDLY MADE?

The first condition is that second entrance should be preceded by an entire year of noviceship. The second condition is similar to this, namely, that profession should not be made before the completion of sixteen years of age. The third condition necessary to profession is that it should not be made from fear such as would affect a constant man. The fourth is that the consent should not have been extorted by fraud, ignorance or deception in grave matters. The fifth is freedom from lawful servitude. The sixth is freedom from the bond of matrimony. The seventh is that the person should not be a bishop. The eighth is that he should not have put on the habit of any other Order, or have in any way been received or incorporated into it. A ninth impediment, at least to the lawfulness of reception, is obligation towards parents in grievous need. The tenth condition is that the subject should not be in debt, or liable to be called to account. Since, however, Scholastics do not, in virtue of their vows, lose all dominion over their goods, although they can no longer lawfully use them as their own property, and since their vows do not render them incapable of inheritance, their debts may often not be such an impediment to their incorporation into the Society as Scholastics, as they would be an impediment to their profession.

V.—WHAT CONDITIONS ARE REQUIRED ON THE PART OF THE SOCIETY, IN ORDER THAT THE VOWS OF SCHOLASTICS MAY BE VALIDLY MADE?

The Society, in the reception of Scholastics does not absolutely bind itself, but reserves and retains the power of dismissing them free from the bond of their vows, if it should deem their dismissal expedient. Such vows, however, cannot be made solitarily or secretly, for vows so made are not vows of the Society, nor would they have force to incorporate men into the Society, and consequently to constitute a religious state.

The first condition which is necessary in an Order, that the vows may constitute its members true religious, and which is found in the Society, is that the Order should be approved by the Apostolic See.

The second condition is that the vows should be made before one who has power to admit into the body of the Society, in accordance with its Constitutions. In the Society this power resides in the General, who can communicate it to others. It is ordinarily communicated to the Provincials, and sometimes it may be communicated to rectors or to superiors, or to other persons of the Society, or even to any one outside the Society, as for instance, a bishop or person of ecclesiastical dignity, if it should happen that in any place there was no member of the Society.

The third and last condition which is necessary, on

the part of the Society in admitting to this profession, is that the prelate should in name of the Society give free consent; since no delivery of oneself is consummated unless it is accepted by the other side, and acceptance does not consist in words only, but requires interior consent.

Besides the person who has power to admit, certain other persons should be present, by whose testimony the reception and incorporation may be proved.

## VI. — CAN THERE BE "TACIT" PROFESSION OR INCORPORATION OF THE SCHOLASTICS OF THE SOCIETY?

Looking to the special law of the Society, and to its Institute, as it differs from the Institutes of other Orders, and to its practice and mode of procedure, there is in the Society no place for tacit profession and incorporation. In the first place, the term of noviceship is not so limited to two years that immediately on their expiry the novice should be incorporated by prescription, but it is committed to the judgment of the superior whether the term should be lengthened or not. Perseverance therefore beyond the two years in any kind of action, is not in itself a sufficient sign of incorporation. Secondly, the power of admitting to the Society does not reside in any particular convent or college, but is, as a rule, committed to the Provincial, and therefore until he expressly gives consent, no one can be considered to be incorporated. Thirdly, there are in the Society various grades after the noviceship, and therefore it has to be determined to which of these grades the novice is to be admitted. Although ordinarily a novice is first admitted to the grade of a Scholastic, he might nevertheless be at once admitted to another grade, and so an express determination of his grade is necessary on the part of him who admits him.

It is a custom of the Society that the Approved Scholastics should every six months expressly renew their vows in the same form in which they first made them, and to this act no one is admitted with them who has not previously been expressly incorporated into the Society. So long therefore as a novice is not admitted with the Scholastics to public renovation of vows, he is not considered as either tacitly or expressly admitted into the body of the Society.

When there has been a previous express admission which from defect of some condition was null, as for instance, if it was made before sixteen years of age complete, the defect may be supplied by tacit incorporation, perseverance in the same state of life being a sufficient sign of consent. But although this may be called tacit incorporation, it is not purely tacit, for it partakes of the express from that which preceded it.

## VII.—In what ways can the Vows of Scholastics of the Society be dissolved?

The bond of the incorporation of Scholastics has all the effects which follow from religious profession, those only excepted which spring specially from the solemnity of vows. This bond and the obligation of the vows may be removed in three ways, by commutation,—by dispensation,—and by invalidation.

If commutation is made into something equal or better, the bond of the religious state is not removed; but neither lawfully nor validly can such commutation be made of this state and grade in the Society without dispensation of the Pontiff.

No bishop, or other prelate inferior to the Pontiff can dispense from the bond of the profession of Scholastics. This is so, not only because it includes the reserved vows of chastity and religion but, even if these were not reserved, because it includes a true religious tradition, or delivery of himself to the Order by the religious, from which no one save the Pontiff can dispense.

The Society or its prelates cannot remove this bond by way of *dispensation*, although they can do so by way of *invalidation*, for these two powers are not convertible.

The power of invalidation exists in no one outside the Society, except of course in the Supreme Pontiff; but he is also Supreme Prelate of the Society, as he is of every other religious Order. The Society possesses this power of invalidation, as appears from the Bulls of the Pontiffs in which it is declared that the vows of Scholastics (and the same applies to those of Formed Coadjutors), are made under the condition that, notwithstanding them, the persons may be freely dismissed. This power of dismissal resides primarily in the Society as a whole, when it is assembled in General Congregation, and otherwise exists of ordinary right in the General, and in other inferior superiors as it is communicated to them by him. In the Society there exists the power to dismiss not only its inferior members, but even those who have been solemnly professed and, in a rare case, the General himself; with this difference, however, that the Professed cannot be dismissed free from their obligations, and therefore their dismissal does not contain an invalidation of the religious bond, but only a separation from the company and cohabitation of the Society.

By the Constitutions of the Society there is always required a just cause for the dismissal of Scholastics. Gregory XIII. declares that the vows cease in no other way save by lawful dismissal from the Society, and that dismissal cannot be called lawful which is made by mere will, and that dismissal alone is lawful which is made with lawful cause, or according to law, for that is said to be lawful which is according to law. If the dismissal therefore is not lawful, it will not hold good.

Again, the state of the Scholastics, and their delivery of themselves, in accordance with the intention of the Society and of the Apostolic See in approving its Institute, is ordained to this that their state should have all the stability and perpetuity which without disadvantage to the Order it can have, and therefore no power should be left to the Order or to any person to destroy the bond simply at his will. Although Scholastics know that they can be dismissed if they behave badly, and although they consent to this, yet they know at the same time, when they deliver themselves to the Society, that they cannot be dismissed if they behave well; and they do not therefore consent to any greater power of dismissal by the Society. Dismissal therefore without cause would be subversive of the force and firmness of the religious bond, and beyond the power reserved to the Society, and would consequently not be valid.

This is the case not only when a Scholastic is dismissed against his will, but also when his dismissal is with his own consent. The reason is because the consent of the religious does not of itself afford a just cause for his dismissal. There has to be considered not only the right of the religious, which he might renounce, but also the good of the Order, and principally the obligation contracted to God; and unless as regards all these there should be sufficient cause, the dismissal will not be lawful.

It might happen, however, that there should be a sufficient cause so far as the Society is concerned, and an advantage to it in amputating a particular member; and yet this cause might not be sufficient as regards the religious in order that he should be dismissed against his will. In such a case his consent might contribute so that his dismissal should be valid and just, which without his consent it would not be; not because he thereby absolutely affords a just cause, but because he completes the cause, or removes an impediment to the sufficiency of the cause. For instance, if a Scholastic should, in consequence of his labours in study or his services to the Society in other ministries, have lost his health, so as to be a burden rather than a gain to the Society, this would not be a sufficient cause for his being dismissed against his will, while it would be sufficient along with his consent.

The causes for dismissal may be either antecedent or subsequent to admission into the Society. If antecedent and known at the time of admission, they will not be just causes for dismissal. If however a person has been admitted conditionally, for the purpose of trial whether in course of time his defects might disappear, or not render him useless for the ministries of the Society, and trial shews that they continue or render him useless, those defects will form a just cause for his dismissal. The cause of dismissal is in this case derived not from the defect as it previously existed or was previously known, but from the defect as it has continued, or as the grave character of it has become better known.

Among just causes for dismissal which arise after entrance, there is the dread of a religious doing damage by bad example in his life, his shewing himself restless, or offending others by words or actions, his not being able to settle down to a life under obedience and according to the manner of the Society, or to correct himself of faults which offend the Divine Majesty, even if they should be hidden. In all these and similar instances the rule is that the defect should be such that the superior prudently judges that it is not well-pleasing to God to retain him in the Society.

In the incorporation of Scholastics there is a *quasi-*contract, from which an obligation arises on the part of the Society, not absolutely and perpetually to retain the subject, but—not to dismiss him without just cause. This obligation is very reasonable, looking to the Scholastic's delivery of himself which the Society has accepted, and which of its nature demands at least this measure of immutability that on neither side can there be dissolution of the religious bond at mere will.

# CHAPTER XIX.

*THE VOWS OF CHASTITY, POVERTY AND OBEDIENCE, AS MADE IN THE SOCIETY.*

I.—OF WHAT NATURE IS THE VOW OF CHASTITY WHICH IS MADE BY SCHOLASTICS OF THE SOCIETY? AND DOES IT ANNUL SUBSEQUENT MATRIMONY?

We suppose, in the first place, that this vow is entire and perfect, as regards both the extent of its matter and the obligation which it induces, for it comprehends the whole of the matter of chastity without any restriction, and it binds to an observance of the whole with all the rigour with which a vow of chastity has force to bind him who makes it.

We suppose, secondly, that this vow is annexed to the religious state, and absolutely inseparable therefrom, so long as that state continues, so that although the Society can remove this vow by annulling the bond of incorporation, it cannot give power to marry on condition that this bond should remain, and on the death of the wife revive as regards its practice.

If a Scholastic, however, should be dismissed free from his vows, and so should be made from being a religious to be not a religious, it is clear that he is not hindered by his previous vow of chastity from lawfully and validly contracting matrimony.

It is certain that before the Decree of Gregory XIII. this vow hindered indeed, but did not invalidate subsequent matrimony; for such an impediment is not annexed to a vow of chastity save by constitution of the Church, and previous to his time the Church had never added this impediment except to an entirely absolute vow. Looking both to the intention of the subject, the acceptance of the Society, and the approbation of the Apostolic See, this vow in the case of Scholastics was, in the beginning of the Society, wholly simple, and did not have annexed to it any impediment which invalidated subsequent matrimony.

It is as certain that after the Constitution of Gregory this vow, so long as it lasts, renders a person incapable of contracting matrimony.

There was in this way provided an expedient remedy for the frauds and injuries which might easily occur, against the divine honour, the common good and the reverence due to the religious state, as well as to the damage of the individual religious. To meet these evils there was at first added to the obligation of the vow the ecclesiastical penalty of excommunication, along with the other penalties which are inflicted on apostates. It was afterwards, however, found by experience that such is the malice of men that those remedies were not sufficiently efficacious since, matrimony once contracted, the Society was compelled, whether it would or not, to dismiss the subject, and so to be deprived of labourers whom with much toil and at great expense it had made able ministers for the service of the Church. So long as Scholastics were *capable of validly contracting* matrimony, they might sometimes be vehemently urged to it by their kinsfolk or friends, and they might also themselves be more inclined towards or easily tempted to a fall, nay, might sometimes deceive the Society by persevering in it in bad faith for a long time solely in order to their progress in learning, and in order that they might, having received their education, more advantageously embrace another state.

II.—Do simple Vows in the Society dissolve Matrimony which has been contracted but not consummated?

These vows do not dissolve *matrimonium ratum*, or matrimony which has been contracted but not yet consummated, for this effect belongs only to profession in the strict sense, or to a solemn vow.

III.—By what means does the Society aid its subjects to the observance of their Vow of Chastity?

The first and principal means is frequent prayer and meditation on spiritual things. This is most necessary in order to obtain the divine grace, without which this vow cannot be observed. It is also very useful in begetting the fear and love of God in the soul, by the aid of which chastity is preserved, and vices which are contrary to it are conquered.

The second means is that subjects should be aided by their superiors to overcome all the difficulties and perils which are wont to occur with regard to the observance of this vow. Next to the divine aid there is no other aid which is more useful and efficacious. A superior can assist his subject in this matter in two ways; first, by the vigilance and providence which he is bound to exercise in virtue of his office; and, secondly, this he can hardly do efficaciously and graciously unless he has a clear knowledge of the needs and difficulties and temptations of individuals, and this knowledge he can scarcely acquire unless his subject sincerely and openly discloses it to him. The religious of the Society are therefore admonished to hide nothing from their superiors in this matter, but to manifest all their temptations and perils in order that they may receive aid from them.

The third means is maceration of the body, and labour or occupation for the prevention of sloth, and modesty and custody of the senses.

The fourth means is to avoid intercourse and conversation or correspondence with women, save for reasons of necessity or with hope of great fruit.

The fifth means is avoidance of familiarity and particular human friendships with the young.

Lastly, the most efficacious means of all is the frequent practice of confession and communion which, while they contribute towards every grace and virtue, contribute specially towards the observance of chastity. By confession, besides the sacramental and internal grace, there is obtained the counsel and aid of the confessor, who if he rightly fulfils his functions and the penitent opposes no obstacle, is directed and enlightened by a special assistance of God to help the penitent in the difficulties which may occur with regard to the observance of chastity. It is a property of the Eucharist, by means of the most pure Body and Blood of Christ to "germinate virgins," as Zacharias says; and St. Laurence Justinian specially attributes to this Sacrament a mitigation of the *fomes*.

IV. — THE VOW OF POVERTY OF THE SCHOLASTICS OF THE SOCIETY DOES NOT RENDER THEM "INCAPABLE" OF DOMINION; AND CAPABILITY OF DOMINION IS NEVERTHELESS NOT INCOMPATIBLE WITH THEIR RELIGIOUS STATE.

It is certain that the Scholastics of the Society are not in virtue of their vow of poverty rendered *incapable of dominion*, or of retaining or acquiring the ownership of temporal goods; for by common law it is only a solemn vow of poverty which has this effect annexed to it, and there is no special law of the Society which adds this effect, as there is in the case of Formed Coadjutors who, although their vows are simple, are incapable of all hereditary succession, and cannot possess any property whatsoever.

A Scholastic's vow of poverty in no way hinders his lawfully retaining the ownership and dominion of temporal goods for a time, and so long as he is not bidden by his superior to renounce them; for he vows poverty according to the Constitutions of the Society, and these declare the kind of poverty which belongs to him. His vow however really concerns abdication of the ownership of all things, since he is bound to this not only in virtue of a Constitution, which of itself does not oblige under sin, but in virtue of his vow, which obliges under mortal sin, whenever the superior shall prescribe and fix a time for his renunciation of his goods.

Hence it is not necessary that the superior should impose this renunciation by way of precept in virtue of obedience, since the obligation does not spring from the vow of obedience but from the vow of poverty, a condition of which is fulfilled by the time being fixed by the superior.

In this vow there is a difference between the retaining and the acquiring of property; and the reason of it is because, although the vow does not oblige the Scholastic not to possess property, it nevertheless does oblige him not to make use of anything as if it were his own. Now, of one's own authority and will and without the knowledge of the superior to accept the dominion of anything is a great act of ownership, and a use of a thing as one's own, and is therefore contrary to the vow. In order to retain dominion which had been already acquired before the vow, no positive act or use of the thing is necessary, and the absence of any act of alienation or donation suffices. But in order to acquire dominion there is required a new act which is in itself contrary to poverty, unless it is made with dependence on the superior; and this dependence is not observed simply by the absence of a special prohibition, but it is required that leave should positively be granted by the superior, so that the thing should be acquired by his authority and will.

There is sometimes acquired a new dominion of things or fruits without a new acceptance of dominion; and as the law of the Society permits or grants to Scholastics the ownership of their former goods, it consequently grants that, if these consist of real property, and are fruitful and increase as time goes on, this should extend to their fruits and increase; and so no new positive leave of the superior is necessary, although it is never lawful to Scholastics to make use of those fruits as if they were their own.

Sometimes, however, the ownership is such that, although acquired in virtue of an old right, a new act of will and acceptance is necessary, as in the case of succession to a paternal inheritance, and then the knowledge and leave of the superior is necessary, in order that the act should be done rightly and in accordance with the vow of poverty. Although without this the act is valid, yet it is not so stable that it cannot be invalidated by the superior, by reason of the general dependence of the will of his subject.

Incapability of ownership is not of the substance of the religious state, for a solemn vow is not of the essence of that state, and a simple vow does not necessarily carry with it this incapability. Again, the whole of that poverty which is necessary to perfection lies within the power of the will of him who embraces it, but to render himself *incapable* of ownership is not always in the power of a man, however much he may desire to do so, but depends on law. Incapability of ownership, therefore, is not necessary to the state of perfection, and capability of ownership is no obstacle to perfection, if the capability is never reduced to actual ownership by one's own free will.

Neither does capability of ownership prevent the religious being said to be dead to the world, for this death, so far as it regards perfection, consists rather in internal affection and renunciation, than in absence of legal capability.

Pius V. declared that the vows of Scholastics are sufficient to constitute them not only truly evangelically poor, but also mendicants.

V.—To whom can or ought the Scholastics of the Society, according to the Rule, to distribute their goods?

It is peculiar to the Society that a religious who is truly united with it should of ordinary right have power to distribute his goods. In other religious Orders this is not lawful, save in a rare case, and for reasons which regard both the religious and the Order. In other Orders, it is only the professed who are true religious,[*] while in the Society there are many who are true religious and who are nevertheless not solemnly professed, and who are therefore capable of dominion, one act of which is distribution of goods. Again, in other Orders, if a religious does not distribute his goods before profession, the whole right to them passes to the Order, if it is capable of the possession of goods; but in the Society, even if the Scholastics

[*] See vol. i. p. 152, note.

have not distributed their goods before making their vows, no right to them is transferred to the Society, or to any College or House of Probation, and the right of distribution therefore remains where it previously existed.

Although this power of distribution of his goods exists in the Scholastic, yet in virtue of his vow of poverty it remains in a manner restrained, and by reason of the religious state it is also in a manner determined to a religious use; and therefore in the Constitutions a mode and order is rightly prescribed with regard to the distribution. It is ordained, in the first place, that the goods should not be given to relatives, simply because they are relatives, although they may sometimes be rightly given to them, because they are poor; for they are not by the fact of their being relatives excluded from the number of the poor; nay, all else being equal, they are to be preferred to other poor persons, and this in accordance with the order of charity. When relatives are rich, there remains only blood relationship as a ground for the distribution being made to them, and although this is not evil yet it is foreign to the counsel of Christ. This ordinance contributes towards the acquiring of perfection, at least by the removal of impediments. It prevents the growth of an inordinate love of relatives, and rather diminishes it, for love is increased not only by receiving but also by giving. It prevents, secondly, an inordinate distribution of the goods. Not only is that distribution called *inordinate* which is contrary to justice or charity, but that also in which the order of charity, and not only that order which is absolutely necessary of precept, but that also which is better and more pleasing to God, is not observed; and this order cannot be observed by him who distributes his goods from carnal affection, and not from pure love of God. The ordinance further prevents all trust being placed in the resources of parents, and transfers it to God. The poverty thus becomes greater and purer, for he who bestows goods on his parents or brethren, in a manner bestows them on himself, since he is as it were one with them by the bonds of flesh and blood, and in a manner retains the goods, as it were, in hope. The same objection applies to all who are connected with him by the bonds of a human friendship, and all in whose case there is no indigence or other ground of necessity, but some other human reason. Besides indigence, however, there may sometimes be a reason which would render distribution of goods to relatives expedient, namely, the avoidance of scandal, or quarrels or enmities which would otherwise arise. The business is to be transacted not by the judgment of the religious, but by that of one or more persons approved for their lives and learning, and chosen by the religious himself with approbation of the superior.

When the goods of a Scholastic are not to be distributed to relatives, no other rule is prescribed except this that they should be distributed to pious and holy works according to his devotion. There is no obligation to give anything to the Society, since it has not acquired any right either in or to the goods of the religious. The Society is not however excluded; nay, a donation to it will, on the contrary, all else being equal, be more in accordance with the order of charity. Every one ought to love those who are spiritually united to him more than strangers, and between a religious and his Order there is a strong and special spiritual bond. How great moderation is observed when the distribution is made for the benefit of the Society is apparent from a rule of Provincials which ordains that, when any goods are to be applied to the Society with leave of the General, the Provincial shall take great care that the goods are realised with edification and charity and not with rigour, and if possible by means of procurators rather than by Ours, and that it is expedient that some alms should be given to the poor of the town in which the property is situated.

### VI.—The distribution by Scholastics of their goods, as regards their Vow of Poverty.

Although the Constitutions do not of themselves oblige under sin, yet by reason of the matter there may arise an obligation of vow. The vow of poverty obliges the religious not to use anything as his own, and distribution of goods is a use of goods, and the greatest use of them, and therefore, in virtue of the vow of poverty, that use only should be assumed which is granted by the Constitutions, since every other use is a use of a thing as one's own.

It falls therefore under an obligation of precept and vow, not to usurp any proprietary use of goods, that is, any use which is wholly by one's own authority and will, and not according to the Rule or to the will of the superior.

He who, after making the three substantial vows, distributes his goods or renounces them without leave of the superior, acts contrary to his vow of poverty.

A testament made by a Scholastic without leave of the superior is not null, although it is capable of invalidation by the superior. To make a testament secretly and without leave of the superior is not a sin against poverty, if it is made with intention to submit it to the superior when death approaches, since such testament is as it were a manifestation of the subject's will, and not an undue usurpation of right. But it would be otherwise, if the testator intended that his testament should be executed by his own will only. A testament is no hindrance to the obligation of renunciation and its observance, for in spite of it the superior can enjoin that the subject should at once and without delay make renunciation of all his goods, and then the testament falls to the ground. Sometimes a testament may be made in good faith, as for instance, if a subject should on a journey or voyage find himself in danger of death, with no superior within reach from whom to ask leave, he certainly would not sin by making a testament, especially in favour of pious works, lest he should die intestate and those who were not in need should succeed to him. To do this, however, in a religious way, he ought expressly in the testament itself to subordinate it to the will of his superior; and he will do this in the most excellent way, if he leaves it to him to alter the testament as may be deemed most expedient.

Further, in such cases of necessity, it will not be a grave sin for a Scholastic to make a testament constituting relations or other similar persons his heirs, if this is done solely to prevent intestate succession and to let the superior know the will of the deceased, so long as it is left to him to change it into other pious works. But if the testament should be made absolutely, leaving his relatives his heirs, or bequeathing legacies other than for pious purposes, he would sin grievously, as usurping a use of goods which is not granted to him, and as consequently using the goods as if they were his own.

The act would, moreover, be well nigh useless, for even if the Scholastic were to die with such a testament, which God forbid, the superior has power to invalidate it in the same way as he can invalidate other donations. The superior is not free, unless this has been expressly granted to him in the testament, to change the destination to another heir, or to other even pious works, he has right and power only to destroy the testament, and it being out of the way, that person of necessity succeeds to whom the inheritance is due by intestate succession. The reason is, because the superior has no right of his own to distribute the goods, but has only the right to designate the matter, mode and time, and to give leave that the subject may distribute his goods and alienate them in accordance with his religious obligations.

As regards a novice who, during the second year of his noviceship, and before making his vows, should make a testament without the knowledge of his superior, he would be acting inordinately, because even a novice should, so long as he remains in that state, observe due subordination to his superior, especially as regards so grave a matter. Novices promise to renounce all their goods after the completion of one year from their entrance, whenever this shall be enjoined upon them during the remaining period of their probation. Although this promise is not properly a vow, it is not merely a purpose, but is a simple promise with the condition understood—If I persevere, and if the superior should enjoin it. The obligation is therefore, not of vow, but springs from filial obedience, and the tacit convention between the novice and the Order when he was admitted to the common life of the religious brethren; and therefore the inordination will not on this ground be a mortal sin, although it could scarcely be excused from venial sin.

## VII. — To what practice or exercise of Poverty are individual Religious of the Society bound, *in virtue of the Rule?*

The practice of poverty by individual religious may be twofold, one positive, and the other negative; and each may be in its manner the matter of a vow. The negative practice of poverty, or the absence of any use of goods may fall directly and substantially under the obligation of the vow of poverty; because since poverty consists in lacking, the poverty will be the greater if it extends to the lacking of certain uses, and so can fall directly under the vow. Positive use, as such, does not pertain to poverty, but to other virtues by which a man is bound to use temporal goods for the preservation of his life and for other ends; but it belongs to poverty to moderate this use, and so far it may fall directly under vow. There are also certain acts which are, morally speaking, necessarily annexed to certain kinds of poverty, such as begging in the case of community poverty, that is, when not even communities in an Order can possess property.

As regards the negative practice of poverty, which is the more perfect of the two, the first observance in the Society is that the religious cannot as individuals possess any of those things which belong to the support of the body, and are included under meat and drink. Not to have a proper and private *ownership* of such things is common to all religious; but not to have a private *possession* of them, either in great or in small quantity, with general leave to use them, is not common to all religious. To many religious it is allowed either by Rule, or by custom which the Rule does not prohibit, to keep such goods in their own cells and under their own custody, and to use them at will, in virtue not of ownership but of general leave. Other religious by Rule and custom profess privation of such use and possession; and there is no doubt that as regards poverty this is best, all else being equal. It is farther removed from the sufficiency of riches, and there are fewer difficulties to be overcome when either the necessity or appetite of the body may be relieved only by means of those common goods which are in the possession and custody of the Order, and that always by the judgment and will of a superior, and with leave asked, the asking of which is the more burdensome in proportion as the matter is more trivial and carnal, and is therefore calculated, of its nature, to put to shame a religious person. This kind of poverty removes also many occasions of intemperance or of superfluous enjoyment, or of useless and idle conversation. It is embraced and observed by the Society, as appears from its custom and rules, and it ought not without urgent necessity and great moderation to be dispensed.

From this there follows a second observance, namely, that if anything is sent to any individual religious, it should not be allowed for his personal possession or use, but should be received and applied for the common use.

A third observance is not to have anything in the way of clothing in one's cell, besides those things which are necessary for actual use.

Fourthly, although from the necessities of study there is granted to the religious a, so to speak, permanent use of the books which he requires, so that he may keep them by him privately so long as he remains in the place, yet there is not granted to him any *peculium* of those books, so that he can carry them away with him, or have the use of them as long as he lives. This is an observance of poverty which presents no little difficulty, since it concerns things which are most necessary to men who give themselves with so much diligence to letters and study, and to which they are consequently likely to be much attached. It may even seem that this kind of poverty might be a great hindrance to progress in letters; and it is perhaps for this reason that many religious Orders, which are otherwise very perfect in poverty, do not observe it. The Society however has deemed that any advantages which might be derived from the perpetual use of books, may be counterbalanced by other means, or are in any case to be postponed to this perfection of poverty. Further, as no one can have books without leave, so neither in those books which he is allowed to use can he write anything, or make any note. No one, when he goes from one place to another, can carry anything with him without leave of the superior; and according to the received custom which is the best interpreter of a law, this leave is not granted except for very small things and for some considerable cause. Among such things are the books assigned to individuals with a view to renovation of spirit, namely, the Constitutions of the Society or a Summary of them, the Following of Christ or some similar pious book, and in some instances a Bible and a summary of moral cases.

The advantages of this observance are partly common to all religious Orders, and partly peculiar to the Society. It prevents solicitude in collecting books, which is sometimes done from curiosity or ostentation rather than from necessity. It avoids also the infinite expense of transporting them from place to place; and it removes the matter of an inordinate love and affection which such things when possessed have a tendency to beget. There exists in the Society a special necessity for this observance, which arises from the end and peculiar profession of the Society, since all the religious should be prepared to undertake any missions or journeys whatsoever, without excuse and even without provision for the way, whenever they are ordered. Since the obligation extends to all, and in a special manner to the more learned of Ours, and to Doctors, they should be unfettered and free, as far as may be, from all ties and impediments.

Fifthly, it is in conformity with the poor appointments of a religious chamber that nothing contained in it should be secured under lock and key; and this is a great sign that nothing is possessed as one's own, but that everything is left to the free disposal of the superior.

Sixthly, by the vow of poverty it is forbidden to a religious to receive anything without the leave of his superior—an observance which is common to all religious,—but it is specially prohibited in the Society to receive anything by way of stipend for any spiritual ministry, so that this is in no way lawful, nor can leave be given for it. It is forbidden to accept for masses, or sermons, or lectures, or the administration of any sacrament, or for any other pious duty such as the Society can perform in accordance with its Institute, any stipend or alms by way of compensation for such ministries. What is lawful to others, as containing neither injustice nor simony, is not lawful to religious of the Society. This obligation arises not from a simple direction of the Rule, but in virtue of the vow of poverty.*

This observance removes all appearance of avarice, and diminishes the desire of temporal gain. In the Society,

* See vol. ii. p. 382, note.

looking to its end and functions, it is almost necessary both as regards its neighbours, for whose spiritual profit and gain the whole Society is ordained, since the more graciously and liberally all ministries are performed for the benefit of our neighbours, the more gladly are they received by them, and the greater the edification and, all else being equal, the fruit; while as regards the religious themselves, who are for the most part occupied in such ministries, if they were to derive gain from them, there would be a peril of the pursuit of gain, rather than piety, becoming a motive of their lives. This observance moreover increases confidence in God Who will not fail to provide things necessary for His ministers, if they faithfully and freely serve Him and their neighbours.

Although it is true that the whole body of the Society is to depend for its support on the donations or alms of the faithful, whether in its Houses or Colleges or on missions and journeys, yet the Society has considered it as a counsel to be observed not to receive those alms for masses, or in compensation for other ministries, but either to accept them only when they are freely offered and given *as alms* and *not as recompense*, or, in case of need, to beg them from the faithful who will give them in the same liberal manner. Although this is more laborious and burdensome, yet the Society does not shrink from this labour, in order that she may the better arrive at the end at which she aims, namely, the profit of souls.

As the Society endeavours to imitate St. Paul in her ministry, so has she chosen to imitate him also in this kind of perfection. The Apostle, after proving to the

Corinthians that it was lawful, and that he had a right to be supported from the substance of the faithful, since the labourer is worthy of his hire, and since those who minister at the altar should live of the altar, preferred nevertheless personally not to avail himself of this right. He observed this counsel, not in order to blame the custom of the other Apostles, or to shew himself better or more perfect than his brethren, but because he prudently deemed it more expedient for the better fulfilment of his office, which was to preach the Gospel to the Gentiles. The other Apostles preached principally to the Jews, and so could without any offence accept from them the things which were necessary for their support; since, according to the Jewish custom, as St. Jerome relates, holy women were wont to minister to their masters of their substance; but among the Gentiles there was no such custom, and they were less trained in divine things, and might have been more easily disturbed if anything had been asked of them. So greatly did the Apostle esteem this observance that he calls it his "glory," and says that he preferred it to his life. The same obstacle to the free course of the Gospel might be dreaded in our own day, in preaching to unbelievers, or controverting with heretics, or in instructing and exhorting the faithful, if this should appear to be done for the sake of any temporal gain, or with any bargaining for stipend. Perchance also the ministers of the Gospel would have less freedom in rebuking vice, and less efficacy to persuade, if they were to receive any recompense from those to whom they ministered.

The Society is not entirely singular in this observance, for the Recollects among the Friars Minor do not accept any alms, or pittances, as they call them, for masses; although in their case this is done solely for the sake of greater purity in the observance of poverty.

Seventhly, it belongs also to the poverty of the Society, that subjects should not have power to give anything away without leave of the superior. This is common to every perfect vow of poverty, but in the Society it is expressly extended to the smallest matters, and not only to donation, but even to lending as well as borrowing, and that not only among externs, but even among the religious themselves.

As regards the *positive* practice of poverty, as it is distinguished from the negative practice which we have been considering, there are various Constitutions of the Society in which special circumstances and certain acts pertaining to the perfection of such positive practice are commended. The food, clothing and beds are directed to be such as become poor men, and each is to persuade himself that the worst things in the house should be given to him, and be prepared to receive them for his greater self-abnegation and spiritual profit. All, moreover, are to love poverty as a mother and, according to the measure of a holy discretion, at times to experience some of its effects.

Only the necessary or becoming use of common things is allowed, so that the rule should be,—that superfluities are always to be cut down, that necessary things are to be allowed, and that comforts and conveniences, although not ordinarily to be rejected, as coming to the relief of necessity, are nevertheless at times to be so moderated and diminished that some effects of poverty may be felt. The Council of Trent declared that the appointments of religious should be such that there should be nothing superfluous, while nothing necessary should be wanting; but this does not negative the expedience of sometimes enduring inconvenience for the exercise of virtue. St. Augustine says that Our Lord in the Gospel shews that neither in abstinence nor in eating does justice consist, but that it does consist in bearing want, when necessary, with equanimity, with ease and serenity of soul, and so carrying into practice the words of the Apostle to the Philippians—"I know both how to abound, and how to suffer want."

To this *positive* practice of poverty there belongs also the exercise of begging, which is practised in the Society in various ways and under various circumstances. The Professed should, in virtue of their profession, be prepared to beg on the Missions, since, in virtue of their vows, they are bound to undertake the Missions without looking for provision for the way. In the Professed Houses also, since in them neither individuals nor the communities possess property for their support, begging is often necessary; and sometimes even in the Colleges it is to be resorted to, should necessity demand it. Since the grade of the Professed is the last or highest grade in the Society, the novices are from the beginning trained towards it by being exercised in begging on the pilgrimages for a month without money, which they make as one of the experiments. Again, before profession the religious are to be sent to beg for three days, as an exercise of self-abjection, and in order that by means of this prelude they may understand the nature of their profession, and may begin to be prepared for it by use and exercise. Further, the Constitutions declare that they should be prepared to beg on the highway, whenever either obedience or necessity demands it.

In this promptitude of spirit the perfection of poverty in great measure consists; and for this reason Pius V. declared that all the religious of the Society, in whatsoever grade of it they may exist, are truly and properly Mendicants.

VIII. — To what practice of poverty are the Religious of the Society bound "in virtue of their vows?"

Hitherto we have been considering the practice of poverty to be observed in the Society, *in virtue of the Rule*. What in this attains to the character of a precept, and when by transgression sin, whether great or small, is committed, is chiefly to be ascertained from the general principle that by the vow of poverty all use of a thing as one's own is forbidden, and also all ownership or dominion, that only excepted which is specially permitted to scholastics.

Although, therefore, none of the observances mentioned in the last chapter can be omitted without imperfection, yet if the omission of them does not attain to this that it includes use along with some ownership, or appropriation, it will not as a rule be a sin against poverty; although, morally speaking, it is never done without some sin, either against obedience or against temperance or some other virtue, because as a rule it proceeds from some inordinate affection; unless in the case of ignorance or absence of consideration when, if there has been a good intention, it may easily be excused from all sin. As to when the possession or use of a thing is *proprietary*, the general rule is that it is *proprietary* when it is possessed or used without the knowledge and consent, either tacit or express, of the superior.

The first four of the observances mentioned in the last chapter belong to the rigorous obligation of the vow of poverty as regards this only that, without the tacit or express leave of the superior, nothing can be received or secretly possessed, or carried from one place to another. If with leave of the superior any of these things are done it will not properly be contrary to the obligation of poverty, although there may sometimes perhaps be less perfection in asking for, or making use of this leave. It may happen, however, that there should be no diminution of perfection by reason of the necessities of office or health, or for other reasonable causes. In obtaining such leave, all subreption must of course be avoided, otherwise the religious will not remain safe in conscience; since the leave would be invalid, as not really representing the will of the superior. Not only deceit and fraud, the causes of subreption, but also any such moral violence as should cause the leave to be involuntary will invalidate it; as for instance, if the subject should either expressly or tacitly threaten to excite disturbance, to give scandal, or to conceive grievous enmity or hatred, if the leave is not granted to him. In such a case there would be a mere permission of the superior in order to avoid this evil, rather than a leave; and this will not render the subject safe in conscience, even as regards violation of poverty. If nothing, however, is hidden from the superior, and nothing false is said to him, and no moral violence is employed, although the leave may perhaps have been granted without sufficient reason and obtained by importunate petitions, or have issued from private benevolence, it will suffice to prevent any sin against poverty, or the guilt of ownership; for if the sin does not suffice to invalidate the leave, when that is given, there is no sin against poverty. The rule is the same with regard to the fifth observance, or the use of a key,—without leave it is not lawful, and with leave it is lawful.

## IX.—The poverty which is proper to Professed Houses of the Society.

The Professed Society is incapable of the dominion of real property, even as vested in communities, but it is capable of some dominion or community ownership of movable goods for actual use, and of the dominion of the real property which consists in dwellings for its own habitation or for purposes of necessary recreation, although not of revenues or possessions from which the religious should be supported. But, although the Professed Houses have the dominion of those goods, they have not the full administration of them, which resides principally in the General. Contracts, therefore, with regard to such goods in Professed

Houses are made not by the convent, or in its name, but by and in name of the General.

Not even for the service or expenses of the Sacristy, or of the Divine Sacrifice, as for ornaments or for the supply of oil, wax, wine or altar-breads, can the Professed Society possess revenues in which it should have a right of property.

Neither can it undertake obligations for the cure of souls, or for the saying of masses; and thus there are excluded also all revenues arising from anniversaries and chaplaincies. On this head the poverty of the Professed of the Society exceeds even that of the Friars Minor.

Looking to the Institute of the Society it is necessary not only that the Professed Houses should be fewer in number than the Colleges, but that, absolutely speaking, they should be few in number. The number of the Professed cannot be great, considering the perfection in learning and spirit which is desired of them. Again, many of the Professed, if they are to respond to their vocation, must necessarily be occupied on the Missions, and in journeying amongst infidels, and if they have a House it is only by way of a camp. Further, great part of the Professed must serve the Colleges, and must therefore live in them. As a rule the Professed are the most noted for learning and erudition, and consequently they must be somewhat aged and well proved. They ought not to be deprived of their profession because they are fit to teach, and the Colleges ought not to be deprived of their services because they are professed; and if they live in the Colleges and serve them, it is clearly only just and right, nay, also necessary that they should be supported from the goods of the Colleges.

In these various ways the number of persons who could possibly be gathered together in Professed Houses is rendered small; and since it is well for the sake of good government that the Professed Houses should be large rather than small, and large houses could be supported only in the more populous and richer districts, the multiplication of Professed Houses is hindered.

X.—To what community poverty are the Colleges of the Society and the Houses of Probation bound?

Although the Colleges and the Houses of Probation coalesce with the Professed Houses to form the one body of the Society, yet they do not, like those Houses, observe community poverty. They are, as it were, heterogeneous members of one organic body.

The Colleges of the Society do not profess community poverty, either as regards movable goods, or as regards revenues and real property, but are capable of possessing these; nay, without them they ought not to be allowed or founded. Every College should possess as much as is necessary and sufficient for the moderate support of the religious, according to the number of religious which is required for its ministries and discipline.

The reason of this diversity may be derived from the doctrine of St. Thomas, that as there are three kinds of religious Orders, namely, *active* Orders, which require some resources for their external and corporal works of mercy—the *purely contemplative* Orders—and the, so to speak, *fertile contemplative* Orders, that is, the *contemplative* Orders which are *communicative* of perfection to their neighbours, so each kind has a poverty which is adapted to its own manner of life. For Orders which are purely contemplative, St. Thomas says that that kind of poverty is best adapted which permits communities to possess real property and revenues.

In the Houses of Probation of the Society the life is contemplative, since they are wholly ordained for the spiritual exercise of Ours, and the chief study in them is prayer and contemplation, and spiritual reading and communication of the Word of God for the instruction and exhortation of the religious, along with so much of external action as may contribute towards their spiritual profit.

In the Colleges also the principal object is contemplation, since every knowledge of the truth, and every enquiry which is ordained towards enlightenment regarding the truth is comprehended under contemplation. The Colleges therefore, for the same cause, require the same kind of poverty. In both cases quiet of soul, and absence of solicitude and care with regard to temporal things is imperatively necessary. Hugh of St. Victor says that three things are wont to hinder study, namely, negligence, imprudence, and misfortune; and that as regards the first one is to be *admonished*, as regards the second one is to be *instructed*, and as regards the third (which includes poverty), one is to be *aided*. St. Ignatius also learned by experience, while studying in Paris and elsewhere, the damage done to study by mendicancy.

Although, absolutely speaking, the Colleges might live on alms, yet it would not be fitting to throw so great a burden on the faithful as that of supporting all the Scholastics before they were occupied in their service. The faithful also would not likely be so interested, or come so readily to the relief of the necessities of Colleges and Houses of Probation, which are ordained for the education, perfection and instruction of the religious themselves, as they would be in the case of the Professed Houses, the inmates of which are occupied for the benefit of their neighbours.

The Colleges of the Society are bound to the observance of a special mode of poverty in the administration of their goods. The administration of those goods is not primarily and principally vested in the Colleges, but in the Professed Society itself, or in the General. That part of the Society which consists of the Colleges is reckoned to be only as yet on the way, and it should therefore be under the care of the Professed Society, as a son is under his father, or rather as a minor is under his guardian, who has the administration of his goods, although the ownership of them remains with the minor.

The Colleges of the Society are deprived of certain modes of acquiring temporal revenues or goods; and this also constitutes a kind of poverty. They are incapable of inheritance, in so far at least that they cannot succeed at law to the religious who make profession or take the vows of the Society in them, as is the case in other religious Orders which are capable of the possession of community property. The reason of this is principally that in receiving religious to the Society account should be taken not of their riches, but of their personal aptitude and capacity for the end and ministries of the Society; also, as far as possible, to remove all occasion of disturbance from their neighbours; and thirdly, lest the Society should be less free, in case of need, to punish or dismiss the religious. The Colleges moreover, cannot receive revenues or alms in view or by occasion of, or with any special obligation to spiritual labours, such as the cure of souls, or saying masses, funerals, anniversaries, chaplaincies and the like. The churches of Colleges, as well as those of Professed Houses cannot have in them any public alms-boxes, for the collection of alms, either for Ours or for others; nor can there be received in those churches the offerings commonly made in other churches at the kissing of relics or the Cross, and the like, and this to avoid all appearance of avarice.*

## XI.—Can the Religious of the Society be bound in virtue of their Vow of Obedience in every matter whatsoever which is good in itself?

The prelates of the Society, like those of other religious Orders, have power by a twofold title to prescribe to their subjects under sin in accordance with the nature of the matter; namely, by *dominative power* in

* With regard to the whole of this matter, see vol. ii. p. 382, note.

virtue of the vows of the religious, and by the *quasi-Episcopal jurisdiction* which they possess over their subjects. Hence there arises an obligation of a twofold character; an obligation of *religion*, and an obligation of *obedience*.

The matter of the vow of obedience in the Society is most extensive; nevertheless, as regards rigour of precept, it has a certain rule and limit.

The power of prescribing is limited by the end which the Society has proposed to herself, and at which all her members profess to aim. This end is rightly to be taken as a rule, and all things necessary to or befitting this end are comprehended within the matter of the vow of obedience, so that they may be prescribed, when expedient. Other things, however, which are either contrary to this end, or have no connection with it, are not comprehended within the matter of the vow of obedience, although they may in themselves be good works; for the religious of the Society do not profess to do every good work whatsoever, or to observe every counsel, but only to live and labour in accordance with the end set before them. Again, not every good action is ordained towards the spiritual aid of our neighbours, which is the end of the Society, nor are all actions which concern our neighbours ordained towards their *spiritual* aid; for the redemption of captives, for instance, is a most excellent work and concerns neighbours, and yet it is not in itself ordained to their spiritual aid, but to the recovery of their personal liberty. The power of the General to send Ours to any place, is limited by this only that it must be with a view to actions such as are proper to the Society in aid of its neighbours. Hence one could not be sent in virtue of the Constitutions, under the obligation of a precept, among the Turks simply to make a pilgrimage, or to visit the Holy Places, or to transact business, or on an embassy which is simply for the welfare of a commonwealth and not for the spiritual profit or conversion of souls, since these are not actions of the Society for the aid of souls. We are speaking, however, as regards rigour of precept, for, as regards counsel, there is no doubt that it is better to obey in all things without dispute. Again, although some of these actions do not appear proximately to pertain to the aid of souls, yet remotely and on occasion they might often contribute towards it. This is what may be in the mind of him who prescribes them, and that it is so is in case of doubt to be presumed, when the contrary does not appear. This excuse therefore is not easily to be admitted in the Society with regard to such missions, especially if they are prescribed under rigorous obligation, although this is rarely if ever done.

With regard to actions which pertain to one's own personal perfection, this end of one's own perfection is in the Society aimed at by means which are proportioned to the adequate end of the Society, and those means are therefore in some way contained within its Institute and Rule; and therefore not all actions which may increase charity or perfection are proportionate matter of the vow of obedience which is made in the Society, so that in virtue of that vow they could absolutely be prescribed.

In this sense the universal expressions in the Constitutions are to be understood, namely, in accordance with the subject matter, and in accordance with that matter those expressions are to be limited.

In the same way the direction—that the will of the superior is to be taken as a rule, is to be interpreted; namely, the will of the superior whose intention it is to rule truly as a superior of the Society, that is, in accordance with the end and Institute of the Society. His will is not limited by the written Rule, for he can prescribe many things which lie outside it, as he may judge expedient with a view to the end which lies within his power; although he never prescribes altogether beyond the Rule, since this is in the Constitutions declared to be in his power, and looking to the end and character of the Institute it is morally necessary. Under those universal expressions, moreover, are comprehended not only those things which can be rigorously prescribed, but those also which may be enjoined as a trial or greater exercise of obedience, and which ordinarily pertain to counsel, and not to precept.

Actions which are very extraordinary or alien to the Institute of the Society cannot be prescribed, but a superior can certainly prescribe an action in which life is exposed to manifest peril for the salvation of a neighbour; since the matter of such an obedience is not alien, but is very conformable to the end of the Society.

It is certain that not only the Professed, but all the religious of the Society can in virtue of holy obedience be bound to the missions.

That which gives measure to the matter of obedience is not its difficulty or easiness, but is its relation to the end and Institute of the Society. Hence many things are comprehended under the matter of the vow of obedience which are most difficult, while others which are more easy are not comprehended.

## XII.—The Counsel of Obedience in the Society, as regards Perfection of Execution.

Besides those things which in the observance of obedience are of necessity of precept, there are others which belong to counsel only, even supposing the vow of obedience.

In the observance of any law or precept, three things may and ought to concur;—namely, execution of that which is commanded—the will to execute or observe the thing prescribed—and a judgment of the understanding which dictates such execution and will.

In the execution of that which is prescribed either to be done or to be refrained from, consists the *substance* of actual obedience; for thereby the precept is substantially observed. This is the proper matter of a precept of obedience, to which it directly obliges.

Besides execution, there are certain conditions which concern the mode of execution; as, for instance, when without waiting for a precept, or any sign whatsoever of the will of a superior to prescribe, execution at once follows. Another condition of execution, in order to its perfection, is promptitude. A third condition is that before execution there should be no excuse.

Excuses may sometimes be contrary to the substance of the vow of obedience, when a precept is given and the excuse is either contrary to that which has been promised, or is not true but feigned or coloured. If, when a religious is ordered to go on a mission, he excuses himself only because provision for the way has not been supplied to him, this is contrary to the promise which he has made. If therefore he excuses himself with the intention of not going, unless the provision should be supplied, he sins grievously against obedience; but if he excuses himself only in order to extort somewhat, he will merely be imperfect in the manner of his obedience. If he alleges a false cause by way of excuse, even although he should be excused by his superior, he will not be excused before God from culpable transgression of his vow. When a *precept* has not yet been imposed, but only *a simple obedience* or *signification of the superior's will* has been given, there may be in such an excuse the guilt of falsehood, but as regards *obedience* there is only great imperfection. The case is the same when the excuse proceeds not from a reason, but from some inordinate affection. When the excuse is founded in a true reason, or in what at least is so considered or is an object of reasonable doubt, there will be no imperfection in the subject's setting his reason before his superior.

Finally, the obedience, in order to perfection in the manner of obedience, should be entire, constant and persevering.

XIII.—THE PERFECTION OF THE COUNSEL OF OBEDIENCE, AS REGARDS THE WILL.

Some kind of will is necessary in order to the *sub-*

*stance* of obedience, and there is another kind of will which belongs to the *perfection* of obedience. Obedience, as it is a moral human act, cannot exist apart from will. It is not sufficient, moreover, that the act should, as regards its substance, proceed from the will of the agent, but it must also so proceed from that will as it is subject to the will of the superior. If a subject voluntarily prays or fasts, ignorant of or in no way attending to this having been enjoined by the superior, he cannot properly be said to *obey*, although materially he does what has been enjoined. He does not of his own intention and will obey a precept, but it simply happens that his will concurs with the precept. As regards his disposition, it is not borne more to observance than to non-observance of the precept. It is necessary therefore that the will should in some way be borne towards the act, as it falls under the will of the superior; otherwise it cannot be strictly and properly called obedience, even as regards execution.

The will may in two ways be borne towards an act as that act is enjoined by a superior; it may be borne towards the *material object only*, or towards the *proper motive* also. The first suffices to satisfy the precept of obedience, so that it should not be sinned against; the second is necessary in order to the exercise of a proper and specific act of the virtue of obedience. In order to such an act of obedience, the motive for doing the action must be—because that action has been prescribed.

The superior, when he prescribes, simply exacts from the subject the debt of his promise which he made to God by his vow of obedience. Not to obey is consequently to sin by non-fulfilment of his vow. It is therefore, while materially a disobedience, at the same time a sacrilege.

To satisfy the obligation of the vow of obedience, it is not necessary to obey formally from a motive of religion or of fulfilling the vow. If the religious does what he has promised from an intrinsic motive of fear, or love, or hope of reward, or affection towards the virtue to which the act prescribed belongs, as for instance temperance, this will suffice to fulfil the vow of obedience, since by that vow he promised not to obey for this or for that motive, but simply to obey.

Where the obligation of the vow is not present, the act cannot possess that peculiar excellence which consists in observance of the vow; since these two, the obligation and the observance, are correlatives, and there cannot be the one without the other.

The vow of obedience in itself and immediately does not oblige to any act, except through the intervention of the precept of a superior. It obliges only to the obeying of the superior, and therefore, until the precept is given, the practice of the vow has no place. The vow has for its matter the precept of a superior, and therefore so long as that is not imposed, the vow cannot properly be exercised, except in affection and preparation of mind, and by manifesting a prompt will for its observance, if matter should be supplied.

If it is argued that, this being so, it would be more advantageous for the religious if they were always commanded by means of a proper precept, because then they would act from vow, which is more meritorious, it is to be answered that in the first place this would not be expedient by reason of the risk of failure; and, moreover, that the merit may be supplied by means of the will of him who obeys. It is supplied both by reason of the more free and spontaneous will which is manifested by anticipation of the precept, and by reason of the intention and preparation of mind gladly to fulfil the precept if it should be enjoined; and because even this kind of obedience can have reference in virtue of religion to the worship of God, and it can moreover by the intention of the person extend even to observance of the vow, so as to participate in its excellence; inasmuch as the subject wills to obey even in those things which are not prescribed, so as to remove himself very far distant from transgression of his vow, and so as to accustom himself to observance of it in the most perfect manner.

True and formal obedience has for its object a proper precept; and by a proper precept is to be understood even a precept which obliges under venial sin only. The reason is because obedience has reference to the superior as he is superior, and not as he is a friend, or prudent counsellor, or the like; and he is constituted in his character of superior by means of his dominative power, or his power of jurisdiction, for, apart from these, men are equal. Obedience therefore has reference to the superior as exercising his dominative power or his jurisdiction; and if he does not exercise either one or other he is not acting as superior, and so *actual obedience* to him has no place, although there may be *aptitudinal obedience*, that is, readiness to obey.

When a superior wills something to be done by his subject, but does not will in any way to bind him under sin, as may be sufficiently manifest from either custom or statute, then he does not really will, or move his subject as he is superior, or as possessing either dominion or jurisdiction over him, but only as he is a moral cause, counselling and morally impelling his subject to do something, not by precept, but by judgment and simple will. In this case the subject who wills to do the work from the precise motive that the superior wills it, does not make a proper act of the special virtue of obedience, but makes an act of charity or of humility. He makes an act of charity if he does the work simply for the sake of union with his head; and this may in a wide sense be called obedience, because it is a movement of the will at the will of another, but it will not be an act of that obedience which is a special virtue. It might be called an *obedience of charity*, in the same way as if one were to know that it was the will of God that he should perform some action, although God did not will to prescribe that action, his willing to be conformed to the Divine will would be not an act of the special virtue of obedience, but it would be an act of charity towards God. In the same way to will works of counsel, on the precise ground that they are more pleasing to God, is an act of charity, not of obedience.

Nevertheless, a specific and formal character of obedience may be added to such an act, and that in two ways. First, if it is done with the view of perfect disposition and preparation to obey precepts when these may be given, and to remove every peril of resistance or contradiction to formal obedience, should it occur. This intention is not merely one which may be excogitated, nor is it an extraordinary intention, but it is one which is ordinary in the religious life; for when subjects act at the nod of their superior, without waiting for a proper precept, they have regard to the first beginnings, so to speak, or shadow of the precept, and so for the better observance of their vow obey, as it were, by anticipation.

Secondly, when a superior simply commands, and does not will to exercise his power of jurisdiction or even his dominative power, he cannot nevertheless divest himself of his authority as superior and head. God, when He wills a thing to be done, without His at the same time exercising His power to prescribe, cannot separate His dignity and majesty from that will which, of the nature of the case, obliges a man on another ground to will to conform his will to the Divine will efficaciously proposed to him; so also the will of the superior, who holds the place of God, and is the head of the body, to wit, the Order, has necessarily annexed to it a peculiar dignity and excellence from the personal circumstance of his superiority; by reason of which his will has a special force of moral motion, which force is greater and of a different character from that which is possessed by the will of a friend. This may be observed in the will of a parent in relation to his child, and in that of a master in relation to his servant, even when there is no intention of rigorously prescribing, and binding in conscience.

From this there appears further to follow in the religious a natural obligation of conforming his will to the will of his head and superior, because natural reason demands that between these two wills there should be conformity and subordination.

Of this we have an example in the rules of an Order which, even if they do not bind under venial sin, nevertheless, existing as they do in a body-politic as the rule of its operations, of the nature of the case oblige in some way to their observance, inasmuch as that part is unworthy which without reason is discordant from the whole. A similar obligation arises from every simple ordinance of a superior.

The matter of the virtue of obedience is wider than that of the vow of obedience, since a man does not vow to observe all precepts, natural and positive, divine and human, but only to obey the precepts of certain prelates; and therefore the virtue of obedience can elicit more acts, especially internal acts, than are promised by the vow.

Since for the substance of obedience there suffices the will to execute that which is prescribed, every affection which goes beyond this, and contributes to the doing of the work more carefully or promptly or gladly, belongs to the perfection of obedience.

First, and principally there belongs to its perfection the pure and formal intention of obedience in order to observance of a precept, and fulfilment of the will of the superior or, higher still, the will of God which in and by means of this will of the superior is applied. Such obedience is exercised under the influence of higher virtues, and is more universal by reason of the universality of its motive, and so better disposes a man to obey in all matters of obedience. This perfection Christ taught when, praying to His Father, He said,—"Not My will, but Thine be done." And again,—"My meat and My drink is to do the will of Him who sent Me." St. Ignatius also says that that obedience is very imperfect and not worthy the name of virtue, in which one does not make the will of the superior one's own, and so agree with it that there is not only execution in effect, but also consent in affection of the will, so that the wills of both should be the same. For this also chiefly St. Thomas sets obedience above all other moral virtues, that it subjects and immolates one's own will to the Divine will.

Secondly, it belongs to this perfection of obedience that the will should not only be absolute, but also entire. That will is *absolute* which is efficacious to operate; and this belongs not only to the perfection but also to the necessity of obedience, because without this there cannot be execution. That will is *entire*, in which there is no conflict or contradiction, or contrary affection or desire. An affection which is at variance with the ordination of obedience may be merely natural, that is to say, compatible with a well-ordered and regulated nature; and this affection does not in itself imply imperfection and, if it does not retard or diminish the efficacious affection to obey, it will in no way diminish the perfection of obedience. Thus we find that Christ in His obedience unto death, permitted to Himself the exercise of the natural affection of shrinking from death, and yet this in no way retarded Him from a prompt will to obey. Again, one may have an affection which is at variance with the thing prescribed, arising from some inordination either of nature or of habit; as for instance when one desires something else from a vehement impulse of the sensitive appetite, or from the too great love with which one is affected towards something which is contrary to the thing prescribed. If, in this case, and notwithstanding this contrary impulse and affection, a man promptly and efficaciously obeys, although the obedience is accompanied with some imperfection in another kind of virtue or affection, it will nevertheless in itself be perfect, nay, may sometimes be even more perfect. Since however, as a rule and morally speaking, the repugnance must in some way retard the will to obey, that obedience is said to be imperfect which is accompanied by such immoderate contrary affections, and it will be the more imperfect the more voluntary these are.

Thirdly, it also belongs to the perfection of obedience that a man should, as far as possible, be affected towards *the thing* which is prescribed, since in that case operation is more voluntary, and this belongs to the perfection of virtue. When the affection for a thing prescribed is merely human and of a lower order, it may easily incline the will to operate from a human motive, rather than from that of perfection of obedience. Still, even if such obedience has in it somewhat of self, as concerning a thing to which a man is himself otherwise inclined, it is nevertheless possible for it to be entirely perfect, because the will can in its freedom, and along with the Divine grace, operate from the pure motive of obedience, notwithstanding that concomitant affection.

Fourthly, affection for the superior himself is also a great aid towards the perfection of obedience; and so St. Jerome counselled,—"Fear the superior of the monastery as a master, and love him as a father;" and St. Ignatius in the Constitutions exhorts us to regard superiors with internal reverence and love, and that we should proceed in the spirit of love, and not with the disturbance of fear. Although true obedience does not spring from friendship for a man, even if it is holy and supernatural, it is nevertheless greatly aided by such an affection as by a most excellent disposition. No disposition of the will, therefore, which inclines it to love or gratitude towards a superior, and which is good in itself, is to be rejected, since it is in itself an aid, and since it does not exclude the true motive of obedience.

Among other perfections of obedience, as regards the will, there is this that the act should be accompanied with gladness and spiritual joy, and that it should be done in humility, and with a constant and persevering spirit.

## XIV.—The Perfection of the Counsel of Obedience, as regards the Understanding.

In the explanation of the perfection of obedience as regards the understanding there seems at first sight to be greater difficulty, since in this mode of obedience the Society demands two things which appear to be contrary, the one to the other; the one seems to be in excess of what is due in virtue, and the other seems to be contrary to the idea of virtue, and to be full of peril.

First, it is demanded that the subject should regard the superior not as man, but as God, so as to receive his precept not as human, but as Divine. The Constitutions declare that it is very necessary that all should give themselves to perfect obedience, recognising the superior, whoever he may be, as in the place of Christ our Lord; and that we should be most prompt at his voice, as if it proceeded from Christ our Lord, and that as Christ's voice we should consider and weigh it, so as wholly to please the Divine Majesty; and that we should regard in the person of the superior not a man liable to errors and miseries, but Christ Himself, Who is Supreme Wisdom, Immense Goodness and Infinite Charity, Who can neither be deceived, nor can will to deceive us.

The other condition which the Society demands in obedience is that it should be blind, and that we should obey persuading ourselves that all things are just, and denying with a blind obedience every contrary view and judgment of our own. This mode of obedience is illustrated by the examples of a corpse and a staff, which without any exercise of judgment permit themselves to be moved at the judgment and will of another.

Still more difficult is the comparison, made by St. Ignatius in his Epistle of Obedience, with the subjection of the understanding which takes place in believing; that as we at once with our whole endeavour and assent set ourselves to believing what the Catholic faith proposes, so should we also be borne to do what things soever the superior shall say, with a certain blind impetus of the will which is covetous of obeying, and without any discussion whatsoever.

Now, between those two conditions of obedience which are demanded by the Society there seems to be a contradiction, for in order to behold God in a man, great clearness of vision and much reasoning is necessary, and how then can obedience be blind, if it requires the eyes of the mind to be so lifted up and so keen?

Again, it appears to be excessive and beyond the idea of virtue, to demand such an apprehension and judgment in him who obeys; since perfection of virtue does not require a false apprehension and judgment, and it is false to apprehend and judge the precept of a man as if it were that of God; because neither in reality and according to truth is it a Divine but a human precept, nor ought it equivalently and by appreciation to be esteemed as Divine.

Further, if the precept of a superior is to be so apprehended that we are to persuade ourselves that he neither is deceived nor wills to deceive us, this seems to be either very false, or humanly impossible. If the blindness of obedience, moreover, requires that one should so judge without examination and sufficient motive, it looks like asking us to see without light.

Nevertheless both conditions, both as regards the language in which they are expressed, and as regards the reality which underlies the language, are taken from the Holy Fathers, and have foundation also in the Sacred Scriptures. Christ Himself said,—" He that heareth you, heareth Me; and he that despiseth you, despiseth Me," and so speaking He speaks to His Apostles who were in

His place to exercise the pastoral care, and in them to all pastors of souls, and St. Basil applies His words specially to superiors of religious Orders. St. Paul also says to the Colossians,—"Whatsoever you do, do it from the heart, as to the Lord and not to men, knowing that you shall receive of the Lord the reward of inheritance. Serve ye the Lord Christ," and again to the Ephesians he says,—"Servants, obey your carnal masters as Christ, with a good will doing service as to the Lord, and not to men."

St. Bernard says,—"We ought to hear him whom we have in the place of God, as God, in those things which are not clearly against God;" and again, "Whether God or a man who is the Vicar of God gives any commandment whatsoever, we must obey with equal care, and defer to it with equal reverence." St. Buonaventure says,—"Whatsoever man in the place of God prescribes, and which is not certainly displeasing to God, is to be received as if God prescribed it;" and again,—"In order that you may be the better able to be obedient, think always when the voice of him who prescribes sounds in your ears, that you hear that voice not as from man, but as from God Himself."

So also with regard to the second condition of obedience which is demanded by the Society, there are innumerable passages of the Fathers which are so conformable to the words of St. Ignatius that he must either have taken his words from theirs, or have certainly spoken by the same spirit.

St. Thomas discussing, Whether there can be election

with regard to a thing which is impossible, because St. Benedict has laid it down in his Rule that, even if the superior prescribes something which is impossible, the subject should attempt to accomplish it? answers that this is so said because the subject ought not to discuss with his judgment whether a thing is possible, or not, but in everything to stand by the judgment of the superior. This explains the meaning of the saints when they counsel that even in things impossible we should obey; that is, either, when the impossibility is not evident, or, that we should certainly at least begin, and do what lies within our power, until we can proceed no farther, since sometimes God opens a way so that that is accomplished which at first sight seemed to be impossible.

It is manifest, therefore, that the doctrine which the Society professes on the perfection of obedience as regards the understanding is not novel, but is most ancient, and is not singular but is most common, and is founded on the greatest authority. It remains that we should explain its true sense and practice.

We suppose that obedience formally perfects the will, since it is a moral virtue, and a part of justice. The will is a power which moves all the other faculties to the free exercise of their actions; and proper obedience is found only in free actions. Hence as the will depends on the understanding in its actions, so does the perfection of obedience depend on perfection of the understanding. The will depends on the understanding as on that which directs and enlightens it, or sets before it its object.

The perfect moving and direction of the understanding requires two things, namely, perfect attention or consideration of the good to be pursued, and removal of every cogitation which might avert or hinder the will from its affection towards or pursuit of that good.

There is therefore rightly demanded in order to perfect obedience, contemplation of God in the superior, and an apprehension of the precept of the superior, as if it proceeded from God. By this there is not demanded from the religious a false apprehension or esteem of the superior or of his command, but only an elevation of the mind to the consideration of the supreme reason and motive for which obedience is given, which is the Divine will and authority. This St. Ignatius declares when he says that obedience is a holocaust by which the whole man, without any diminution whatsoever, is immolated to his Maker and Lord in the fire of charity, and by the hands of His ministers.

He who so obeys does not judge that the superior is God, but that he represents God, as God's vicegerent, which is most true, for St. Paul said of all magistrates that they are the ministers of God, and have their power from Him. Neither does the subject judge that the precept of the superior is Divine, that is, given immediately by God Himself, since it is evident that the superior is a man; but he judges that the *reason* or *motive for obeying* is *Divine*, namely, the will of God which is fulfilled when the will of the superior is fulfilled, and which ought to be the primary reason or motive of obedience. In a religious also there is another and a peculiar reason for the Divine worship, which in his obedience he should keep in view, namely, the special vow by which he has consecrated himself to God, and by reason of which the precept of a superior is in a manner made equal to a precept given immediately by God Himself; in a way similar to that in which the same Divine worship is given to Christ and to the image of Christ, for Christ is adored in the image, and by reason of the same excellence of Christ, His image is co-adored.

Similarly, he who so obeys does not judge or esteem that his superior cannot be deceived or err, either from ignorance or from malice, for it is expressly added that obedience is to be given only where no sin is manifest. This exception supposes that a superior can err by prescribing something which is unlawful, and if he can do so from invincible ignorance, he can do so also from culpable negligence, or even from depraved affection; for as he has no special privilege to prevent him in the one case so neither has he in the other.

But if a religious in his superior contemplates Christ, while he does not suppose that the superior cannot err, he, nevertheless, when no manifest evil is apparent in the precept, holds it for certain and judges that the superior does not err; and this is not a rash judgment, but one which is founded in sufficient authority and reason. The subject conforms his judgment to that of his superior by a human faith, which is however founded in a manner on the hope of a Divine providence with regard to the superior by reason of his superiority.

Notwithstanding this, reasons may occur which urge a contrary line of action, and in that case perfection of obedience does not prevent these reasons from being set before the superior, with a pure intention in so doing, and not from an affection of excusing one's self from the burden of the precept, but from a desire that that should be done which is most expedient for the end aimed at by the superior. If, however, notwithstanding these reasons, and even if they appear evident to the subject, the superior should still persist in his precept, it is, since it is not evil in itself, to be fulfilled.

That this should be done to perfection, it is not necessary to judge that the thing is useful, but it is necessary only to judge that it is useful for the subject to undertake it, and to do it as far as he can. This is the practical certainty which is not incompatible with previous speculative doubt. But in order that this practical certainty may be more constant, and consequently that the obedience may be more prompt, the best counsel is not to discuss the fitness of the matter in itself, but, as far as may be, to suspend the judgment with regard to this, and to judge that what is prescribed is just.

It may be taken as a general rule that whenever it is lawful to obey, it is always better and more perfect to obey, even if the obligation of the precept could on some ground be excused; and this especially when the absence of obligation does not arise from defect of power, but from defect of will, that is, when the superior does not intend to oblige, although it is in his power to oblige.

Hence also we see the sense in which blind obedience is to be given by perfect religious to their prelates. Since blindness consists in privation of sight, and is transferred by metaphor to spiritual things, it is certain that it is not so transferred in a sense to signify privation of all knowledge and judgment. A man is to obey not like a brute, or in a stolid way, but as a man of right reason, for the Fathers who use this phrase require at the same time lynx eyes in the perfectly obedient religious, by which he may discern God in his superiors, and whereby he may also discover sin if it should exist in a precept. Religious blindness should exclude the human reasons by which we might be moved to obey a superior, namely, because he is learned or prudent, or because he commands things which are pleasing to us, rather than solely by reason of the will of God. It should exclude also the human reasonings by which the subject would examine why the superior should so prescribe, or why he should prescribe this or that to him rather than to another.

In one word, this blindness excludes the prudence of the flesh, but it does not exclude the prudence which is spiritual and supernatural. Since obedience is a most perfect virtue it no less requires, in order to a perfect act of it, the guidance of prudence, than do other moral virtues; but this is proper to it that the prudential judgment which directs it should be founded more in an extrinsic principle, and in the judgment of the superior than in one's own judgment. As it excludes one's own judgment, it is called a blind obedience; and it excludes one's own judgment so far as that judgment is vitiated or imperfect, but not so far as implies all use of one's own understanding. As a blind man is led by another, and sees, as it were, with another's eyes, so is it with a subject in his relation to his superior.

An obedience of this nature is necessary in order to all well-ordered government, whether it is political, economic, military or otherwise; for if a servant or a soldier ought always to understand or perceive the reasons and causes which move his leader or master to command him, all government would be rendered difficult and morally impossible. Further, a superior is often moved to prescribe by higher and more universal reasons, which a subject either cannot perceive for himself, or which it is not expedient for him to know. In the process of building, the inferior masons are moved and directed by the architect, and it is necessary that they should obey although they do not understand the cause and reason wherefore they are moved. The greater the concord between superior and subject in judgment and will the better, both as in itself desirable and as useful for every work; and this is to be procured by the conformity of the subject to the superior, and not by the conformity of the superior to the subject.

Obedience of judgment is also more perfect because it is necessary in order to all the other perfections of obedience, such as promptitude, alacrity, perseverance and the like, which could scarcely co-exist with divergence of judgment. It embraces in itself also the exercise of many other virtues, to wit, of humility, reverence and confidence in God; and by it are also prevented all cogitations and reasonings which might hinder the perfection of obedience. Hence it appears that this blindness is rightly counselled as a perfect mode of obedience. St. Bernard gives a most excellent rule when he distinguishes between things which are wholly good, and therefore to be done, especially if they are prescribed; and other things which are wholly evil, and therefore not to be done, by whomsoever they may be prescribed; and other things again which, according to the circumstances of place, time, person and mode, may be either good or evil. He concludes that with regard to them there need be no discussion, and that the only prudence which is necessary is that which suffices to the discerning of the wholly evil; and that for that but little discussion is necessary, since the things that are wholly evil are in themselves and at once evident.

With regard to the example of faith, which is made use of by the Fathers, namely, that as the understanding is led captive to the obedience of faith, so also should the understanding be, as it were, blinded in order to the grace of obedience, this is to be understood by way of similitude, and not as if the cases were precisely parallel. The subjection of the mind which is made by obedience is not founded on infallible authority, nor on the truth of the thing proposed, as is the captivity of faith; but only on the power of him who prescribes, and on the practical certainty which may arise therefrom, supposing no incompatibility as regards the matter. Even if the judgment of the superior should be really false, the subject will be excused by reason of his invincible ignorance, and will at the same time merit by the virtue of obedience.

The extraordinary examples of obedience which we read of in the lives of the saints, such as obeying a command to walk on the water, or to capture a lioness and bring her to the superior, or to plunge one's hand into boiling water, are proposed only in order that by means of them we may understand how much the virtue and simplicity of obedience is pleasing to God. This was the end of those actions which was intended by the Holy Ghost, as distinguished from the actions themselves, or from the matter prescribed; and for this reason He, in nearly all these instances, confirmed the command by miracle. We are not to imitate those actions as regards all their particular circumstances, but we are to imitate only the perfection and simplicity which was displayed in them, and that in accordance with the common and ordinary laws of obedience. Sometimes the Holy Ghost moves just men to act in a marvellous manner, and outside the common and ordinary course of virtue; and this mode of operation is set before us, not in order that we should imitate it, but in order that moved by admiration we should strive at least to attain to perfection of virtue. So, for instance, Samson and Apollonia who, led by a special instinct of the Holy Ghost, inflicted death upon themselves, are proposed to us as examples of fortitude, not that we should imitate them in their acts, but that therefrom we should learn to despise death. In the same way, in those cases of obedience in which peril of life or grievous injury was imminent, there was a special instinct of the Holy Ghost which influenced both the superior and the subject.

XV.—Is THE PROMISE TO ENTER THE SOCIETY WHICH IS MADE BY THE APPROVED SCHOLASTICS, WHEN THEY MAKE THE THREE SUBSTANTIAL VOWS, A TRUE VOW BEFITTING THEIR STATE?

In the incorporation of Approved Scholastics, after the religious has made the three vows he adds—And I promise that I will enter the same Society, perpetually to live therein, understanding all things according to the Constitutions of the Society.

This promise is a true and proper vow, and is distinct from the three vows which precede it. Although it is expressed by the word *promise*, while they are expressed by the word *vow*, yet this word *promise* is coupled with *to the Divine Majesty*, and hence the promise is a true vow; for what is a vow save a promise made to God?

This vow is distinct from the three preceding vows, for something different is promised by it. Although it is the same Society *in* which these vows are taken, and entrance *into* which is promised, yet in the two clauses the word *Society* is used in a different sense. It means, in the case of the three vows, the body of the Society taken as a whole and absolutely, while in the case of the promise, entrance is understood as to be made into an inner part or farther grade of the same Society; in the same way as if one, standing inside a house but in its outer chambers, should promise both to remain in that house, and to enter farther in, there would be two distinct promises.

Although the grade of a Scholastic in the Society constitutes a true religious, yet any farther or higher grade is absolutely better and more perfect; otherwise a vow could not rightly be made to pass from the one to the other, and the promise itself would not be a true vow as not concerning a *better* good.

Although this promise is not properly a vow of religion, since it already supposes the religious state, yet it is a vow of greater perfection within the same state. The Scholastics of the Society are so constituted in the religious state by the three substantial vows that they are not constituted in the final term of that state; and so, although they are outside the condition of novices, they are not wholly beyond probation and trial. Hence they vow to pass to a farther grade, because they are tending towards that grade, and it is most necessary for the Society that they should attain it, since the welfare of the Society would not be sufficiently provided for if they, desiring to remain in the state which they had embraced, would proceed no further; and this strictly speaking they might do without sin, unless they had specially promised to proceed. Although a precept of obedience might suffice to oblige them to proceed to a farther grade, supposing this to be matter of obedience, yet the obligation is induced in an easier and better manner by their own promise, voluntarily made to God in their entrance on their state, as it is made in the Society.

XVI. — WHAT EFFECTS DOES THIS PROMISE OF SCHOLASTICS TO ENTER THE SOCIETY PRODUCE?

This vow does not oblige in any way to *procure* the entrance which is promised, or to any diligence for that end, but only to accept the entrance when it is enjoined. Herein the vow differs from a vow to enter religion, or to pass to a stricter Order, for here there is one Order, one head, one Rule, and as the vow concerns a better good, supposing the institution and providence of the Order, it is better to leave this care and solicitude to superiors, and to be prepared to execute what they may enjoin, than to be solicitous about one's grade and state, and to either petition for or procure it. Hence in the Constitutions this is counselled as better adapted for the preservation of humility, obedience and internal peace, which might be in great measure hindered if leave to petition or procure were given, and much more if this formed any part of the obligation of the vow.

Looking to greater perfection in virtue of the Rule and Institute, the indifference of an Approved Scholastic should extend even to his being admitted only to the grade of a Formed Temporal Coadjutor; for both the Rule and perfection of obedience demand that one should accept an inferior ministry, in place of a higher or more honourable ministry; and therefore at least in virtue of the Rule and of perfection one would be bound to accept such a grade.

No change can be made from the grade of the Professed to that of Coadjutors, for this would not be to enter farther, but to go back; and the four solemn vows, once made, cannot be diminished or made into simple vows. A spiritual coadjutor, on the other hand, can be admitted to solemn profession, and although this is rarely done yet it is done, and it is not prohibited by any law of the Society, and it may even sometimes be expedient; since in the course of time either the religious himself may make greater progress in learning and spirit, or his talent and capacities may become better known, and he may be judged useful to the Society in its highest grade; and in such a case he will be bound to accept the grade of the Professed.

# CHAPTER XX.

*THE SCHOLASTICS OF THE SOCIETY, AND THEIR STUDIES: AND THE PUBLIC SCHOOLS OF THE SOCIETY FOR EXTERNS.*

### I.—Is a religious state in the Society rightly destined for study?

It was an error of some, and among others of Wicliff, that the study of letters is foreign to the religious state. The reasons alleged were that studies take up time, and distract the mind from the proper duties of religious; that religious perfection does not number among its goods those things which stand midway between vice and virtue, since it does not consider it enough for a thing not to be evil, unless it also makes a man good and better; because religion flies from glory, and does not display but exercises virtue, while science puffs up, and ministers to ostentation rather than to virtue.

Nevertheless it is certain that the study at least of Sacred Letters is most befitting to the religious state. This is a truth of faith, which St. Thomas confirms from the words of the Psalm,—" Teach me goodness and discipline and science," from which it appears that not only goodness but also science belongs to the perfection of the soul. But if science is useful, it is not to be looked for from God by way of infusion, for that would be superstitious; neither is it to be sought solely by one's own genius and labour, for that would be presumptuous and full of peril; and therefore it is most fitting that a religious should at an opportune time give himself to study and learning.

Study, especially of Sacred Letters, is necessary in order to the perfection both of the active and of the contemplative life, and therefore it is most fitting for the religious state. Science is in itself a perfection which is in the greatest accordance with the nature of man, and it can therefore for even the sake of its own perfection be rightly desired. To desire a perfection which belongs to and is an adornment of nature, is in itself good; that is to say, it is good apart from any bad end, or other accidental moral peril, or impediment to necessary good, and these are extrinsic, and can easily be avoided in the religious state. If this is true of science generally, much more is it true of the science of God and of the things which belong to God, since the bliss of man consists in this knowledge, or chiefly depends on it, as Jesus said —"This is life eternal that they should *know* Thee, the only true God."

Contemplation consists in consideration of divine truth, and this cannot be acquired by natural means and without risk of error, without previous reading and study; and therefore, all the Fathers who treat of the contemplative life teach that, before all things else, assiduous reading and study is necessary for that life, of which they also reckon these to be parts.

In that religious state the end of which is not only to contemplate divine things, but also to communicate to others what has been contemplated, it is necessary to possess no ordinary science, but a perfect science of all things which belong to faith and morals; and therefore it is necessary that the religious should give themselves to the perfect acquirement of such knowledge in their religious state. No one can teach others if he himself is ignorant, for how could he enlighten minds which are in darkness, or confute heretics, or give a reason of the faith that is in him, or solve the moral difficulties which occur, and satisfy all, unless he has been sufficiently instructed in theological doctrine both positive and scholastic, speculative and moral? St. Paul therefore exhorts Timothy to give heed to *reading*, as well as to exhortation and doctrine; and by reading is to be understood every study of sacred doctrine which is necessary in order to any ecclesiastical or religious function, or which is adapted for the admonition or instruction of men in all things which pertain to their faith and morals. In this way only and not otherwise could a minister of the Gospel fulfil in every matter the precept of the Apostle to Titus —" Speak the things which become sound doctrine."

All the members of the Society cannot be at their reception men who are advanced and already sufficiently instructed to be able to exhort and teach others; and the necessary doctrine or science is not to be sought or expected from God by way of miracle, for such signs and extraordinary works are not now necessary in the Church; the necessary learning must therefore be acquired by means of labour and industry with the aid of divine grace. St. Jerome says—Learn that you may be able to teach, and offer to Christ a reasonable sacrifice, lest you be a soldier before you are a recruit, and a master before you are a disciple; and Innocent I.—It is wretched for him to be made a master who was never a disciple; and St. Chrysostom speaks of St. Paul as admonishing all in the person of Timothy, and asks,—If he who raised the dead gave such admonitions, what shall we miserable men say? If therefore Timothy required a teacher, what wonder that religious, and especially those who are to be ministers of the Gospel, should stand in need of teachers, study and learning?

Hence it is evident how excellent it is that young religious should give themselves to the study of Sacred Letters, since it is necessary for the purpose of every end at which the Order aims, and is in no way contrary to the perfection of the religious state. St. Thomas says that such youths are the best fitted for progress in learning, since they are so far separated from carnal affections and secular cares.

Most fittingly therefore has there been instituted in the Society this first grade of religious, of which the members give themselves to study. The grade of Scholastics is ordained with a view to the grade of the Professed, and its proximate and intrinsic end is to dispose and render the members of it capable and apt for the grade of the Professed. This disposition consists chiefly in two things, namely, in virtue and in learning. Instruction and exercise in virtue begin with entrance on the noviceship; while for further study and exercise of virtue the Second Probation is specially ordained.

Study is pursued in religion with such moderation

that proper and sufficient time is reserved for the higher works of religion; for all things have their time, and the state of religion so disposes and ordains all (hence the name of Order) that there should be no confusion of time. Neither is the time given to study spent without spiritual profit, since the whole of the study is a great service of God, both by reason of the end to which it is ordained, and by reason of the charity and obedience from which it proceeds. Again, study does not in itself distract the mind from thinking of God or of some good thing for the sake of God, but rather collects the mind, and is a means for the hindrance of evil thoughts, and consequently for the hindrance of the concupiscences of the flesh, and the other lower desires. Even if during the time of study the mind should be distracted from the actual thought or contemplation of God, this is simply because our mortal condition will not permit us to be always actually thinking of God, and next to the thought of Him nothing better can be imagined to think of than that which pertains to sacred learning. To think of other things for the sake of God is virtually to think of God Himself; and the knowledge of things in their own proper nature, when it is referred to the praise of the Creator, partakes of the divine light; and finally, the religious mind is never so absorbed in literary study, even at those times at which it gives itself thereto, that it does not frequently recur to God by renewal of the intention, by petition for aid and light, and by thanksgiving for understanding of the truth.

The study of letters, regarded by itself or as embraced for its own sake only, might be reckoned among inferior goods, and so be not greatly esteemed by religious; but regarded as it is an instrument of virtue and of actions which are ordained as means for the salvation of souls, it is to be reckoned among the greater goods, since it shares in the goodness of the end to which it is ordained. It is not undertaken by religious men for the sake of ostentation or vain reputation, and so it is in no way at variance with religious modesty; and if any contrary motions arise they are accidental, and can be conquered with the aid of the divine grace. Neither is it always reprehensible in a religious occasionally to do somewhat for the display of his erudition and progress in letters, for this does not end in mere display to gain only the opinion of others, which would be vain ostentation, but is referred to the end of the salvation of souls. St. Augustine says,—To us our life is necessary, to others our fame; and again,—Thy conscience to thyself, thy fame to thy neighbour. St. Paul also says to Timothy,—Meditate on these things, be wholly in these things, *that thy proficiency may be manifest to all;* attend to thyself and to doctrine, be earnest in them, for in doing this thou shalt both save thyself and *them that hear thee* (1 Tim. iv. 15, 16). St. Chrysostom likewise would have our progress, not only in rectitude and sanctity of life, but also in sincerity and fulness of doctrine, made manifest to all.

The study of letters is therefore and rightly appointed as the proper function, and therefore as the proximate end of this first grade in the Society.

## II.—Is the study of, and skill in the Classics, in Languages and in Liberal Arts becoming to Religious of the Society?

The enemies of religion in the time of St. Thomas greatly condemned the study by religious of inferior arts, and said that it belonged to the preachers of Antichrist rather than to the preachers of Christ. Nevertheless it is clear and certain that erudition in languages and the liberal arts is most necessary for labourers in the Gospel, and is not at variance with the religious state. It is right therefore that the Scholastics of the Society should be diligently instructed in these, before they give themselves to sacred learning in Scholastic Theology, or to the interpretation and understanding of the Sacred Scriptures.

St. Clement exhorts the religious, whom he calls in a special manner his disciples or fellow-disciples, first to poverty and obedience, and then to understanding of the Scriptures, which he says are to be interpreted not in a private sense, but according to the tradition of the Fathers, and in agreement with other passages of the same Scriptures; and he adds that somewhat of the common erudition and the liberal studies which were pursued in boyhood may contribute towards the maintenance of true doctrine. Hence also Eugenius ordained that in all bishoprics there should be appointed Masters and Doctors to teach assiduously letters and the liberal arts; and he gives the reason,—because in these divine things are manifested, and the commandments are elucidated. St. Paul did not disdain to make use of profane authors, quoting to the Athenians a saying of their own poets,—"For we also are his offspring" (Acts xvii. 28); and in his Epistle to Titus, Bishop of Crete, he adduces the testimony of one of their own prophets,—"The Cretans are always liars" (i. 12). St. Jerome speaks of his own employment of secular wisdom as a means in order to beauty of language and eloquence of speech; and he confirms it by the examples of Origen, Methodius, Quadratus, Aristides and many others both Greeks and Latins, and he says of them,—You know not which first to admire in them, their worldly erudition or their knowledge of the Scriptures. St. Augustine also insists on the necessity of these arts for the understanding of the Scriptures, and sums up that three are necessary—an understanding of *signs*, a knowledge of *things*, and the method of *solving doubts* and *difficulties*. To the first, he says, a knowledge of languages contributes; to the second, philosophy and mathematics lend aid; while to the third dialectics supply method and great light. Besides these three which are necessary in order to understanding, he requires eloquence, not as absolutely necessary, but as very useful in order to proposition; all four being employed of course with due moderation. Clement of Alexandria also speaks of the Greek philosophy, and other branches of learning, and liberal arts, and says that one ought to take from each of them that which contributes towards the truth. He adduces the example of Abraham, who was skilled in astrology and astronomy, and made excellent use of them in order to knowledge of the truth; and of Moses who, as St. Stephen declared, "was instructed in all the wisdom of the Egyptians," and this not without a special providence of God, in order that he might confute those by whom he had been instructed.

That human erudition, acquired with due intention and moderation, which is evidently so very useful and morally necessary for a preacher of the Gospel, is not at variance with the religious state is evidenced by the cases of St. Jerome and St. Augustine, who were both of them religious, and who everywhere display the highest erudition in human learning. We may say the same of St. Athanasius, St. Basil, St. Gregory Nazianzen, and many others. Reason also confirms this, since such learning is sought after as a means towards the highest end, and an end which belongs to the most perfect religious state. A sufficient knowledge at least of the Latin language is necessary, as well as mediocrity at any rate in dialectics and philosophy, for without these one could not save rashly and without the necessary skill approach to Theology. To acquire the latter with exactness, a knowledge of languages, and proficiency in all the liberal arts, and especially an exact comprehension of dialectics, philosophy and metaphysics is most useful. Hence Clement V. among other ordinances for the improvement of the Divine worship, ordained that in each of the monasteries, the resources of which would admit of it, there should be maintained an able master, who should diligently instruct the monks in "primitive" sciences, meaning thereby those which are the preambles to Theology. Trithemius in his book of the illustrious men of the Order of St. Benedict, relates that it was a most ancient custom of that Order to instruct the younger brethren in the various branches of Scholastic learning, such as rhetoric, dialectics, arithmetic, philosophy and the like, so that being sufficiently instructed in these they might be introduced to the study of the Sacred Scriptures. If this was an approved custom in monastic Orders, much more must it be commendable in those Orders which have been instituted for spiritual ministries to their neighbours, as St. Thomas rightly concludes.

In the Society, therefore, it is manifest that such instruction is absolutely necessary. This is evident from the end of the Society, for among all the Orders which are ordained for the salvation of their neighbours, the Society without doubt excels in its mode and principal intention of seeking the salvation of souls, to which end it undertakes the three principal functions,—of propagating the Church among infidels and the most remote nations,—of defending it against heretics and labouring for their conversion,—and of exhorting and teaching catholics, and co-operating to their sanctification and perfection. Hence it requires proficiency in languages and in the whole of philosophy and metaphysics, not only in order to an understanding of Theology and the Sacred Scriptures, but also in order that in other ways it may use this proficiency for the service of the faith. As the Holy Ghost bestowed upon the first preachers of the Gospel the gift of tongues in order that they might sow the faith in divers nations, so since these signs ceased an Order which shares their office must with all due diligence and industry prepare itself to be a fit instrument therefor, and to become, as far as may be, universal. Hence the necessity for a knowledge of languages: and apart from miracle or an extraordinary providence of God, a preacher of the Gospel could not with force and efficacy of reasons confute errors which are contrary to the natural light, if he were not accurately instructed and well versed in the various branches of philosophical learning.

Although it would be difficult or morally impossible that all these studies should in their perfection be united with theological learning in the individual members of the Society, yet eminence and excellence in all of them may be and is to be procured in the whole body of the Society. This may be easily done if in each branch of learning there are one or more who give themselves to special study for a longer time and with greater diligence.

### III.—The Method of Study in the Society.

St. Bernard expounding the words of St. Paul to the Corinthians,—"If any man think that he knoweth anything, he does not yet know how he ought to know" (1 Cor. viii. 2) says—The usefulness and fruit of knowledge is in the mode of knowing; and the mode of knowing is that you should know in what order, with what study, and for what end you ought to know. To these three points St. Ignatius has paid most diligent attention. As regards order, he commands that primarily and principally a due order should be observed between the study of virtue and the study of learning. In the Constitutions he says that, after a fitting foundation of self-abnegation and progress in necessary virtues appears to have been laid in those who have been admitted to probation, the edifice of learning is to be taken in hand. He prescribes also the order in which the various branches of learning are to be pursued, namely, that first there is to be a solid foundation in the Latin language, before the study of the liberal arts; and in these before the study of Scholastic Theology; and in it before the study of Positive Theology; and that the Sacred Scriptures may be studied either at the same time, or afterwards.

By Positive Theology he means the reading of the Holy Fathers, the Councils, the Decrees of the Church, and Ecclesiastical History. To all these the perfect theologian should give himself with the greatest diligence, but this after he has laid a solid foundation in Scholastic Theology. There may also be comprehended under Positive learning all the erudition which is necessary for preaching to the people. Those greatly err who, before they have made great progress in Scholastic Theology, distract themselves with that kind of study, since they confuse all things, and do not learn anything with solid foundation, while they study many things not without peril of error. Some study of the Scriptures in order to a literal understanding of them is necessary for Scholastic learning itself, and therefore certain principles or some elements of such study must accompany Scholastic Theology. It is probably for this reason that St. Ignatius distinguishes the understanding of the Sacred Scriptures from Positive Theology, under which it is commonly comprehended.

As regards the second point, St. Bernard asks—With what study? and answers that that is to be studied the more ardently which more vehemently excites to love. He refers to mystical science, which is in great part practical, and is ordained towards love; but his words may be applied also to the speculative arts and sciences of which we speak. These are ordained, so far as the learner is concerned, towards Divine love, as their end; and therefore the more nearly they approach, and the more they move towards Divine love, with the greater affection and study are they to be embraced and pursued.

But although, as regards the *affection* of the learner, this is true, yet as regards the *effect*, and application of labour, every branch of learning is to be pursued with the greatest study, and that in proportion as the difficulty and arduousness of it demands. The proximate measure of study is not love, but the arduousness and necessity of the work. Hence St. Ignatius says generally of all these studies, that the religious should resolve seriously and constantly to apply their minds to study, and should persuade themselves that they will do nothing more well-pleasing to God in the Colleges than with due intention to expend themselves diligently on their studies. He says, Let the Scholastics be assiduous in the hearing of lectures, and in diligently preparing for them, and, after they have heard them, in repeating them, asking explanations of those things which they have not understood, and noting other things as may be necessary. He lays it down as fundamental that this literary labour requires *the whole man*, and he declares that, if it is done with due intention, it is not less but more pleasing to God than any other labour whatsoever, during the time of studies. He adds that the labour of study undertaken from obedience and charity is a work of great merit, and that therefore the fruit of it is not lost, even if it should never arrive at the effect aimed at, as for instance, by reason of a premature death.

As regards the third point, or requisite for studying rightly, St. Bernard asks,—For what end? and answers, —Not for vain glory or curiosity, or the like, but only for the edification of oneself, and of one's neighbour. For there are some who desire to know with this end only that they may know, and this is a *base curiosity*; and some who desire to know that they may themselves be known, and this is a *base vanity*, and they cannot escape the grinning satirist (Persius) who sings of such men,—To know is nothing unless another know that you know; and some who desire to know that they may sell their knowledge for money or for honours, and this is a *base quest of gain*; but there are some also who desire to know that they may edify, and this is *charity*; and some likewise who desire to know that they may be edified, and this is *prudence*. Of all these it is only the last two who abuse not knowledge, those namely who desire to understand in order that they may do well.

All these words apply most excellently to our present subject, and to begin with the last, the Society seeks learning chiefly for this, that it may do well, that is to say, that it may benefit first itself, and then its neighbours. It procures its own perfection primarily, and then the perfection of its neighbours. Although in this labour of learning, we may say that for the most part the principal end or aim of the Society is the benefit of its neighbours, since in order to its own perfection a lesser erudition, and a smaller number of languages and sciences would suffice, nevertheless the end of its own perfection is never to be excluded even from the labour of study; not only because, since it is meritorious, it always more and more sanctifies the soul, but also because it in itself more and more enlightens a man with regard to the knowledge of God and that moral perfection which is always and principally to be aimed at.

But although this is the general end to be kept in view in such studies, yet in every branch of learning its proximate and peculiar end is to be observed, in order that, in accordance therewith, the measure and mode of its study may be determined. The proximate end also for which any particular study is undertaken should be considered, for he who is to employ philosophy as a proximate instrument for the conversion of infidels, must study it in a far different manner from that in which he studies it who enters on it only as it is a disposition for Theology.

The same idea of the proximate end it is also most necessary to keep in view with regard to the reading of books. Every one is to read those books which are useful or suitable for the office or end set specially before him; otherwise reading might rather be for the satisfaction of curiosity than from a motive of religion. For some the reading of pagan or infidel books will be necessary, in order that they may confute their errors and answer their arguments; while for others such reading would be useless or harmful. Similarly, for certain persons it will be a religious work for them to give themselves, for instance, to the study of astrology, while in the case of others it would be useless and idle. St. Thomas says that to study magic is good in order to refute it; but that if the person is so circumstanced that this knowledge does not pertain to him the desire of it will be inordinate.

From a consideration of these three ends in the pursuit of science we gather what St. Bernard condemns. The first end is not evil in itself, but in a religious it is inordinate by reason of his state and condition. Since science is naturally desired by the highest inclination in man, to seek it is in itself good; for, as it relates to the adornment and perfection of the mind, to seek science for its own sake is not in itself evil, even if thereby nothing else should be aimed at save knowledge of natural truth. But in a religious man this will be reprehensible, and for two reasons; first, because by reason of his state he is bound to be occupied in those things chiefly which contribute towards perfection, and science by itself contributes nothing; secondly, because those who with this intention only immerse themselves in studies, seek, as a rule, not those studies which are most useful, but those which are most pleasurable. Rightly therefore may such study be called in a religious man, a base curiosity; for although there may not perhaps be always sin in an individual case, it will always be very imperfect, and open to great and frequent peril of sin.

The second end is in itself and intrinsically evil, and although by reason of its object the malice is not mortal, yet it may easily be the occasion of many grievous sins, such as ambition and vain glory, as St. Thomas observes. From this end there chiefly springs a desire to display singular knowledge, and consequently to give utterance to novelties, which are most of all to be avoided in theology. Novelty, says St. Bernard, which presumes at variance with the usage of the Church, is the mother of rashness, the sister of superstition, and the daughter of levity.

The third end condemned by St. Bernard should be very foreign to Scholastics of the Society. Although to seek science for the sake of gain, whether in money or in honour, is not in itself intrinsically evil, it is nevertheless inordinate in the Society, since it is contrary to the Rule and Institute. No one of Ours is permitted to receive any stipend or temporal gain for his ministries, and by the Institute the way is closed to honours and dignities through literary excellence. Degrees in letters are permitted, but only in so far as they are necessary for the sake of others, to the greater glory of God, and fruit of souls. A certificate of knowledge, and the honour which flows from it, is sometimes necessary in order that the knowledge itself should be useful to others, for, as the wise man says,—Wisdom which is hidden, and a treasure which is unseen, what use is in them? Although therefore one should not learn in order to be esteemed wise, it is nevertheless not wrong in itself to display the learning which has been acquired, and to desire to have a good reputation for learning, not resting this desire in fame or honour, which would be vain, but in order to be useful to others. Hence Rabanus, treating of the parable of the talents, says that those are blamable who from an immoderate humility conceal their learning, and do not use it for the benefit of their neighbours. For this end, therefore, to display perfection of learning by means of Public Acts, and to accept the insignia of the same or honours arising therefrom, is not wrong, nor is it contrary to due order or intention. St. Thomas says that a man may laudably seek his own glory for the advantage of others, even as Christ said,—" Let your light so shine before men, that they may see your good works;" and he proves that religious may lawfully receive Degrees, even in secular Universities. He explains the words of our Lord— "Be not called Rabbi," to mean neither a precept nor a counsel not to exercise the office of a Doctor or a Master, for this would be contrary to the office which Christ Himself and His Apostles exercised, and for which there is promised a special crown in Heaven; and he proves that by these words the title or other insignia of Doctor or Master are not forbidden, for if the office is not evil neither will its title be evil, nor the insignia of it, which are ordained not in order to elation but for the manifestation of authority. Hence St. Paul, in both of his Epistles to Timothy, calls himself a Doctor and a Master. St. Thomas concludes that what Christ forbids is the ambition and elation which is in the desire of those degrees or titles solely for the sake of one's own honour or reputation.

As regards the means which are provided in the

Society towards progress in learning, they are various; and of them some are corporal and others spiritual; and of the spiritual some belong to the understanding and others to the will; some are divine, and others human; some are positive, and others privative, or such as may remove hindrances to progress.

Among the corporal means those may be called *positive*, which are necessary for the support of the Scholastics, who in the Colleges have all that is necessary for their fitting sustenance, in the way of food and clothing, and also what is needful for purposes of study, so that they are free from all care and solicitude on this head. The *privative* means are those which remove or prevent corporal hindrances to study. It is ordained in the Constitutions that special care is to be taken that the Scholastics should not study at times prejudicial to health, that they should have as much time for sleep as is necessary, and that they should observe moderation in mental labours, so that they should be able to persevere longer both in study, and in the fruit of study, the communication of their learning for the glory of God. It is also to this end provided that they should be freed from the hindrances of external occupations and labours, both in domestic duties and other ministries, that they may have more time to give to study.

Among spiritual means, the principal and more divine are those which preserve the soul in purity and peace, and draw down aid and light from God; for the knowledge which is chiefly aimed at by means of those studies, is supernatural, and greatly depends on the aid of divine grace. St. Athanasius says that without a pure mind, and imitation of the saints no one will comprehend the words of the saints; and St. Augustine says that study should begin from faith, and should strive by good living to arrive at that at which it aims; and again,—It is faith which first subjugates the soul to God, and then by observance of the precepts of right living our hope is confirmed and charity is nourished, and then that begins to shine forth which before was only believed.

But since even in exercise of piety there may sometimes be excess which may hinder progress in letters, St. Ignatius has provided a remedy, by counselling due moderation, and by enjoining on superiors great care and vigilance with regard to this matter. He says that as it has to be guarded against, that in the fervour of study love of solid virtues and of the religious life should not grow cold, so also during the time of study much place is not to be given to mortifications and prolix prayers and meditations.

Individual selection is specially committed and commended to superiors and rectors, so that every one may be set to that for which his nature and talent is prudently considered to be sufficiently adapted. Further, because it may sometimes seem hard and difficult to certain persons to apply themselves to this or to that science, which is at variance perhaps with their own inclination or will, those who are to be Approved Scholastics in the Society are, at the outset, in the Examen before their entrance, interrogated whether they are willing to allow themselves to be led with regard to what they ought to study and the method and time of study, as it shall seem good to their superiors.

On superiors there is enjoined solicitude, vigilance and care that both teachers and Scholastics should fulfil their respective functions with all diligence, and that nothing should be wanting to them which is necessary as a means in order to this end.

It may therefore not unreasonably be hoped that the Scholastics of the Society should become conspicuous for learning, if they use the means which are lawful to them in accordance with their Institute, and which are without doubt well-pleasing to God. They are bound also by no slight obligation strenuously to labour in their studies, both because they are supported from ecclesiastical goods for the sake of study, and because study is for the time being their special function and their own appropriate Divine service, to which they have been deputed by God Himself through their pastors. As Aristotle says,—A little error in the beginning is a great one in the end ; and so he who is negligent in his studies will afterwards be useless as an instrument for the conversion or cure of souls and, what is still more grievous, will frequently expose himself to peril of error.

IV.—DOES IT BECOME RELIGIOUS OF THE SOCIETY TO HAVE PUBLIC SCHOOLS AND UNIVERSITIES, AND TO TEACH IN THEM ?

By Public Schools, we mean those which are intended not only for the instruction of the religious of the Society, but for the instruction of all whether laymen, seculars, or religious of any other Order. These Schools are styled Universities when they are endowed with

Pontifical and Royal privileges, so that the students may proceed in them to literary degrees.

Such Schools and Universities have been condemned by heretics, as for instance, by the Emperor Licinius, as public pests ; and Julian the Apostate, who recognized their efficacy, forbade the Galileans, as he called Christians, to learn poetry, rhetoric or philosophy, endeavouring by this means with a diabolical malice to uproot religion, so that the Holy Fathers accounted his persecution more bitter than that of the tyrants who by force and torments compelled men to deny the faith. Moved by the same spirit, Wicliff declared Universities, Schools, Colleges, graduations and masterships instituted by the Pope and bishops to have been introduced by a vain gentilism, and to profit the Church no more than does the devil. Luther afterwards embraced the same error, and called the Christian Schools Sodoms and Gomorrhas, and sinks of all wickednesses.

This error is not only contrary to faith and the universal consent and tradition of the Church, but also contrary to all natural reason and the evidence of experience.

Schools and Universities are necessary not only for the ecclesiastical, but also for the civil community and its welfare, and therefore in all well-ordered kingdoms and provinces they have flourished, as for instance, at Rome and Paris, at Oxford in England, Salamanca in Spain, and Coimbra in Portugal.

The function of teaching in Public Schools and Universities may be excellently adapted to the religious state ; and it has been undertaken by the Society lawfully and to the great advantage of the Church. In proof of this it is sufficient to cite the approbations by various Pontiffs of the Colleges and Universities of the Society, such as those of Paul III. Julius III. Pius V. and Gregory XIII. According to the common Pontifical Law, only Civil Law and Medicine are excluded from the number of subjects which may be becomingly taught by religious men; and these are also prohibited by the Constitutions of the Society from being taught in its Universities, at least by the Society itself. To teach Canon Law, or to study it, or to take degrees in it is not forbidden to religious by common law; and in the Constitutions it is comprehended under Positive Theology which the professors of the Society may teach, so far as it aids to the end of the salvation of souls. The only restriction is with regard to that part of it which refers to litigation, for this, though not forbidden to secular clerics, since it is not profane but ecclesiastical and necessary for ecclesiastical government, is nevertheless alien to the religious state, to which all forensic causes, even those which are ecclesiastical, should be foreign.

The lawfulness of religious publicly teaching is confirmed by the practice of religious men, notably in the School of Alexandria, in which there was a continuous succession of such teachers. The argument moreover is the same whether the doctrine is delivered by word of mouth or by writing, and certainly the bulk of theological writing, whether that of the Fathers or that of the Scholastic Doctors, has been the fruit of the labours of religious men. St. Athanasius, St. Gregory Nazianzen, St. Basil and many other Greeks were religious and monks; among the Latins, St. Augustine, St. Jerome and others were religious; and, among the Schoolmen, St. Thomas and St. Buonaventure. Many Universities owed their foundation to the efforts and erudition of religious men, and among others the University of Paris, which was founded by monks.

Hence a religious Order might well be instituted for the purpose of publicly teaching any branches of learning whatsoever the teaching of which should be becoming to the religious state. Whatever there is in this ministry is holy in itself and adapted to foster charity in oneself and towards one's neighbours. Before teaching there is required, on the part of the teacher, sacred reading and assiduous meditation on Divine things, and on other things which conduce to an understanding of Divine things. This is not only good, but belongs to the Contemplative life. Again, the act of teaching, especially when it is done with religious intention, has in it many excellences and advantages. It is, in the first place, useful to one's neighbour, who is taught and enlightened, especially with regard to good morals and the life eternal; and so it is of its very nature a spiritual act of mercy, and an act of charity, both to him to whom the benefit is done, and to God for the sake of Whom it is done. It is also an act of religion, because it is done for the service of God and from zeal for souls, than which no sacrifice can be more well-pleasing to God.

The religious state is also itself in a special manner adapted for the office of teaching, both because religious are free from the cares and solicitudes of the world, and are therefore better disposed for reading and study and consequently for teaching; and also because teaching is then more fruitful to disciples when it is conjoined with good morals, and a religious in virtue of his state professes not only good but also perfect morals, observing not only the precepts but also the counsels.

It may also be rightly instituted in a religious Order, as for instance in the Society, that it should have its own Universities, under its own care and government and teaching; this being of course always done in a proper manner, with due order, and not by its own but by Pontifical authority. The whole work is one of piety and public beneficence, and of itself has in it nothing unbecoming or foreign to the religious state, and any inconveniences which may occur are purely accidental, and the religious state greatly serves to their avoidance; while any results of human frailty are counterbalanced by the abundance of fruit. "They that explain Me (that is, true wisdom) shall have life everlasting" (Eccles. xxiv. 31) and in the Book of Daniel it is written,—"They that are learned shall shine as the brightness of the firmament; and they that instruct many to justice, as stars for all eternity" (xii. 3). These words shew of how great merit and esteem it is before God to teach others in order to salvation; and they may be specially applied to the fruit of Universities.

Further, the more closely Universities are connected with a well-instituted religious Order the more will their erudition be to salvation. St. Thomas argues that as a religious Order may be instituted to defend the Church by corporal warfare, much more may an Order be instituted to defend her with her own proper arms, which, as St. Paul says, are spiritual rather than corporal, and which in great part consist in learning. As moreover it belongs to a military Order not only that the members of it should severally fight, but also that they should lead, assemble and direct armies, so also it belongs to a spiritually military Order to do in like manner. To this end Universities are instituted, in which, and by means of general learning, public war is waged against the devil, and many warriors and leaders are trained who may in other places and in various ways fight against him. Again just as a religious Order may be instituted for the care of the sick, not only by the private exertions of individuals, but also by the erection of public Hospitals, the whole charge of which is undertaken by the religious, so similarly may religious have charge of institutions for the exercise of spiritual mercy, such as public Schools and Universities.

Besides its own Universities and Colleges, in which the Society publicly teaches both its own members and externs, the Society is not in virtue of its Institute forbidden to exercise the same ministry in general Universities, should this be offered to it, provided the poverty which it professes may be observed, and all occasion of ambition and secular business be removed.

It was declared by the First General Congregation that public Chairs in Universities or elsewhere, the appointment to which depends on votes or competition, should not be allowed; but that if these should be spontaneously offered by the Universities or their Rectors, and if the teaching should be gratuitous, they might be accepted on consulting the General.

For the same reason it is conformable to the Institute of the Society that sometimes certain persons should be promoted to the Degree of Master or Doctor, everything being always observed to avoid damage to poverty and humility, as for instance the prohibition to Doctors of Ours of places reserved according to seniority or other prerogatives. Professors of Ours may sometimes receive degrees in Universities which do not belong to Ours, since this is not at variance with the religious state, or with the Institute of the Society, and it may be sometimes necessary in order to the exercise of their ministry with profit. In those Universities it is necessary to follow their order and custom with regard to places, because it is not in our power to change it, since they are not subject to our jurisdiction, and also because in a matter which is otherwise and in itself indifferent, and harmless to religion, it becomes a member to conform to the custom of the whole body.

Another condition is that Ours should not incur expenses which do not become poor men, in the obtaining of such Degrees. A Doctor of the Society should also neither hope for nor receive any temporal emolument or stipend by reason of his Degree; and a religious of the Society cannot procure a Degree, for that could not be permitted without great damage to humility. To preserve humility it is also a custom in the Society that Degrees should not be conferred as honours or personal rewards, but only as the necessities of its ministries may demand, and that Degrees should not be multiplied amongst Ours more than these require.

To the Mendicants, in virtue of their institution and

state as approved by the Apostolic See, the office of lecturing and teaching belongs, *not by ordinary*, but by *delegated* power. This delegation however is not personal, but is to the whole Order; and it proceeds not from a private bishop, but from the Universal Pontiff, and as it were from law, by reason of the Approbation and Privileges of the Order. It therefore belongs to the Order in virtue of its state and Institute.

The religious state never hindered Clerks Regular from teaching, as it at one time hindered monks except by authority of the bishop; and since the institution of the Mendicants, many even of the monastic Orders share in the power or delegation to teach.

V. — HAS THE SOCIETY FITTINGLY UNDERTAKEN THE EDUCATION OF BOYS?

The whole of the learning which is imparted by Universities may be divided into three parts, — the lowest, the intermediate and the highest. In the highest division there is Sacred Learning and what intrinsically belongs thereto, such as cases of conscience; and this is imparted not to boys, but to adults. In the intermediate part there is the curriculum of Arts, which embraces Mathematics, and to a certain extent Ethics; and this also does not belong to boys, for it demands a sufficient development of the faculties and genius, and the perfect use of reason, and it has also a great affinity to Theology. The learning which belongs to boys is that of languages, beginning from the first elements of grammar up to perfect eloquence, along with the aids and ornaments of other languages, especially of Greek; and excepting only Hebrew, the study of which belongs rather to adults.

We can, says Cicero, do no greater or better service to the commonwealth than to teach and instruct youth; and Diogenes Laertius says that the education of the young is the foundation of the whole commonwealth.

So far as the young are concerned, it is most expedient that they should be instructed by religious, and that as regards both their progress in learning, and their life and morals; for both depend in great measure on the qualities and gifts of their masters. The first depends chiefly on the master's learning and erudition, and so far it little matters whether he is a religious or a secular, a good or a wicked man, since a secular who is also a wicked man can excel in erudition and learning. Nevertheless, since the progress of a disciple depends not only on the knowledge of his master in itself, but on that knowledge as applied to the teaching of the disciple, that is to say, on the master's care and solicitude entirely and perfectly to fulfil his office, not for gain or ostentation, but for the advantage of his disciple, the life and good conscience of the master has much to do with even the literary progress of the disciple. For the same reason the religious state in a master can of itself contribute much towards the better instruction of his disciples, for in virtue of their state religious ought to be more diligent and faithful in the fulfilment of their office, and they are also likely to be more honest and independent if they receive no stipend from those whom they instruct. Since their office is undertaken from a motive of charity they will also take care to profit all and every one, according to the capacities of each; and since their lives are more free than are those of seculars from solicitude and worldly cares, they can the better give themselves to their work, besides imploring the Divine aid for themselves and for their scholars.

Of still greater moment is progress in morals which are most easily imprinted in those tender years, and to this progress the religious life of a teacher greatly contributes. First, there is the example of the religious, and this is of the greatest efficacy, for as is the master so are the disciples, especially at that age when they can hardly discern between good and evil, and the conduct of the master, if it is bad, is to the disciple a tacit leave, or rather an inducement to follow him. Secondly, there is the intention, and the industry which is begotten of it; for a religious teacher aims more at the good education of his pupil in morals than at his progress in learning, and therefore strives diligently to prevent whatever might teach him bad morals, whether in the books which he reads or in his companionships or otherwise, and omits nothing which may tend to train him in good principles.

The Sacred Canons which frequently prescribe that in every Church there should be a master to instruct boys in grammar and the lower branches of learning, at the same time exhort that with great care there should be chosen for this office one who is likely to profit his scholars by his life and morals.

But further, that religious should teach boys is expedient not only for the latter, but for the religious themselves. The Society has been blamed for giving itself to this ministry, on the ground that it is a ministry which is mean and unbecoming religious men, and which is also hurtful to them, both by reason of the distraction and disquiet which a multitude of boys must necessarily occasion; and because of the labour and occupation hindering not only their own spiritual progress, but also ministries which are of greater moment, and which might bring forth greater fruit to the Church; and because of the many perils which surround this ministry. There is also brought forward the example of other religious Orders, none of which occupy themselves in this ministry for the benefit of seculars, and it is argued that to depart from their footsteps and introduce a novelty in a matter so grave, is not laudable.

Nevertheless, this ministry is not a novelty and it is not foreign to the religious state, and looking to the necessities of the times it is most conformable with the end and institution of the Society. From ancient history and the Fathers it is evident that the education of boys was undertaken by religious men, as a work which was both pious and very useful to the Church, and how can that be reckoned unbecoming which was undertaken and approved of by most grave and holy men? and why should it be considered a humble rather than an honourable ministry? It is on the contrary most becoming to the religious state; for otherwise it would not be becoming for religious to take care of the sick, to wash the feet of pilgrims or in charity to serve one another, as St. Paul exhorts. If for other even abject and laborious works of charity religious Orders are rightly instituted, why not for this which, although very laborious and not so honourable as are some other ministries, is nevertheless and without doubt most serviceable to the Church? It is itself so useful and necessary to the Church that it ought not to be set aside even if it should seem in a measure to stand in the way of greater ministries. Even if it appears small it is virtually great, since on it both the moral life of the Church and the higher branches of learning in great measure depend, so that to it may be fittingly applied the parable of the grain of mustard seed, which in size is of the smallest but virtually is great. Further, while for the higher sciences there are found many masters, both religious and secular, few are inclined to devote themselves to the education of children, and so a very great necessity of the Church is supplied by those who undertake it; and even if it should seem among men to be of lesser dignity, it may perchance be before God of greater merit. Moreover, although this work may hinder individuals from higher ministries, yet the whole body of the Society is not thereby hindered from these ministries, but is on the contrary aided, both as regards preparation of the pupils for higher subjects, and as regards the ministers themselves who ascend by degrees from lower to more perfect ministries. "The body," says St. Paul, "is not one member, but many. . . . And those that seem to be the more feeble members of the body are more necessary" (1 Cor. xii. 14, 22.)

This labour and solicitude cannot hinder the increase of substantial perfection, both because the work is one of the highest charity and being undertaken by obedience greatly increases and perfects charity itself, and also because, the whole Order being ordained for this amongst other functions, this function is not without a special providence and approbation of God; and therefore there is ground for hope that there will not be wanting a special aid from God for this function that it may be fulfilled with fruit to others, and without damage, nay with great profit to those who undertake it. Whatever peril, therefore, may accompany it, it can generally speaking without great difficulty be overcome by means of divine grace and the vigilance of superiors, and the other works of the religious life, and those especially which belong to the contemplative life. Such perils, moreover, are not in themselves connected with this ministry, but are very accidental and extrinsic, and one can scarcely imagine any human actions in which similar or greater perils may not be found.

In these times and in this Order (whatever may be the case as regards other times and other Orders), this means has proved very opportune for the Church, and it has been established not without a special providence of God; for all the reasons and circumstances which concern the constitution of the Society and its other ministries to its neighbours may be applied to this special ministry, and the experience which has approved the Institute no less approves and confirms this ministry. The fruit is incredible which has redounded from this ministry. In catholic provinces where the faith has been preserved intact, the morals not only of the young but of persons of all states and conditions have been reformed by this means, for from the ranks of the young who have been educated by the Society, many religious, and many excellent priests, and many just rulers of the commonwealth have sprung. When at a tender age they conceive the fear of God, and are accustomed to Divine things, they always, generally speaking, retain the odour of them, for, as the Wise Man says,—"A young man according to his way, even when he is old he will not depart from it" (Prov. xxii. 6). In regions infected with heresy, not only the young but also their parents have often by this means been preserved from heresy, and have sometimes been recalled from heresy to the faith. Heretical princes and other patrons of heresies have, in order to the dissemination and propagation of their errors, striven that the young should imbibe them from the very beginning and along with the first principles of learning; and in more modern times the Lutherans have written verses and elegant compositions against the Pontiff and the Catholic Church, in order that children reading them might drink in their spirit; and they have used the utmost diligence that the teachers of the young should be infected with their errors, and drawn towards themselves. It would therefore be absurd and scandalous if heretics were, for the upholding of their falsehood, to busy themselves in preoccupying the minds of the young, and the Church were to be found negligent in similar efforts for the truth and the salvation of souls. Hence God raised up St. Ignatius, and gave to him this mind and counsel, without the motive of the example of other religious Orders, and it has been approved by the authority of His Vicar, and by many manifestations of His grace. To these has been added the most weighty testimony of the Cardinals of the Congregation of the Council of Trent, who, declaring that masters instructed in grammar and music are to be sought to educate the boys in seminaries, add —and if Jesuits can be got, they are to be preferred to others.

So much had St. Ignatius at heart the education of the young that he thought it not unworthy of or foreign to his Institute to teach even reading and writing. But although this is, as he says, a work of charity and, being undertaken in order that from their earliest school days the young should know nothing save goodness and religion, a really great and religious service of God, yet by reason of our lack of numbers he would not have it undertaken save rarely, and for some grave cause and general necessity, lest the Society should be overburdened by the multiplicity of its occupations. Moreover, the results of this labour would be more remote from the literary studies, and the higher sciences would less depend upon it than in the case of grammar or other liberal arts, and it would so far be less connected with the Institute of the Colleges; and seculars might easily be found to teach what is more a mechanical than a liberal art, and is therefore more frequently taught by laymen than by clerics. There is the further consideration that as a rule at that age children are not yet fit for moral instruction, and so our ministry is less necessary for them; and what is necessary may be supplied by sometimes visiting their external schools, and instructing them in christian doctrine and morals according to their capacities, a care which, as proper to Ours when it can conveniently be carried out, the Society does not lose sight of.

## VI.—The means employed by the Society in the education of Externs.

Two things are aimed at by the Society in the schools, namely, progress in learning and in morals; and although learning is as it were the proper matter of this ministry, and the proximate effect of the Colleges, yet the principal end which is aimed at is goodness of morals.

The first means which is employed in our Colleges for the preservation and promotion of the young in virtue, is frequent confession, or at least confession once a month; since a pure conscience is the seat of wisdom. This means was approved by the Council of Trent for those who are being educated in seminaries. By the words *at least* it is insinuated that it would be better to confess more frequently, and so this is to be counselled, although it is not to be exacted, or laid down as a rule, especially for the younger secular scholars. For the same reason perhaps nothing is laid down in the Constitutions with regard to the communions of the extern scholars; but that is tacitly understood which the Council expressly declared in the case of seminarists, namely, that according to the judgment of the confessor they should receive the Body of our Lord Jesus Christ. This can be more easily observed in the seminaries because in them the youths are kept under a more severe ecclesiastical discipline.

The second means prescribed is the daily worship of God, and since God is best worshipped in the Sacrifice of the Mass, the students are daily to hear Mass, as the Council of Trent ordered also in the seminaries.

Thirdly, since general sermons addressed to the mass of the people are less suited to the capacities of the young, and are therefore less useful to them, the care of instructing and exhorting their pupils to virtue in various ways is commended to the preceptors of the Society. The pupils are to be well trained in Christian doctrine, and are to have a lecture upon it once a week, and they are themselves to learn and repeat it. There is also once a week to be an exhortation, by which all may be stirred up to increase of virtue; and to preceptors it is commended that during their lectures they should, when occasion offers, move their pupils to the service and love of God and of virtue; and this also they should do in private conversations.

The fourth means is the excellent custom of public prayer at the beginning of schools or lectures. We read of St. Thomas that he never gave himself to reading or writing without previous prayer. The pupils are to be taught in this brief prayer to do two things,—first, to refer all their studies, and in particular the present time and action to God,—and secondly, to beg of God grace to make progress in study.

The fifth means is the avoidance by preceptors of all books which contain anything hurtful to morals. The reason is clear, because under the veil of eloquence, and the sweetness of the Latin tongue, and through the pleasantness of fables, evil thoughts are suggested and bad morals inculcated, and the mind is excited to the incentives of lust. Origen compares such books to a golden chalice in which poison is presented. St. Augustine, speaking of Terence in particular, says,—I accuse not the words, which are vessels elect and precious, but the wine of error which is presented in them by drunken doctors. St. Basil says that the books of the Gentiles are to be read with the discretion of bees,—bees do not settle on all flowers, nor from those which they approach do they strive to take all away, but they take only so much as is fitting, and they leave the rest; so we, that we may be sober and wise, should pursue in those books what is fitting for us, and akin to truth, and pass by the rest; and as in gathering roses we avoid the thorns, so also in such books let us take what is useful, and what is hurtful let us avoid.

Since this selection cannot be made by boys, such books are not to be read, either at all, or until they have been purged from all evil expressions.

With no less prudence have the necessary and fitting means for the promotion of the young in learning been defined and ordained in the Society. The statutes in which these means are contained form a part of the Rule which is to be observed by the religious in order to the acquiring of perfection; and they are therefore to be as accurately observed as is any other rule of perfection, because the divine good pleasure and counsel are equally set forth thereby.

The first and principal means is the sufficiency and diligence of the masters themselves. Without the approbation and leave of the Provincial, no one can teach publicly, save for a time, by reason of necessity, and in the lower classes. The teachers must be in sufficient number; and according to the number of the pupils the classes must be divided and arranged.

The second means is order and method, both in delivery of doctrine, and in disputations and all literary exercises, and in the repetition of lectures and private study.

The third means is that general one which is most necessary in every commonwealth in order to the promotion of morals and arts, and the repression and extirpation of vices, namely, rewards and punishments; and these ought to be proportioned both to persons and to actions. Corporal punishment is to be administered not by the preceptors themselves but by a corrector appointed for the purpose. If the correction does not suffice, and there is risk of damage to the other scholars, and but little chance of profit to the delinquent who is incorrigible, he is to be expelled.

# CHAPTER XXI.

*THE PROFESSION OF FOUR VOWS WHICH IS MADE IN THE SOCIETY; THE PROBATION WHICH PRECEDES IT; AND THE SIMPLE VOWS WHICH FOLLOW IT.*

I.—Is Profession rightly deferred in the Society for a long time?

For just causes the date of solemn profession is not defined by any law in the Institute of the Society. The Constitutions require certain conditions in order to profession; first, those who are to be professed of four vows must be priests; and with regard to this there is no dispensation, for if, for any urgent cause, it should be necessary to admit any one to profession before his promotion to the priesthood, the solemn profession of three vows will suffice; and this the Society, although rarely, allows.

Secondly, there is required age exceeding twenty-five years, and therefore a greater age than that which is required for the priesthood which, by ordinary law, requires the twenty-fifth year to have been begun.

Thirdly, there is required more than mediocrity in learning, and proof of a conspicuously good life and morals. This necessitates the lapse of a considerable time.

A religious may be admitted in two ways to solemn profession in the Society, namely, either after having passed through the grade of a Scholastic, or immediately after the noviceship; for, although this is rarely done, because rarely are persons found who are immediately capable of this grade, or causes for immediately granting it, it is nevertheless in itself not at variance with the Institute.

For solemn profession of three vows there are required at least seven years of religious life in the Society, and according to ordinary law no one is to be admitted to this profession immediately after his noviceship, but only after his probation in the grade of a Scholastic.

When a person, by reason of his condition and peculiar gifts, is to be admitted to profession immediately after his noviceship, he should be such that he may worthily be admitted to the profession of four vows. Although this profession is of greater dignity, yet the passage to it immediately after the noviceship is easier than is the passage to profession of three vows.

Two years are assigned as the shortest time necessary for profession, in virtue of the Rule; but this does not hinder the General from abridging it by dispensation, although it cannot be abridged for admission to the grade of a Scholastic. To do this would be less expedient than to abridge it for solemn profession; for although the latter is a more indissoluble bond, and is proximately ordained to a higher end, and therefore of itself requires greater probation, yet as a rule and nearly always the vows of Scholastics are made immediately after their noviceship, and their two years are required primarily by reason of the age at which they are received, and the duties to which they are proximately admitted. It is therefore expedient that for Scholastics the door of dispensation in order to their incorporation should be entirely closed, lest occasion should be given for frequent dispensation, and because it is scarcely possible to imagine a cause which should demand it. But admission to profession immediately after the two years is and must be most rare, since it is necessary either that some extrinsic cause should demand it, and this can scarcely ever oblige to shorten the two years; or that the person should be so mature and worthy that a shorter time will suffice for satisfaction of all concerned. For this rare case therefore dispensation is not forbidden, lest thereby entrance into the Society should be rendered more difficult for such grave persons.

Although the period of two years of noviceship can be shortened for solemn profession, an entire year of probation cannot be dispensed with by the Society; since not by the special law of the Order, but by the common law of the Council of Trent, an entire year is necessary in order to validity of profession even in the Society.

The term of two years is laid down as the minimum, and therefore as of ordinary law to be held sufficient; but not as the maximum, for it may be prolonged. Although many persons may be received to the noviceship who do not need the discipline of Scholastics as regards learning, they may nevertheless frequently need a longer time for religious discipline and for greater and more exact probation of their morals, and talents for the exercise of ministries to their neighbours. They may also need greater instruction in the practice of the exercises and actions of the Society. Even in those who are already advanced in age a longer probation, as regards learning and even as regards morals, may often be desirable, by reason of the to them special difficulty of accommodating themselves to the mode of procedure in the Society, especially in humble obedience and subjection, and in laying aside their own judgment, and in conforming it to the dictates of superiors and of the Society.

The Council of Trent specially excepts the Society from the rule which it prescribes for other Orders, that on the completion of the term of probation, the person should be admitted to profession; and the Institute, which the Council confirms, lays down no other term save the full satisfaction of the Society or its General in the Lord.

Having regard to the Institute of the Society, and the variety of persons who may be received in it, no fixed term could be conveniently assigned. Either it would have been short, as for instance, seven or nine years; or lengthened, as twenty years or more. The short period would not as a rule have been expedient, since the Institute demands long and manifold probations. It ordinarily requires after the two years of noviceship, at least the whole term of the studies, which is wont to be nine, or ten or more years. After the noviceship two or three years are commonly spent in the study of humane letters and in acquiring a more perfect knowledge of languages; and to these are added three or four years (according to the custom of the country) for the course of philosophy. Then come the four years of Scholastic theology; and sometimes there is granted to the more advanced one or two years for the repetition of what they have learned, and for the reading of the Fathers, and for giving some specimen of their learning in public acts and disputations. It frequently happens also that the course of study is interrupted by teaching the lower branches to externs, for it is often necessary for Scholastics thus to bear the burdens of the Order and to satisfy its public duties. Hence it not rarely happens that fifteen years or more are consumed, and they should be followed by the third year of probation. Now, since moral laws should be made in accordance with that which is of most frequent occurrence, and should have regard to the whole body of the Society, and not to the convenience or custom of one or other province, the period before profession, if it had been necessary to fix it, could not have been prescribed as much under twenty years; and to fix so prolonged a period was in those times and in this Order not expedient, for although some of the old monks were proved for thirty years, this would not be in accordance with the spirit of modern times, especially if so long a period should be assigned as fixed and necessary. Moreover, considering the very great variety of persons who are received into the Society, and their great diversity of age and condition, so great a delay would often be incongruous, burdensome to subjects, without lawful cause, and useless and even hurtful to the Order. The period therefore could not be conveniently limited, and was rightly left to prudent judgment.

All the causes which have moved the Society to

ordain a long probation, apply equally to the satisfaction of the Society, which is the end of that probation; for probation would be useless if, without its end of the satisfaction of the Society having been attained, profession were nevertheless to be given. There cannot be certain satisfaction as the result simply of the lapse of a determinate time, and in the case of some persons a brief space of time might suffice, while in the case of others, and most frequently, a longer time would be required.

There are other advantages which arise from this uncertainty or indeterminateness, for if the time of profession were certain and determined by law, human frailty might thence take occasion for remissness and negligence, as regards progress both in virtue and in learning, and in application also to the ministries of the Society, and in endurance of the labours which are proper to the Professed. This occasion is removed by the uncertainty of the time of profession; nay, since all understand that what merits profession is not seniority, but those gifts and conditions which are demanded for that grade in the Society, they will, morally speaking and as a rule, be induced to greater care both in observance of the Institute, and in the studies and other exercises and ministries of the Society.

That a thing should be novel would be but of little consequence, if it was suitable for the convenient government of a new Order, if it was instituted in a proper and special manner for a special end, and if it should have been deemed worthy of Apostolic approbation. But, as matter of fact, this ordinance is not novel, especially as regards the spirit of it, and the end aimed at by it, namely, that the most important ecclesiastical ministries and the sanctification of souls should not be committed save to worthy persons, of whom it might be hoped that they would exercise their functions with security to themselves and fruit to others, and in a manner worthy of religious life. We learn from Cassian that the probation of the juniors for the monastic profession was wont to be made by means of many trials, without any determination of time. Again, in the old times when the monks, as a rule, were not clerics, but might be promoted to that state, no time was determined for this, but the merits of individuals were kept in view; hence St. Jerome says,—So live in the monastery that you may deserve to be a cleric. Pope Gelasius required two conditions for the promotion of a monk to the priesthood, one, that he should appear worthy of it by the merit of a venerable life, and the other, that the Abbot under whose rule he waged war for Christ the King should ask for his ordination. Since therefore the Society is an Order not of any persons whomsoever, but of priests to whom ministries with regard to souls are committed, what wonder that the rule of profession should be not a certain length of time but a certain degree of merit? Hence both for the priesthood and for profession the time is indefinite in the Society, and is to be determined by the judgment of the superior. A longer time is required for profession than for simple priesthood, for profession supposes the priesthood, and adds a greater obligation, and requires a greater capability for all the functions of the Society, and for the principal government of it, which is committed to the Professed.

Although certain times are assigned for the reception of the various orders, no certain time is fixed for elevation to the episcopate. The priesthood has not so necessarily annexed to it the *pastoral* office, as has the episcopate, and therefore although it requires innocence of life, much more perfect virtue is demanded in a bishop, who is therefore said to be in the *state* of the perfect. His promotion, consequently, is to be measured not by time but by merit. Now the Professed of the Society, although they do not attain to the grade of bishops, share it nevertheless so far as regards the preaching of the Gospel, and procuring the salvation of souls, and so no wonder that in the Professed life and doctrine are required rather than a certain lapse of time.

If Ours are true and solid religious they will have but little fear with regard to this matter, for they will not desire profession as if it were a title of honour, or as giving capacity for higher functions either within or outside the Order, for that would be ambition. As regards solemn profession constituting a closer bond with God they need not be solicitous, since already they are true religious, and have dedicated themselves wholly to the divine service, and they are prepared to straiten the bond if and when they are bidden. As regards comparison of themselves with others, every one, if he is truly religious, should account himself more unworthy of this grade than is his neighbour. The Society should, on its part, take care that all equity and due distribution should be observed; and it may reasonably be believed that this is done, both because the matter is transacted by those to whom is committed the government of the whole Order, and because it is not determined without diligent examination and the counsel of many, and these prudent and religious and conscientious men. Even if sometimes through error or human affection there should be any lack of equity, that is a *private* disadvantage which is not of such moment as that in order to avoid it the *public* advantage which results from the arrangement in force should be interfered with.

## II. — For what reason is a third year of probation required of Scholastics of the Society before Profession?

The third year of probation is not demanded as of the substance, or as wholly necessary to the validity of profession, for neither the Constitutions nor the Bulls require this. Hence it is certain that the General can dispense, and he does sometimes for just causes dispense from it; although the Constitutions by their silence with regard to such dispensation sufficiently indicate that it ought not to be easily granted.

This third probation consists principally in abstaining from studies and ministries to neighbours, so that the Scholastics may give themselves during that time more intently to God and their own personal perfection, with that "holy leisure which the love of the truth delights in."

When the numbers are small this probation may take place in the same House with the novices. If there are ten Scholastics they will be proved in a separate House, under one instructor, who shall have authority to govern them. He will take care to form them in spirit, and will explain to them the whole idea of the Institute of the Society on certain stated days in every week, and will expound to them the methods of promoting the salvation of their neighbours. He will also enjoin penances and mortifications, but privately among themselves, which he shall judge conducive to their progress; and he will, if need be, absolve from reserved sins. But he will not impose anything which regards external discipline without consulting the Rector or Minister of the College, if their separate habitation forms part of a College. If any of them is not satisfactory in his probation he will be dismissed, and his probation will be deferred to another time. On the completion of the year both the Instructor and the Provincial will fully inform the General with regard to every individual whether he has rightly made his probation or not.

The proper idea of this probation consists not so much in formal probation, as in spiritual exercise, and the disposition necessary for profession, which is the primary and in itself sufficient idea of the probation, even if there were no other, although the idea of experiment and probation is not to be lost sight of.

The Society is a perfectly mixed religious Order which so aims at action for the benefit of its neighbours that it also principally gives itself to contemplation so far as is necessary that there should be no relaxation of its own perfection, and that its ministries to its neighbours should result in greater fruit. Although therefore ordinarily the life of the Society is mixed, yet certain times are specially set apart for the exercise of the purely contemplative life; and among other times there are principally these two,—the two years of noviceship and the third year of probation. This last is fixed at a most fitting time, and it ought not to be shortened; and it cannot be shortened, if the effects which are desired are, ordinarily speaking, to be obtained.

The first period of noviceship should be longer, because in it the foundations of spirit are laid, and persons then begin to exercise themselves in divine things who have previously had no practice and almost no knowledge of them. In the third year the religious have been already instructed and exercised in spiritual things, of which they have a larger knowledge and more ready practice through their learning and acquaintance with the Scriptures, and so for them a period of one year is sufficient. That length of time is however necessary because in the noviceship, as a rule, this mystical and spiritual science can never be perfectly learned, nor the degree of interior meditation, prayer and contemplation be well attained to which is necessary for perfect or advanced spiritual men. What was lacking in the noviceship can rarely be acquired during the time of studies, nay, it is rather to be feared that what has been acquired in the noviceship, will during the time of studies be in some measure lessened, or at least grow tepid. Most fittingly therefore is the third year of probation placed *after* the studies, not only in order that any loss may be repaired, but also in order that the actions of the contemplative life may be exercised in a higher and more perfect manner. By this means he who aforetime knew and thought and prayed and spoke as a child may, after he has become a man, put away the things of a child, and begin in a new manner to cleave to God, to despise the world, and to contemn himself and all temporal things; and if learning has led, as is its wont, to aught of elation or ambition, this may be cast out by a higher knowledge and consideration of divine things.

Besides the advantages or necessity of the third year of probation as regards the time past, we see that they are not less if we look towards the time to come. The beginning or foundation of every good life, or reformation of life springs from internal cogitation and consideration; and so the mixed life is to be begun by acts of the contemplative life, to which are at the same time to be added those actions which are ordained for the moderation of the affections and the purging of the heart, by which a man is made more capable of acts of perfection of the contemplative life; and by these again he gains strength and forces for the more perfect exercise of acts of virtue, and so by degrees he makes progress in both of these lives. Again, contemplation is necessary in order to that perfect action which is spiritual, and which consists in the enlightenment and sanctification of souls, and which, says St. Thomas, is derived from the fulness of contemplation, and of which the perfection consists in this that by means of it that which has been contemplated is delivered to others.

This order Christ Himself has commended to us by the example of His life, for not only from the moment of His conception did He engage in the highest contemplation through union with God, but before His public preaching He retired to the desert for forty days, to give Himself to God alone. He willed the same order to be observed by His Apostles, not only teaching them to pray before He sent them out to preach while He was still with them, and often retiring with them for the purpose of prayer, but also before His departure commanding them to remain in the city till they were endued with power from on high; a command which they fulfilled by assembling in the supper room and there persevering in prayer before, being enlightened and strengthened in the Holy Ghost, they began their apostolic labours. St. John the Baptist also exercised himself for thirty years in the contemplative life before he began to preach, and of him St. Bernard says that he first burned within himself before he began to shine forth to others, as Christ also declared when He said,—"He was a burning and a shining light." A man burns by contemplation, and he shines forth by teaching, and it would be very inordinate if he were to begin to teach before he had himself learned. Finally, if contemplation were not to precede a life of action, it could scarcely if at all be acquired during a life of action, and much less could it accompany, and continually pervade the life of action.

Hence we see the reasons and wonderful wisdom of St. Ignatius in his education and instruction of his offspring. First he will have them sufficiently exercised in the acts of both lives during their first noviceship, and in this order that they should begin with the foundations of the contemplative life by means of spiritual exercises, along with that part principally of the active life which contributes towards their mortification of themselves and the acquirement of virtue, so that the time of noviceship belongs wholly or almost wholly to the contemplative life. This kind of life continues throughout the whole time of their studies, since learning is a species and part of contemplation. This mode of contemplation however is not contemplation in its perfect and highest degree, although it may dispose thereto, and therefore he has ordained that before the Scholastics go forth to labour in the vineyard of the Lord, they should return to the school of the contemplative life, in order that they should be, as far as possible, made perfect. Although one year may seem to be but a very short time for so great a work, yet, looking to the frailty of humanity and to the shortness of life, it must be held sufficient. It is not allotted as if within the limits of it the whole of perfection could be acquired, but as in order that during it more solid and sufficient foundations should be laid, and that, as Gregory XIII. has said, the spirit should warm to the love and pursuit of perfection.

Besides this proper and primary end, there is another principal reason for the institution of the third year of probation, namely, that it is of great service, and is morally necessary in order to the perfect probation and knowledge by experience of those to whom the functions which belong to the Professed are to be, as it were, by office and special obligation, committed in the Society.

Finally, this period of probation is called the Third Year, because a year is the minimum; but the period may be prolonged, and all the rest of the time up to profession, when it is delayed, belongs in fact to the period of probation.


### III.—Does the special form of Profession in the Society induce a special obligation with regard to the teaching of children?

Besides the three vows which are of the substance of profession generally and in other Orders, profession in the Society adds two things;—first, a special determination of the vow of obedience as regards the teaching of children; and secondly, a special vow of obedience to the Supreme Pontiff as regards the Missions.

There are two modes of solemn profession in the Society. One, and the ordinary one, is the profession of four vows. This is what is understood when *profession* is spoken of in the Society, since those who are professed of four vows are the principal members of the body, and the General Congregation which represents the whole Society is composed of them, and to them there belongs an active and passive vote in the election of the General, and the government of the Society, as regards its Provinces and Professed Houses, can ordinarily be committed to them alone.

The other mode of solemn profession is when three solemn vows, namely, the three substantial vows of religion, and these only are made, without the vow of obedience to the Pontiff. In the mode of making the vow of obedience as regards declaration of the function of teaching christian doctrine, those who are professed of

Three Vows are identified with the professed of Four Vows; while, as regards the absence of the fourth vow and of all its consequences, they are identified with the Formed Spiritual Coadjutors, with whom they are almost the same as regards the ministries to which they are appointed, and the gifts or qualities which are required in them. They are, in fact, Spiritual Coadjutors whom the Society deems worthy of some special prerogative.

There are two kinds of instruction of children (and under children are comprehended all uneducated and ignorant persons), namely instruction in letters, and instruction in the faith or christian doctrine. The Society undertakes both, but the first is not so proper to the Professed, and belongs to the Colleges of the Society; while the other, although common to all the members of the Society, is in a peculiar manner annexed to the profession of the Society, and is expressed in the form of making profession.

This ministry has been rightly undertaken by the Society as one of its principal ministries, and as one of those which are to be exercised with the greatest care and perfection. This is evident from the Constitutions, which no one can lightly esteem, by reason both of the sanctity and prudence of their author, and the practice and consent of the whole Order, in which there have been so many religious and wise and prudent men, and chiefly also by reason of the Pontifical approbation, and that not only in general, but in particular.

Although this ministry may not appear to be in itself a very lofty one, it is nevertheless, as it is a seed and virtually, very great, because on it in great measure depends the good and holy life of the faithful; since faith is the foundation of all justice, and the children are taught not only what they ought to believe, but also what they ought to do, and to what end they ought to ordain their lives ; a knowledge which is most necessary from the very beginning. Not only are they enlightened with regard to these matters, but they are also stirred up and by various means, proportioned to their age, allured and induced to works of piety. Again, by occasion of the instruction of children it often happens that persons of greater age, and sometimes old men who have never been sufficiently instructed in the things of faith, are taught, while others also who have forgotten them learn them anew. Many likewise who will not come to graver discourses, or who do not sufficiently understand them, are by this means of christian doctrine moved to do penance and to follow after virtue. Hence, since the majority of men are uneducated and unlearned, it may be hoped that by this means more persons may make progress in faith and virtue than by means of other more excellent and higher ministries ; and so Paul III. says with such asseveration in his Bull, that no other occupation is more fruitful for the edification of our neighbours, as well as for our own charity and humility. This ministry may profit all who can possibly be profited by other ministries, while other ministries may not profit all who can be profited by this ministry.

This ministry is also most efficacious against errors and false doctrine ; and for this reason it commended itself so greatly to St. Ignatius, by means of whom God prepared the Society principally to wage war against the heresies which arose in his time.

This ministry is rightly set forth in the vow of obedience which is contained in the form of profession which is in use in the Society; although this is done not so much in order to impose a new obligation, as specially to commend the ministry itself, in order that it may be devoutly cared for as a singular service to God, through the aid which it affords to souls, and because it might more easily be neglected and fall into desuetude than other ministries which are more brilliant.

In the First General Congregation this ministry was specially commended to the Professed; and it is recorded that our father Ignatius enjoined on each of the Professed that he should perform it for the space of forty days. The Congregation signified that this was enjoined by St. Ignatius as a perpetual observance in the Society; but, lest this should not have been sufficiently explained, the Second Congregation declared that every one of the professed should be bound, after his profession and within the year, to teach christian doctrine to children and uneducated persons, for forty days, either continuously or with interruption.

This ordinance however is only a direction in order to the better executing or beginning of that which is expressed in the profession, and it is not a law which obliges under sin; neither is it a determination of the matter of the vow. Not even of counsel are the Professed bound absolutely to exercise this ministry for forty days, unless it should be enjoined on them by the superior; or at least unless leave should be given, for it is not the intention of the decree to exempt subjects from the obedience of their superiors, but to render them ready to execute this ministry, or even to procure it from their superiors, and to admonish superiors that they should not only permit it, but also take care that it should be observed by the Professed. If superiors therefore should either expressly or tacitly excuse any of the Professed from this ministry, on the ground that they are otherwise lawfully hindered, they will in no way sin.

To the same end of imprinting the importance of this ministry more deeply on the mind, and causing it to be held in greater esteem, St. Ignatius imposed a similar charge on the Rectors of Colleges, that they should themselves teach christian doctrine for forty days. This they ought to do within their first year of office; and if any impediment comes in the way, they are to communicate with the Provincial in order that this duty may be fulfilled by another. In so many ways, and by so many signs has the usefulness and necessity of this ministry been commended, in order that all of the Society may be more and more warmly affected towards it.

In order to teach and explain the rudiments of the faith no ordinary knowledge is often necessary, both in the expounding of doctrine and especially in the expounding of morals; and in such knowledge the Scholastics of the Society are certainly not supposed to be yet sufficiently instructed; and therefore in this ministry the industry, and solicitude and learning of our religious, particularly of the more advanced, can greatly profit the Church through the grace of God, as experience has shewn. Rightly therefore in the Profession of the

Society is there made special and express mention of this work, in order that not only to the Scholastics but to all the labourers in the Society it should be commended, and in order that the Professed should understand that in a special way it belongs to their state and office.

## IV.—Is the vow of obedience to the Supreme Pontiff, which is made by the Professed in the Society, a solemn vow, and distinct from the three substantial vows?

The Professed of the Society who make a fourth vow to obey the Supreme Pontiff, do a holy thing, and by so doing they are bound in virtue of their vow to something to which religious of other Orders are not bound in virtue of their profession. The matter of this vow is not the whole of that which can be the matter of religious obedience, even according to the Rule of the Society; but is only the matter of the Missions. This includes, however, not only proceeding to the Missions, but also remaining in them in any part of the world, according to the intention of him who prescribes.

The Professed are bound, in virtue of this vow, not only to go to the Missions, but also faithfully and strenuously to perform all the actions or functions to which or for which they are sent; for by *Missions*, according to the true sense and common use of the word, are meant not merely journeys to, and residence in certain places, but the actions also and ministries for which those journeys are ordained.

In practice the obligation will be in proportion to the precept which is actually imposed. It may often be prescribed to one of the Professed to go to India, while the work which he is to do there is not prescribed, but is left in accordance with the Institute; and in this case, if he obeys by going, even if afterwards he should be negligent or should otherwise sin by ill performance of his duty, he will not sin specially against this vow, because a precept such as to cover the whole matter of his vow was not imposed upon him.

The words—"for the profit of souls, and the propagation of the faith"—which declare the end of the vow, substantially limit its matter; for the Professed, for instance, are not bound, in virtue of this vow, to visit the Holy Places by way of pilgrimage. Under the end expressed by these words are comprehended all spiritual works of mercy, such as the procuring of peace between hostile princes, the relief of those who are in any peril of soul, the sowing of the seeds of faith, the confuting of heretics, and the aid of catholics by means of any spiritual ministry whatsoever, whether of doctrine or sacraments. Works of corporal mercy, such as the redemption of captives, or the like, although they are not directly comprehended under this vow, are nevertheless, if they are such as become clerics, not excluded from it; since all of these may be ordained towards spiritual profit, and the Institute of the Society embraces them. The defence of the Church, and the resistance of infidels by force of arms and war, although they are works of charity, do not nevertheless belong to priests, and therefore it is clear that they are not comprehended; although from the work of the Missions those ministries on land or sea are not excluded which are for the aid of christian soldiers or leaders who are fighting for the Church, since they belong immediately to the spiritual end of assisting the souls of the faithful, and are ordained ultimately to the peace and universal spiritual good of the whole Church. Hence under this vow are comprehended all the spiritual ministries which the Society exercises for the benefit of its neighbours, since for all of these the Pontiff can send Ours whithersoever he wills; while if we are already in a place to which he might have sent us, he can prescribe to us to remain there for the performance of any such ministry. If there should be any doubt as to whether a ministry belongs to the profit of souls, or only to the temporal or civil advantage of our neighbours, such as, for instance, the teaching in any particular place of grammar or philosophy, the resolution of the doubt certainly remains with the Pontiff.

To the matter of this vow belong also certain circumstances of great importance and no small difficulty. The first is that, when the Professed are sent, they are bound to go without waiting for or demanding *viaticum* or provision for the way. This condition is connected with the vow of poverty, but it also falls under the vow of the Missions. Wherefore if a professed religious of the Society should, by occasion of viaticum or from fear of indigence, refuse a mission, he would sin directly against this vow. He is bound not only to go but also to remain, without looking for viaticum or relief from the Pontiff, and relying on God alone and the alms of the pious, from which to support himself in accordance with the poverty which he professes.

Secondly, obedience without tergiversation or excuse falls under this vow. This condition however, is to be understood in accordance with the Constitutions and with right reason. Perfection of obedience does not, when a just excuse occurs, exclude its being set before the superior in a proper manner and with due reverence, for this is just and in conformity with right reason. It is lawful not because it is permitted by the Rule, but it is permitted by the Rule because right reason demands it. Silence on the part of the subject might sometimes be very contrary to the intention of the Pontiff in prescribing, and to the end which he has in view. In one word, there is excluded by this vow all excuse of the will, but not excuse of the reason; or, certainly, there is excluded every excuse which includes an absolute purpose not to go, but not such an excusing as consists solely in setting forth a reasonable impediment. Even when the excuse seems reasonable, it is not lawful absolutely to resolve not to obey and in this sense to excuse oneself, for if, notwithstanding the difficulty proposed, the Pontiff should insist on his precept, it must be obeyed in virtue of the vow. If a subject were by tergiversation arising from frailty, without deceit and fraud, to insinuate his difficulty and beg to be excused by removal of the precept, being prepared at the same time to obey if the superior should not condescend to his petition, then there would not be grave sin, although there would be great imperfection, and perhaps also venial sin.

The third circumstance which belongs to the matter of this vow of obedience with regard to the Missions, is that it should be universal and indifferent to all places and peoples, whatsoever their religion or opinions, whether, as the Bull says,—to the Turks or to any other infidels whatsoever, even in the parts which they call the Indies, or to any heretics or schismatics whatsoever, or to any of the faithful; and, add the Constitutions, the Society has not understood any particular place, but that Ours should be scattered throughout the world to all its various regions and places. For this cause chiefly has the whole body of Society decreed by this vow to place itself specially in the power of the Pontiff, because since it desires the greater service of God and of the whole Church in the assistance of souls, and since also it is ignorant where it can be employed with the greatest fruit, it has judged that this matter should be committed to the Vicar of Christ; both because he, as Head of the whole Church, will have a greater knowledge of its affairs and necessities, and also because it is rightly to be hoped that his distribution of the ministers of the Society will be the best, and made with the most abundant aid of the Holy Ghost.

Hence also in virtue of this vow, the Professed of the Society are bound, if it should seem good to the Pontiff, to have no fixed domicile, but to go hither and thither, and, if need be, to live outside the houses of the Society for a lengthened period, as may be expedient for the good of souls. This mode of life is not accidental or foreign to the Institute, as it would be in other religious Orders;

but it is in itself comprehended within the limits of the Institute, and has itself been chosen in order to the end of the Society.

Under the matter of this vow is comprehended also the returning from, as well as the going to the Missions, and also the not going to certain places, the reason of the prohibition being the advantage of souls; since all this belongs to the distribution of the Professed, which should be wholly in the hands of the Pontiff.

This vow is pious and holy since it concerns an excellent thing, and is made for an excellent end; for what ends can be more excellent than the common good of the Church, the salvation of souls, and the defence and propagation of the faith?

Certain persons have calumniated the Society as ambitious of the special favour of the Apostolic See by reason of this vow, since by it, as they say, the Society in reality vows nothing new, and has only for the sake of adulation and from human respect invented this singular mode of profession. This calumny cannot have been conceived by prudent men, but must have been hatched by such as rashly judge others, since neither from the matter nor from the end of the vow is such an intention or any suspicion of it apparent, and since in the Constitutions the right intention is frequently declared, and it is also set forth by the Supreme Pontiff in the Bulls. Such an ambitious intention could not morally have place in individuals, as is evident, since by means of this vow they are not made more known to the Pontiff, nor do they expect any temporal gain from this vow; while to intend that the whole body of the Order should be specially under the protection of the Supreme Pontiff, and that it should be defended and aided by him, would not be ambitious, but would be very much in conformity with reason and charity. St. Francis specially promised for himself and his Order obedience to Honorius III. the Supreme Pontiff and to his successors, and St. Buonaventure says that by reason of its singular poverty the Order of the Friars Minor is committed in a special manner to the care of the Pontiff as to that of a parent, and this is not ambition, but a holy intention; and so even if the Society had intended this, it would have done right well. In reality, however, this is not the intention of the vow, although it may be a fruit or effect which is a consequence of the vow.

By no higher authority, and by no greater direction of the Holy Ghost could the ministers of the Society be sent,—" And how shall they preach unless they are sent?" (Rom. x. 15)—than by the Supreme Pastor of the Flock of Christ, to whom it belongs by his office to watch over the spiritual welfare of the sheep. The most excellent mode, moreover, in which they can be sent is by obedience, which is a holocaust most pleasing unto God, and especially when it has been consecrated by vow.

These Missions are made by the Supreme Pontiff, either by his asking for religious, and leaving the selection of them to the General, or sometimes by his sending particular persons and occasionally even the General himself, as in the case of Laynes who was sent to France, and Borgia who was sent to Portugal for the good of the Church, and others of the first companions of St. Ignatius. Even if individuals are not known to the Pontiff, it is important for him to know that the whole body of the Society is consecrated by a special vow to this duty, and will be obedient to him at his nod in all things which he may command for the good of souls. Since he is Generalissimo of the whole ecclesiastical army, it may be useful for him to have at hand auxiliary bands of soldiers whom he can freely distribute, as he deems expedient. For this reason our Father St. Ignatius has, in the Constitutions, most wisely provided that the General should, when a new Vicar of Christ has been established in the Apostolic See, be bound within a year from his creation and coronation to declare, either in person or through another, to His Holiness the profession and express promise of obedience to which the Society has bound itself by a special vow with regard to the Missions for the glory of God. Even if the Pontiff cannot know all the professed of the Society, he can easily have knowledge of some of the more distinguished of them, and of such as he might more conveniently use as his instruments. He must know such persons either by reputation or personally, since they often come to Rome, and many also live there, and from these he can as he pleases gain sufficient knowledge of others; and this is enough and more than enough that the vow should not be reckoned useless, but that it should rather on the contrary be considered very serviceable.

The General is the principal minister whom the Pontiff will necessarily ordinarily employ in arranging the Missions; and the General is bound in virtue of his office, and also in virtue of his own vow of the Missions, faithfully to execute and ordain whatever His Holiness may order, and in accordance with his intention.

This vow induces a *special* obligation which the general vow of obedience of other religious Orders does not include; for a monk is not bound in virtue of his vow of obedience to be ready to go to India, or to the Turks, whenever he may be ordered by the Pontiff; for in such a case he is no more bound to obey the Pontiff, than is any secular, since this does not belong to his profession.

A religious of another, and even of a mendicant Order can only be obliged to migrate to distant regions, so far as he can be transferred by his own General from one province to another for his own greater good or for that of the Order; but a professed religious of the Society can, in virtue of this vow, be sent by the Supreme Pontiff simply for the sake of preaching, or of in some other way ministering to his neighbours in spiritual matters, and this even if it is necessary that he should go where there is no House or Province of the Society. In virtue of his vow he can be sent where he will have to live in perpetuity outside the Houses and Colleges of the Society; and to this religious of other Orders cannot in virtue of their vow of obedience be compelled. The Professed of the Society are also bound to go, so to speak, at their own expense, that is, without viaticum, and begging if need be, whereas other religious, since they do not profess this, cannot be bound to it with so great rigour. Finally the Professed of the Society are liable to such Missions, as it were, by office, so that they can be sent without any special necessity, because they have professed this mode of life; whereas other religious can be bound only accidentally, or by the common law of charity, justice, or christian obedience, or for the sake of some special service to their Order.

With regard to the alleged novelty of this vow, since the Society in its Institute and mode of life was itself new, what wonder that it should also have professed something which was new? When the Order of St. Francis began to profess community poverty this was probably something new. To profess military service or the redemption of captives was at one time a novelty. Not every thing which is new is reprehensible, but only that new thing which is at variance with antiquity, and not that new thing which, in accordance with the circumstances and necessities of the time, is introduced in order to perfect those things which are old.

With regard, moreover, to the singularity of the vow, as the Society is a special Order distinct from other Orders, so it should have some special and proper mark by which it may be distinguished from them; and the distinguishing mark of the Society is its ministry for the salvation of souls *under the special obedience of the Supreme Pontiff.* This is its special scope or end and aim to which it has been called and ordained by God. This singularity therefore has been conceived not by human reason merely but by a special grace of the Holy Ghost, for the dissemination of the faith in so many of the most remote regions, and for the defence of the Church against so many assaults of heretics.

Although this vow is of a thing which is very arduous and difficult, and which looking to human frailty is encompassed with perils, yet it is not therefore imprudent or rash. In the first place, it is not by human strength but by the grace of the Holy Ghost that the vow is to be accomplished; and He who has begun and inspired the good work will Himself perfect it if we do not stand in the way, for that is the special grace of this vocation, which is more powerful than all perils and difficulties. Again, by this vow we do not promise to expose ourselves to perils, or to go to these or those regions, or to perform these or those actions, but to obey the Vicar of Christ; and there cannot be any more certain means of not erring in the way of God. There has also to be taken into account the providence of the Order, both in training and proving the persons sent, and also in the selection of them. Besides, in the Constitutions and Bulls we are frequently admonished that no one should procure his being sent to this or to that place, but that every one should permit himself to be moved, although it will not be wrong for him to shew his readiness.

Such a vow adds a greater intensity of obligation, even if it does not extend the sphere of obedience; so that a Friar Minor who should disobey the orders of the Pontiff would sin more grievously than a religious of another Order would sin by so doing; and one of the Professed of the Society would sin more grievously, by refusing a mission which had been enjoined on him by the Pontiff, than would a Coadjutor or Approved

Scholastic, although these also would sin against obedience by refusing a mission.

Approved Scholastics are not bound by the Constitutions to proceed to the Missions without viaticum, or without seeking or procuring it, and they have not, moreover, professed this kind of poverty, except at most in case of necessity and when their going is necessary. Coadjutors are bound by reason of their vow of poverty the obligation of which is greater than that of the vow made by Scholastics. The Professed, on the other hand, are bound not only by reason of poverty, but also *by reason of obedience*. In comparison with Scholastics therefore there is in the Professed a greater obligation as regards the matter; while in comparison with Coadjutors their obligation is greater in the same matter, by reason of the bond of a new vow, or promise of obedience.

Neither Scholastics nor Coadjutors are expressly bound to obey as regards the Missions without excusing themselves; and so in some cases they might without grave sin make excuse, when the Professed could not excuse themselves; as for instance if the business should be too arduous, or attended with imminent danger of death, and if one of the Professed was at hand who could equally well be sent. This we say that the Professed may recognize the greatness of their obligation, since they are, as it were, *by office* bound to expose themselves in this special duty, and they have expressly vowed to go without excusing themselves, so that their excusing themselves would neither be reasonable nor colourable; and not that the other religious should extenuate their obligation, and take occasion to excuse themselves, for besides this being never without great imperfection it can hardly be excused in a particular case, since a private religious cannot have knowledge of all the reasons which move the Pontiff or General to send him rather than another, and the hindrances which occur to the sending of others, and chiefly because in one's own case one is often deceived, either dreading where there is no cause for fear, or judging that an injury is done to oneself by one's being sent rather than another.

Finally, the Professed are, in virtue of their profession, laid open to a greater number of affairs and missions than are others because, since profession should not be given save to men who are conspicuous for prudence, learning and the religious spirit, from the fact of their being admitted to profession, they are judged fit for all the ministries for which such gifts are necessary. Similarly, when they themselves accept profession they offer themselves to all these ministries as the superior may judge fitting, and so in them a lawful excusing of themselves can scarcely find place.

The vow which is made by the Professed of the Society of obedience to the Pontiff with regard to the Missions, is made to the Pontiff, not only as he is Supreme Prelate of the Society as of every religious Order, in which sense the general vow of obedience to the Society includes obedience to the Pontiff as its Supreme Head; but to the Pontiff himself and directly, and just as if he were not a Prelate of any religious Order. Hence there exists in this vow a special property, namely, that when the General sends any one of the Professed in virtue of this vow, the General is properly the vicegerent of the Pontiff, and by means of special power bestowed by the Pontiff, exacts the promise made to the Pontiff; whereas when he sends or prescribes by reason of the general vow of obedience, he then acts in virtue of his own right and his own acquired dominion. Hence a precept of the first kind is graver, and of greater obligation, in the same way as the same law, given by the Pope and given by a bishop, is graver and demands greater reverence when it is imposed by the Pope than when it is imposed by a bishop.

The Supreme Pontiff thus acquires a proper and special right to the whole Society which is in a special manner subjected to him. Although only the Professed Society lies under this proper obligation, yet since all the other grades of the Society are ordained in order to this its highest grade, either by co-operating with it, or by preparing subjects for it, it follows that when it is specially bound to the Pontiff, the whole Order becomes also specially subject to him.

We believe that it was by a special providence of God that this counsel was conceived and embraced, that at the time when heretics were assailing the Apostolic See with a special hatred, one religious family should approach that See with a special reverence, and devote itself wholly to its service, and so specially recognize its supreme authority.

This vow is *solemn*, and its solemnity consists in the irrevocable tradition attached to the promise, by which the Professed specially delivers himself to the dominion and power of the Pontiff, as regards this effect of the Missions; so that as regards this he remains not his own master, and not even the property of his own Order, but the servant of the Pontiff.

### V.—Is Profession made in a fitting manner in the Society?

In the form of Profession as made in the Society, all those things are most distinctly contained which are of the substance of the religious state, so that in no way could a more express profession possibly be made. First, the tradition, or delivery of himself by the religious, is made expressly by the words,—*I make profession;*—and then the several vows are singly expressed, declared, extended and limited; and finally it is also insinuated that all this is done in a religious Order approved by the Apostolic See, when mention is made of its Letters.

The Profession is to be made publicly before those of the household and externs who are present at Mass. The Mass is to be said publicly by him who is to receive the profession. Having finished the sacrifice and holding in his hands the Blessed Sacrament he will turn towards the religious to hear his profession. After the general confession the religious will read with a loud voice so as to be heard and understood by those around, the form of profession, which will be in writing both for greater solemnity and certainty, and in order that the words may be more accurately and securely uttered.

This done he will receive the Holy Eucharist at the hands of him who admits him. The priest afterwards receives from him his written profession; and there follows a mutual embrace. The profession, with all its circumstances of persons, place and time, is to be recorded in a book kept for the purpose, so that evidence of it may remain to the glory of God.

VI.—THE SIMPLE VOWS WHICH FOLLOW PROFESSION; AND FIRST, THE VOW NOT TO ASSENT TO RELAXATION OF POVERTY.

After Profession and the making of the four solemn vows, other and simple vows are made, as prescribed in the Constitutions; not so publicly however or in the church, but in the sacristy or some similar place, before the same superior or other priest who has accepted the profession, and in presence of certain of the household and sometimes of externs.

These vows induce grave obligation, since the matter of them is sufficiently grave, and they are truly and most properly vows.

One of them is a vow not to admit any relaxation as regards revenues or any possession for proprietary use, either for the sacristy, or the fabric or for any other purpose which is unconnected with the Colleges and Houses of Probation.

St. Ignatius says that Poverty is the firm wall of religion, and is therefore to be preserved in its purity, and he also calls it the bulwark of religious Orders, which preserves them in their state and discipline, and protects them from many enemies. St. Thomas says that poverty is the first foundation for acquiring perfection. The enemy of human nature will endeavour to weaken this bulwark, and to change what has been well ordained by the first founders of an Order; for since his desire is to destroy the whole Order, he strives to uproot its foundations and to overthrow its wall, for if that is demolished, he will easily be able to overcome the whole Order. Although the vow of poverty is the lowest among the three substantial vows of religion, and although also its observance is the easiest, for it is easier for us to abandon our goods than it is to abandon ourselves whether in soul or body, yet violation of poverty has done greater damage to religious Orders. The reason may be, either because violation of poverty is of more frequent occurrence on account of the greater assaults of the devil in that direction, and its wickedness being less apparent or more hidden, so that it is more easily dissembled and permitted on the part of superiors (since shame interferes on behalf of chastity, and the superior, whose interest it is that he should be obeyed, on behalf of obedience), or because by means of it may be procured the comforts of the body, or because ownership is so much at variance with religious regularity.

Hence the end of this vow is that the foundation should remain firm, and the wall entire and uninjured, so that the edifice may be supported, and the city defended. With the same end in view several Pontiffs have imposed the most grievous penalties on the violators of religious poverty; and the glorious Fathers St. Francis and St. Dominic have left a special malediction on such of their religious as should transgress the poverty which was instituted by them.

There are two kinds of alteration of religious poverty, of which one is intrinsically evil, and consists in a transgression of the substantial vow, while the other is not intrinsically evil or even evil as prohibited, since it is not a violation of law but an alteration of the law made by him who has the power to do so. Other founders or protectors of religious Orders have, by means of penalties or maledictions, guarded against the first, but they have not provided against the second. Consequently many Orders, and perhaps without fault although not without some relaxation of their first fervour, have moderated the rigour of their first institution as regards the observance of poverty, by procuring Apostolic Indults. Of such an Indult, even although it was spontaneously offered, St. Clare refused to avail herself. St. Ignatius did not think fit to add as a means in order to observance, so long as its obligation lasts, of the poverty which is promised in the Society, any special penalty or malediction; but he has taken pains to provide that no relaxation should ever be made in that law of poverty itself which he laid down for the Society. This he could not do by means of commination or malediction, because such an alteration would not be in itself evil; and therefore he has done it by the addition of a new obligation through this vow, of which the matter is—not to procure or consent to any relaxation of poverty being made in the Society, even in such a way as might, under other circumstances, be without sin.

This vow is distinct from the vow of poverty, for it is one thing not to possess property, whether revenues, chaplaincies and the like, which are the matter of the vow of poverty in the Society, and it is another not to admit relaxation in this institute of poverty. The matter of this vow is most excellent, both because perseverance in the first spirit of the Order is in itself a greater good, and also because relaxation of poverty is wont to be an occasion of falling away from the rest of the rigorous observance of an Order.

The Professed alone make this vow, because to them chiefly the government of the Society belongs, and it is only the Professed who have votes in a General Congregation, in which alone such an alteration could be made.

This vow is purely negative, for it does not oblige to the doing of anything, but only to the not doing of a certain thing. Those of the Professed therefore will not sin against this vow who see others procuring a relaxation of poverty, and do not oppose or dissuade them, although they might do so. Although by this omission they may sin against the charity which is due to the Society, in the same way as one of Ours who is not professed might sin in a similar case, yet they will not transgress this particular vow, because by it they are not obliged to resist or hinder, but are obliged only not to do anything towards relaxation.

Two kinds of actions are prohibited in virtue of this vow. The first and principal one is to give a decisive vote for the relaxation of poverty; and the second is in any way to procure that it should be made or allowed by the Society. This forbids all counsel, or any vote, even if it is consultative only, and not decisive; and still more all positive favouring or procuring of such relaxation, although simple permission of relaxation is not excluded by the vow.

Since a vow can concern only a better good, and since it cannot be a hindrance to a greater good, so this vow will not oblige when the matter of it has from circumstances become so changed that it cannot be observed without hindering a greater good; but this change as regards the matter must be certain and evident. In case of doubt it does not seem that it would be against the vow to agitate and discuss the matter, and to set forth the reasons for and against, and to prefer that which appears most likely or probable, for this seems necessary to the common good, and to avoid peril of any damage to the whole Society. In such an event even if the truth and necessity of the matter could not be known with certainty and evidence, it would not be contrary to the vow to set the whole matter with all the arguments before the Supreme Pontiff, in order that he might ordain what he should judge to be best for the whole body of the Society. This would be done with the greater security if the Pontiff's leave should first be asked that, notwithstanding this vow, each one might freely declare what he felt or thought.

Without question the Supreme Pontiff would have to be obeyed if he should ever prescribe a relaxation of poverty; for since he had it in his power at the first to approve only a more moderate measure of poverty, so is it also in his power to prescribe relaxation of poverty, as he may judge expedient from the necessities of the time and for the common good; and his precept is always to be presumed to be just, when the opposite is not evident. He has power to do this, not only as he is Supreme Pontiff, but also as he is Supreme Prelate of the Order, in virtue of obedience; because it would not be contrary to the vow or to the Rule, but would be a reasonable alteration of a particular rule ordained for the better observance of the whole Rule.

If the Pontiff should not prescribe a relaxation of poverty, but should grant it to the Professed Society by way of indulgence, as the Council of Trent granted to nearly all the religious Orders that they might possess real property even if this was not previously permitted to them, this vow not to assent to relaxation of poverty would not oblige the Professed of the Society not to accept the grant of the Pontiff. When the Fathers of the Second General Congregation renounced the grant of the Council of Trent, they did so not of necessity, or from the obligation of this vow, but as it were voluntarily, and as spontaneously confirming it anew. The Professed cannot now recall their renunciation of that privilege; but if the Supreme Pontiff or another General Council were in the future to make a fresh grant of similar leave, the Professed Society would have the same liberty as before either to accept or to renounce it.

The obligation of this vow extends to the whole matter of poverty as it falls under the vow made in the Society, in whatever grade or state of the same it may be made; and it extends to the Colleges and

Houses of Probation as well as the Professed Houses. The Professed promise not only for themselves or their Houses, but for the whole body of the Society, the principal care and government of which lies upon them.

VII.—THE VOW WHICH IS MADE BY THE PROFESSED OF THE SOCIETY NOT TO SEEK DIGNITIES.

The desire of prelature, as it regards honour, pre-eminence and superior power, and every pretension which proceeds therefrom, contains within it the evil of ambition and vain presumption. A vow therefore which restrains this vice and inordinate desire, is manifestly most excellent, and very expedient for a religious Order. No vice could be more pernicious to a community, and particularly to a religious community, and specially to the Society. From this vice spring the envies, dissensions, contentions and calumnies which are the pests of every community. In a religious community not only the salvation, but also the perfection of individuals, depends in great measure on the life and example of the superior, and the whole good of the Order depends on obedience, and this is greatly disturbed by ambition. A religious who, forgetful of his profession, is ambitious of dignities begins to look backwards. There is, in fact, nothing which so bars the way to perfection, nay, to virtue, as does ambition. It is, says St. Bernard, a subtle evil, a secret virus, a hidden pest, a maker of guile, a parent of jealousy, a root of vices, the fuel of crimes, the rust of virtues, the moth of sanctity, a blinder of hearts, creating diseases out of remedies and engendering languor out of medicine.

For this cause St. Ignatius has provided with so much solicitude that the way should be entirely barred to this vice in the Society by means of this special vow of the Professed. It is especially adapted for the Professed, both because inside the Society the principal government belongs to them, and because they are likely to be the best fitted for positions of dignity outside the Society. For this cause also such a vow may be more necessary in this Order than in other Orders, since the Society might be more easily assailed by this vice from the fact that the Professed are to be, as far as possible, men of learning, and fit for all ecclesiastical ministries whatsoever, and well exercised in them; and so it might easily happen that they should be on familiar terms with princes and the prelates of the Church, and in the esteem and favour of these dignitaries. All these and many other things might easily provoke and promote ambition, and so not only is this vow useful after profession, but it is of service even to those who are being instructed in the noviceship; since by means of their consideration of it, they are from the beginning imbued with the spirit of it, and conceive that nothing is more contrary to the end at which they aim in the Society than is the inordinate affection of ambition. Hence also in nothing is the providence of superiors more vigilant than it is in the extermination of this vice, both by the committing of all prelatures within the Society to the General alone; and also by procuring with due reverence that the election of any one to a dignity outside the Order, when it is contemplated by the Pontiff, should not take effect ; and in this the Society has by the divine grace been more than once successful. As regards the Generalate itself, one amongst other reasons for its perpetuity is declared by the Constitutions to be that all thought and occasion of ambition, which is the pest of such offices if there is an election at stated times, might be farther removed.

But further, by this vow is prohibited not only that which is in itself and of its nature evil, namely, to seek prelature for the sake of pre-eminence and power, but also that which is in itself indifferent, and which may be justified. To seek prelature for the benefit of others, and because of the watchings and labours which are attached to it, is not wrong in itself, nay, it has an appearance of good, for as St. Paul said to Timothy— He who desires the Episcopate desires a good work. Hence to procure the Episcopate, if it is done with a well-moderated affection and for the foresaid end, and with other due circumstances, is not in itself evil, and it might sometimes perhaps be meritorious, if a particular bishopric or prelature were such as to entail great labour, and bring with it but little honour or temporal advantage, so that few if any, who were also worthy, would accept it. But in the Society the Professed are bound by this vow not only not to procure their prelature, either inside or outside the Society, with any ambitious or base intention or pretension, but also not to procure it even if the pretension should appear on any ground or title to be justified. To desire prelature solely by affection and interior desire, although otherwise evil and forbidden, is not contrary to this vow. Neither is the doing of anything with this desire, such as studying diligently so as to be more capable or worthy of prelature inside or outside the Society, contrary to the vow, so long as there is no negotiation or inducement of others; although he who should do so would be accounted ambitious before God, and his endeavour would be imputed to him as sin.

Outside the Society there may be understood by *prelature* the Episcopate, and by *dignity* the Cardinalate, which is thus distinguished since it has not attached to it in itself any *ordinary* power of jurisdiction; but besides these the vow extends to every prelature and ecclesiastical dignity whatsoever. Inside the Society these two words *prelature* and *dignity* signify one and the same thing; since in the Society there is no proper *dignity* apart from a prelature, for all the other posts are rather onerous offices, and if they have any honour attaching to them it is not so great as to suffice to the idea of *dignity*, and arises rather by reason of the gifts or qualities which are supposed in or manifested by the persons, than by reason of the offices themselves. The office of Assistant is not a *dignity*, and much less is that of Consultor to the Provincial. By *prelature* in the Society is signified the office of a superior who as such has proper and spiritual jurisdiction over subjects, either *ordinary*, as in the case of the General, the Provincials and the Rectors of Colleges or Houses of Probation, or *delegated* as in the case of a Vicar-General, Commissary or Visitor. The other ministries of inferior government under the Rectors or local superiors, such as the offices of novice-master, minister and the like, are not properly prelatures; such persons being only officials of the Rector, and not having *ordinary* jurisdiction, but only so much as may have been committed to them by the Rector.

One of Ours might sin against this vow by pretending to any extraordinary dignity in the Society, as for instance to have, as of proper and personal right, a vote in a General Congregation on any ground not prescribed by the Constitutions; or by procuring any title or kind of dignity, by reason of which he should have some share in government, with certain special prerogatives, in a way similar to that in which, according to the custom and observance of some Orders, there are Masters of the Order, Definitors, and others who are distinguished and privileged after having held the higher offices.

As regards the penalty for violation of this vow, none is fixed for those who seek dignities outside the Society, for this reason perhaps that that sin would be more a private sin, and not so hurtful to the body of the Order. But for those who directly or indirectly procure prelature within the Society, the penalty is incapability and disability for any prelature whatsoever within the Society; not however *ipso facto*, but after conviction.

VIII. — Is A VOW NOT TO ACCEPT THE EPISCOPATE, WITHOUT A PRECEPT FROM A SUPERIOR, FITTINGLY MADE IN THE SOCIETY?

The third simple vow which is made by the Professed of the Society is not to consent to their election to the Episcopate, so far as lies in them, unless compelled by obedience to him who has power to prescribe to them under pain of sin.

These words widen the previous vow, and constitute as it were a new vow, of which the matter comprehends every prelature and dignity outside the Society. The intention of the Founder was not that prelatures should not be possessed *inside* the Society, for that would be subversive of its government; and so the promise is not, as concerns these, *not to accept* them, but *not to pretend* to them; but his intention was that prelatures should not be held *outside* the Society, and so he would have the Professed bound as strictly as they can be bound, *not to accept* them. They could not be bound simply and absolutely, because they could not lawfully resist the precept of a superior, and a vow must always concern that which is lawful; but since, apart from a case of precept, they are free not to accept, they could also be bound *not to accept* in every case in which there should be *no precept*.

A purpose not to accept the Episcopate, so long as non-acceptance can be without sin, is, according to St. Thomas, most excellent, and consequently may fittingly be confirmed by vow; or otherwise—not to accept the Episcopate is an act which is of its nature better than to accept the Episcopate, so long as both are lawful; and therefore it may be the becoming matter of a vow.

St. Augustine says that nothing in this life and especially in times such as his is more difficult, more laborious and more perilous than is the office of a bishop; and St. Gregory praises the humility of him who from his heart flees from the pinnacle of government, and who when it is laid upon him obeys reluctantly. History also supplies us with many examples of the saints who by flight, by hiding themselves, by their prayers and in other ways have resisted their election to the Episcopate, such as for instance Saints Gregory Nazianzen, Basil, Martin, Cyprian, Ambrose, Augustine, Chrysostom, Gregory the Great, Antoninus, Laurence Justinian, Malachy, and others. St. Augustine says of himself—"I so dreaded the Episcopate that, after my fame began to be of some moment among the servants of God, when I knew that in a certain place there was no bishop, I would not go there. I was on my guard and did what I could to be preserved in a humble sphere, lest in a high sphere I should be placed in peril. But, as I have said, the servant ought not to contradict his master." He then only accepted the Episcopate when he understood acceptance to be the will of God. St. Gregory also grieved over the burden of the Episcopate which was laid upon him; and he complained of his friends that they congratulated him as if it were a piece of good fortune. In their endeavours to avoid the Episcopate, even when invited to it by the Supreme Pontiffs, some have succeeded, as did St. Bernard, St. Thomas Aquinas, and several members of the Society.

Although the Episcopate is the most perfect state, yet it supposes and does not confer perfection, and since it requires perfection in him who embraces it, lest it should expose him to many perils, so long as a man can without sin refuse it he will do better, morally speaking and for the most part, by refusing than by accepting it; for he will act more securely for his own salvation, and his attitude will be more humble and farther removed from presumption. He, on the other hand, sufficiently provides for the welfare of others, if he is prepared to accept the burden, whenever either charity or obedience may oblige him.

If the necessity of the Church or that of neighbours is not so great that charity itself should oblige a religious under sin to accept the Episcopate (a case which is certainly excepted from this vow, for a vow cannot oblige to anything which is contrary to charity), every other necessity or advantage is sufficiently provided for by acceptance in obedience to the precept of a superior, by which there are avoided the many and grave disadvantages and perils which might otherwise arise. The care of the common good belongs more to a superior than it does to a subject, and what will conduce to the common welfare is better known to him, as well as how far this particular person may be necessary to promote it; and the superior can also more easily and without suspicion or peril of inordinate affection come to a judgment in the case.

There is a difference between prelature within and prelature outside an Order; for outside the Order the prelature will have in it more of self, while inside the Order it will have less of peril. This especially applies to religious who ascend to the Episcopate, because they not only gain honour and power, but they seem to flee from the practice of subjection and poverty. Moreover, it is necessary to an Order that some of its members should be prelates within it for the purpose of its government; while it is not necessary to this that any of its members should be prelates outside it, nor is it as a rule to its advantage, since it may thereby be deprived of the better and more learned religious, who are most fitted for its own ministries as well as for the government of the Order. Hence, as a rule, it is not expedient or opportune that religious should not accept prelatures within their own Orders unless they have been compelled by rigorous precept, since this would impede ordinary government. It suffices that they should shew themselves not easy but somewhat difficult with regard to such ministries, always however with that moderation which prudent reason and an intention of the greater service of God dictates.

If it is true of the members of every religious Order that they should not accept prelatures outside the Order, apart from a precept of their superiors, with special reason is it most certainly true as regards the Society.

In the first place, by reason of the Institute and ministries of the Society, this Order stands most of all in need of learned and religious labourers, and it would be deprived of these if they, being invited to the Episcopate or other dignities, were easily, and without being compelled by a precept, to accept them.

Secondly, in this Order the more peril there may be of ambition, the more necessary it is wholly to preclude all the occasions of it. And therefore it has been well decreed that dignities should not only not be procured, but that they should not be of one's own accord accepted.

Thirdly, morally speaking and as a rule, the learned and religious Professed of the Society will be more useful to the Church by remaining in their own humble state, and faithfully exercising the ministries of the Society, than by their accepting bishoprics. It is related of St. Dominic and St. Francis that, when it was set before them by Cardinal Ugolino that it would be well if the Episcopate were bestowed upon the more distinguished of their friars, both replied that they would never consent to this. St. Dominic said that his brethren had already a sufficiently exalted state as preachers; and St. Francis,—My friars have been called *Minors*, in order that they may never desire to become greater upon the earth, and that being content with the submissiveness of their own vocation they may be better able to serve to the welfare of the Church. St. Ignatius also by means of these and similar reasons induced Paul III. to preserve the Institute of the Society intact on this point, and this Gregory XIII. afterwards confirmed.

It is most necessary for the spiritual welfare of the whole Order, that there should be a definite law by which it should sometimes be lawful to accept the Episcopate, and not otherwise; else every one would according to his own judgment and will conceive necessities of acceptance, and would easily be led to judge acceptance to be better and a greater service to God. To avoid this no better rule could be laid down than that the precept of the superior is to be waited for; since thereby both the welfare of the Order is provided for, and every necessity which can arise in the

Church is sufficiently met. So long therefore as the Pontiff does not interpose his precept, and there is no certain and evident obligation of charity, a professed religious of the Society can securely judge that it is not better for him to accept the Episcopate; not only because he may always fear peril to his own salvation, but also because, in accordance with the due order of charity, he, as a member of the Society, is bound to have regard rather to its common good than to the advantage of the faithful who are external to it. The Professed of the Society can, moreover, remaining in their own state, lend assistance to the bishops, and in this way sufficiently relieve the necessities of the faithful, or contribute towards their welfare.

After making this vow, the Professed not only may lawfully judge, but they are bound to judge it to be a greater service to God not to accept the Episcopate, so long as it has not been prescribed. Even if in a particular case there should appear to be doubt, the vow removes it, its claim being in possession and therefore in doubt to be preferred; nay, even if, regarded apart from this vow, it should appear clear and certain that it would be better to accept the Episcopate, after making this vow it is not to be accepted without a precept, for there is no necessity of doing otherwise since it is easy for the Pontiff to impose a precept if he should really desire acceptance. Even the Patriarchate of Ethiopia or the Bishopric of Japan, in which there is much labour and burden, but little honour, and scarcely any temporal gain, and which therefore it might seem a good work and an excellent to accept, are not to be accepted by a professed religious of the Society without a precept; and, so far as the Society is concerned, such appointments are to be resisted.

IX.—The vow which the Professed of the Society make to listen to the counsels of the General, if they should happen to be raised to the Episcopate.

Since it may happen that a professed religious of the Society should be compelled to accept the Episcopate, St. Ignatius has provided a means for his spiritual welfare, for his greater union with the Society, and for the greater edification of his neighbours, in another vow which the Professed make after profession.

They promise that, if it should happen that they are promoted to the Episcopate, they will never refuse to listen to the counsel of the General which either he himself or some other of the Society whom he may substitute for the purpose, deigns to give; and that they will always comply with such counsels, if they shall judge them to be better than those which occur to themselves.

A professed religious who is promoted to the Episcopate is thereby exempted from obedience to his own Order. Although his solemn vow of obedience is not removed, or invalidated or properly dispensed, its obligation remains only with reference to the Supreme Pontiff, and the religious bishop is exempted from subjection to any of the prelates of his Order. Hence a professed religious, even of the Society, who has become a bishop, is not bound to obey the counsels of the

General, nor is this vow made in the sense that he should have any one of the Society as his superior.

A person, however, who by reason of jurisdiction is superior, can as regards his own actions voluntarily submit himself to the direction and will of another. He can also bind himself to this by vow, inasmuch as it is a better good, at least in order to his own spiritual good, because hereby religion and humility and obedience are exercised, without damage or injury to any one. By ecclesiastical law, however, this is not lawful without leave of the Pope, to whom the bishops are immediately subjected; and individuals cannot renounce their right of exemption, and voluntarily promise or retain an obligation of obedience to any inferior, from which by law, or in virtue of their state, or by the demands of their dignity they have been set free. This especially applies to obedience with regard to actions which concern the government of souls; since the care of these is committed to the bishop and not to any extern, and therefore he cannot so place himself under the will of another in this matter as to be entirely dependent upon that other's will, for this would be in a manner to alter the order and rule laid down by the Pontiff. Hence St. Ignatius prudently not only would not have the Professed of the Society who become bishops, bound in virtue of this vow to obey the General as their superior, but he would not have them bound even to follow his judgment or counsel; since this would be a virtual obedience by which their episcopal government would be reduced, and in a manner subjected to the General. He would have them bound then only to follow the counsel of the General when they themselves should judge it to be better than their own.

The first advantage of this vow is both counsel and admonition, and that from a person of whom it is morally certain that he will perform this duty with charity and prudence.

Prudence, says Aristotle, is the virtue which is proper to those who govern, and it almost suffices in order to right government; and St. Chrysostom says that nothing is so necessary for the administration of affairs as is prudence. But an upright and sound judgment of prudence chiefly depends on wise counsel, for there is no man who suffices for himself, and especially amid the variety and difficulty of the matters which occur in public administration.

If this is true of every government, much more is it true of the government of souls, which is, says Innocent III., the art of arts. All the wise, says St. Bernard, are wont in matters which are doubtful to trust to the judgment of others rather than to their own; and those who easily elucidate the difficulties of others are accustomed more scrupulously to hesitate in their own. St. Clement exhorts a bishop that he should not by reason of his age or birth fail to accept useful and salutary counsels, even from the meaner and the less learned; and St. Augustine declares,—I, an old man and a bishop for so many years, am ready to learn from a young fellow-bishop and from a colleague of only a year. It is then a great part of prudence to make use of the counsels of others, and, as Aristotle says, it is easier to see with many eyes than with two only.

The second advantage of this vow arises from its being ordained not for the enlightening of the understanding, but for the confirmation of the will as regards the doing of that which the understanding sees to be better and more pleasing to God; and it serves also to make the bishop dread becoming faithless or blinded by private affection.

The bishop will be said to refuse to *listen to counsel* when he either will in no way hear the counsel, or when he takes it so bitterly as to signify great displeasure. The counsel however must concern matter which has relation to the vow. The Professed does not promise to listen to the General's counsel on temporal matters, such as household affairs, or the administration of temporal goods, or his literary studies, but only on such matters as concern either the salvation of his own soul, or the due administration of his Episcopal office.

Although the Professed of the Society when made bishops are bound to hear the counsels of the Society, the Society is not bound in its turn to admonish them, or to take the charge of their souls and offices, by any special obligation save that which belongs to the law of charity, which may however be more binding on it as regards them by reason of their greater union with it.

A bishop or cardinal of the Society will not sin against his vows by procuring or accepting a still greater dignity without the obligation of a precept; nor will a bishop be bound to renounce his episcopate, or to ask leave to renounce it. He may however, be admonished by the General not to seek another dignity or even to renounce what he has, and he will be bound to listen to this counsel, and to follow it if he shall judge it to be for the greater service of God, and more for the salvation of his soul.

The Supreme Pontificate is not comprehended within the matter of this vow.

The obligation not to accept dignities without leave belongs at common law to all religious, by reason of their vow of obedience, but certain points are special to the Society. First, the leave is reserved to the General, while in other Orders it is not as a rule so reserved. Secondly, the General himself cannot give leave unless compelled by obedience to the Pontiff. Thirdly, not only the inferior religious, but the General himself, if a dignity is granted to him, cannot accept it without the consent of the Society, and the Society is to wait for such a precept of the Pontiff as will oblige under sin. This is not demanded in other Orders, and in them it suffices that the Pontiff alone should consent or give leave.

If an Approved Scholastic should, through the favour of some prince, be elected or nominated to the Episcopate, even he could not, in virtue of the Constitutions, accept it without leave of the General. Since, moreover, according to common law it is grievous presumption in a religious to accept election without the consent of his prelate, and since in the Society and by its Constitutions the General is declared to be the one prelate to whom this belongs, therefore to accept election without his leave will be a grievous transgression, not by reason of a vow, as in the case of the Professed, for this the Scholastic has never made, or in virtue of the Constitutions alone, for they do not oblige under sin, but, supposing them, in virtue of common law.

## X.—The vow made by the Professed of the Society to manifest to the Superior those who procure dignities.

Still farther to prevent all ambition for dignities and prelatures, whether within or outside the Society, St. Ignatius was not content with obliging the Professed by a special vow not to procure them for themselves; but added another vow whereby they promise to manifest to the Society or its superior the whole matter, if they should come to know of any one who procured or pretended to any dignity or prelature.

Although charity might of itself suffice to impose this obligation, yet the peculiar obligation of religion arising from a vow is more clear and express, and it more strongly moves the conscience of a religious man. This vow, moreover, obliges not only when it supposes an obligation of charity to manifestation, but absolutely, whenever the manifestation can be made justly, even if it should not have been otherwise prescribed. It may often happen that one might rightly reveal the sin of a brother to the superior, and yet that one's doing so should not be under precept.

A vow therefore which so obliges not only when the necessity of charity compels, but also when the prospect of greater good suggests and justifies the act, contributes greatly to the welfare of the Order.

Such ambition as would be a mortal sin against the vow not to procure dignities, either within or outside the Society, is matter sufficient in order to the obligation of this vow.

## XI.—Why are these vows simple and not solemn?

These vows, of the intention both of those who make them and of the Society, are *simple*; for although the intention of him who makes a vow is not sufficient in order to its solemnity, it is nevertheless necessary in order to its solemnity.

These vows although made before a Prelate and witnesses, by reason of their importance and in order that the Society may have evidence of them, are not made publicly in the Church or with the other solemnities which accompany profession.

Finally, these vows have no moral effect added to them by positive common law or by the special law of the Society, but have only the obligation which they themselves induce; whereas a solemn vow always produces some such moral effect. Hence the Professed of Four Vows have the first place in the Society, and they alone have of ordinary right an active and passive voice in the election of the General; while the Professed who do not make the fourth solemn vow, although they make the five simple vows, are not constituted in that grade, nor do they possess the said vote; and so those vows have no moral positive effect, and are altogether simple.

# CHAPTER XXII.

## THE PROFESSED OF THREE VOWS; AND THE FORMED COADJUTORS OF THE SOCIETY.

BESIDES the Professed of Four Vows, there are in the Society other religious priests who are received to aid the Professed in their spiritual ministries, and who are incorporated into the Society by another kind of profession or union, and are constituted thereby in a final religious grade. These are the Professed of Three Vows, and the Formed Spiritual Coadjutors.

In accordance with the Institute of the Society it was very expedient that certain priests should be incorporated into it by means of three vows only, and so as always to remain in that final grade of the Society which such profession establishes. The expedience of this rests in the first place on the authority of the Pontiffs who have approved the Institute. Again, there are demanded in the Professed of Four Vows many gifts not only of grace, virtue and spirit, but also of sacred learning and philosophy, and of all the erudition which is necessary in order to teach, preach and explain matters of faith, and to defend them against adversaries, and to solve moral questions and cases. Such gifts cannot be found in all or even in the many. And therefore those who are endowed with those gifts, or who are above mediocrity in the possession of them, would not by themselves suffice for the bearing of all the burdens of the Society, even in its spiritual ministries. Other well-proved religious priests are consequently necessary to the Society, who, although less conspicuously gifted, are nevertheless sufficiently capable of aiding the Society in its spiritual ministries, or in certain temporal ministries which may be more becomingly exercised by means of priests. Such persons could give assistance in hearing confessions either of externs or of Ours, in visiting the sick and prisoners, and in exercising other works of mercy, or by fulfilling the office of Minister, or that of Procurator of a House or College, or of the Province. They could also assist in the Colleges, either in their government, as Rectors, or in teaching humane letters or liberal arts, or in hearing the confessions of the scholars and taking charge of their spiritual progress. Further, in the Houses of Probation they might hold the office of Rector, or that of Master of Novices. Many priests are adapted for certain ministries of the Society who are not fitted for absolutely devoting themselves to the Pontifical Missions, or for being exposed to these by the Society, and therefore they are rightly incorporated without the fourth vow. There are many who, although they might be sent to the Missions, should certainly not be sent as heads of Missions, but as companions of the principal ministers; and therefore it is sufficient that those only who are fit to be sent in principal positions should consecrate themselves to this duty by special vow, leaving the others as regards this matter to the obligation of the general vow of obedience.

The expedience of this manner of institution may also be confirmed by ancient examples, for Christ our Lord when about to send preachers into the world, chose a few who were to be the principal heads or chiefs of that ministry, and afterwards added many others who should be their fellow-workers. He first called the Twelve Apostles, and He afterwards added the Seventy-two Disciples, to be their companions and coadjutors. St. Paul says to the Philippians with regard to Timothy —"I hope in the Lord Jesus to send Timothy to you shortly, that I also may be of good comfort when I know the things concerning you;" and again—"Now know ye the proof of him, that as a son with the father so hath he served with me in the Gospel." He also speaks to them of Epaphroditus and says—"I thought it necessary to send to you Epaphroditus, my brother and fellow-labourer and fellow-soldier, but your apostle, and the minister to my wants;" and finally he entreats his sincere companion—"Help those women who have laboured with me in the Gospel, with Clement and the rest of my fellow-labourers, whose names are in the Book of Life" (ii. 19, 22, 25; iv. 3). Of St. Luke "the brother whose praise is in the Gospel through all the churches," he writes to the Corinthians,—"he was also ordained by the churches companion of our travels;" and of Titus also he speaks in like manner—"He is my companion and fellow-labourer toward you or our brethren, the Apostles of the churches, the glory of Christ; wherefore shew ye to them, in the sight of the churches, the evidence of your charity and of our boasting on your behalf" (2 Cor. viii. 18, 19, 23, 24). St. Mark is called by St. Jerome the "companion and helper of Peter;" and Popes John III. and Leo II. call St. Clement the "coadjutor of Peter."

The Apostles could not by themselves accomplish all things, and they could not always go together, and it was neither becoming nor expedient that they should travel alone, and so they required companions and coadjutors, and it became these to be in a manner inferior to them in their ministry, and subordinate to them, that all things might be done more fittingly and in order. The Society, therefore, since it shares the function of the Apostles as regards travelling throughout the world to preach the Gospel, has certain men to whom this ministry principally belongs, and that in virtue of their profession, and whom therefore it is fitting to bind to this ministry by special vow; while at the same time it stands in need of certain others who should be only, as it were, their companions and coadjutors, co-operating with them either on the Missions or in the Houses and Colleges.

Some of those coadjutors, however, or religious priests who do not make the fourth vow, are rightly admitted to a *solemn profession* of the Three Vows. It may not be expedient for them to make the fourth vow, since they do not have all the gifts which are necessary for the ministry to which it relates; and yet they may be most worthy to be received to solemn profession, by reason either of their singular sanctity of life, or of distinguished deeds or works by which they have merited well of the Society.

Sometimes also it may be expedient in order that there should exist in the Society a mode of dissolving *matrimonium ratum*, or marriage which has been contracted but not yet consummated, but without making the profession of *four* vows; or again, in certain cases, in order that the bond of union with the Society should be rendered absolutely perpetual on both sides.

This mode of Profession of Three Vows is not however in itself and principally intended by the Society; nor does it constitute a grade distinct from that of spiritual coadjutors. It is, within that grade, a special exception or dispensation, ordained to meet special occasions and causes which may occur.

The religious who is to be professed of Three Vows must have lived for at least seven years in the Society, and he must after lengthened probation of his talent and religious life have given no mediocre satisfaction to the Society, and further there must be in every particular case a concurrence of special causes of no small moment.

By this profession a religious is admitted to perpetual union with the Society, and to its spiritual ministries; and the Society binds itself to him in a special manner, and absolutely, and accepts him without any understood condition. Hence on the first ground there are required in him at least all the gifts which are necessary in Formed Coadjutors; and on the second, there is required some excellence, either by way of evidence of special sanctity, or of spiritual services done to God, to the Church or to the Society, or of some other cause which seems to demand this kind of gratitude on the part of the Society.

The Professed of Three Vows, however, cannot of ordinary law become Provincials, or Superiors of Professed Houses. This is in accordance with right and reason, for as the prelate of an Order should be *expressly* professed in the same Order, so also there should exist a due proportion between him and those over whom he is to preside. He ought therefore to be either in a superior grade, or at least in an equal grade of profession, and for this reason both the Provincial and the Superiors of Professed Houses should be in the most perfect grade of profession which can be attained to within the Order, namely, in the grade of the Professed of Four Vows.

For the same reason the Professed of Three Vows can be superiors in the Colleges and Houses of Probation, because in these they are in a higher grade than are their subjects. Since in the Colleges both Formed Coadjutors and even Approved Scholastic Priests may be Rectors, much more may the Professed of Three Vows who are in a higher grade. Even if in the Colleges there should be many who are professed of Four Vows, this will present no incongruity, since they are there only, as it were, accidentally.

The Professed of Three Vows have no suffrage, active or passive, in the election of the General, neither are they created assistants of the General, nor are they called to the Provincial Congregations, or elected Procurators for the whole Province to go to Rome for the Triennial Congregations; that is, in virtue of their *profession*, for they may be called in virtue of their *office*, as Rectors, Procurators of the Province and the like.

### THE SPIRITUAL COADJUTORS OF THE SOCIETY.

Some members are received into the Society to aid the Professed in their spiritual ministries, although they are not established in an equal grade with them. These are called *Spiritual Coadjutors*, and they constitute a special grade in the Society. They are *finally incorporated* into the Society by means of the *three simple vows only*. The reason why their vows are *not solemn* is because they are not made as *absolutely perpetual*. They are perpetual only on the part of him who makes them, while on the part of the Society which accepts them there is the condition understood that they endure only so long as the superior judges it to be for the common good that those religious should be retained. Hence in the tradition, or delivery of themselves which is made by the vows of Spiritual Coadjutors, there is not a mutual obligation of the same nature on both sides; although it is only in a rare case and for the gravest causes that the Society remains free to dismiss them, and they are in that case dismissed free from every obligation, and not bound by any vow. This contract is just and holy, and it has been expressly approved and confirmed by Pontifical Bulls. The nature of it is however at variance with the solemnity of vows, for solemn vows must be either wholly immutable, or mutable by dispensation alone. Moreover, the vows of Spiritual Coadjutors do not have force to dissolve previous matrimony which has been contracted but not yet consummated, an effect which is inseparable from the profession of solemn vows.

It was not without good cause that St. Ignatius ordained and instituted this grade, and among other reasons which moved him was this that he judged it to be to the great advantage of the Order to retain power to dismiss all who should not accommodate themselves to its end and method; so that it might be the better preserved in its purity, and might with greater security and usefulness minister to its neighbours, which is its scope, and that the religious might be preserved in greater carefulness, and live with greater vigilance. He considered it also to be most convenient that those who were to be dismissed, should be dismissed free from, and not bound by their vows, for thus less inconvenience is caused to both sides; to the Society, for it would be always a grave matter for an Order to expel one who should yet remain truly a religious of the same; and to the subject, for it is a grievous thing to be deprived of the advantages of religion, and yet remain beneath the burden of its yoke.

There ought however to be in the Order certain principal members who should be as it were its columns and foundations, and in the persons of whom it should be immovable, and who should therefore be bound to it by an indissoluble bond; while it should also in the most perfect manner bind itself to them, and should not be able to dismiss them free from their vows. Such members exist in the Society, and they are the Professed of Four Vows. Apart from these, it was the mind of St. Ignatius that all others should remain always dependent on the power of the Society; and only by way of dispensation did he permit certain of the Spiritual

Coadjutors to be admitted to profession of three vows; and that for certain grave causes which might occur, and in so doing he had regard rather to their personal devotion, than to the general idea of the Institute.

The Spiritual Coadjutors are not deprived of any merit before God by this condition of their vows; nay, they in a manner increase in merit since they bind themselves more liberally, without looking for a similar obligation on the part of the Order. Moreover, so far as lies in them, they equally with the Professed deliver themselves to God and to the Society in perpetuity, nor is there any risk of the perpetuity and stability of their state, if they are determined to conduct themselves in a proper manner. They are not deprived of any spiritual good by not being admitted to solemn profession, but are on the contrary aided by being thus admonished to be faithful to religion, and fulfil their functions. For the observance of due order throughout the body, it is expedient also that every one should recognize his own grade, and know to what ministry he has been called, and because these Spiritual Coadjutors are not the principal labourers, but their assistants, they should be united to the Order in a different manner, and with dependence and subordination to the higher grade of its principal labourers.

The grade of Spiritual Coadjutors in the Society is not to be argued against from the customs of other religious Orders, for the Holy Ghost is one and manifold, and has distributed different institutes to different Orders, in accordance with their various ends. In other Orders, in the admission of persons who are fit for profession and the religious state, there is considered only their aptitude as regards their own perfection, or at most as regards choir and the ministries of the divine worship, or the exercises of the contemplative life; but in the Society there is considered, as a principal point, the aptitude of its members for ministries towards their neighbours, and therefore even if a religious should appear to be personally excellent, he is not at once admitted to solemn profession. By reason also of the peril which may accompany such ministries, greater difficulty attaches to an absolute and perpetual obligation on the part of the Order, so that as a rule such an obligation is not contracted except with those who are, as it were, its foundations and principal members.

There is no reason however to dread from this any division or diminution of concord, since in the same body the various members have different offices and therefore different places, and a different mode of union with the whole, and yet all are perfectly united with each other so as to constitute one body. As in the One Mystical Body of the Church there are various grades in the hierarchical order, which not only do not hinder the unity of the body, but greatly preserve it, so in the Society, which most closely imitates the ecclesiastical hierarchy, this variety does not hinder union of souls, but rather perfects it; and this chiefly because it is founded in humility and charity, for those who have received greater gifts of God, and who have therefore been established in a higher grade, do not despise others, but on the contrary honour them, and love them as their fellow soldiers and fellow-labourers, and venerate them as the ministers and servants of God. They also, who have been called to the grade of Coadjutors, embracing their own lot, serve God in purity and humility of life, and esteem the others as their fathers. Neither in this distribution of grades should there enter ambition on the part of subjects, or acceptance of persons on the part of prelates, since there is to be considered not the honour, but the burden, and the greater service of God, and the assistance of neighbours.

Between the vows of Approved Scholastics and those of Formed Coadjutors there can be no *substantial* difference, since there is no such difference even between simple and solemn vows; but there is a *moral* difference as regards certain effects, or conditions which belong to the two states of life. Scholastics although they are true religious are yet in a manner on the way and on probation, and their state, therefore, should not be perpetual, but should have a term or end; while in Coadjutors there is required a state which is final, and finally approved. Again, as regards the vows, and their effects, there is a difference in the vow of poverty which, in the Society, renders Coadjutors *incapable* of dominion and inheritance, an effect which it does not produce in Scholastics, as declared with regard to both cases in the Pontifical Bulls from which this effect of *incapability* chiefly results. There is no difference of effect in the vow of chastity, since the vows of both states oblige to perfect chastity, and *disable* from contracting matrimony, although the vows of neither state *dissolve* previous matrimony contracted and not consummated, this being an effect which is proper to solemn profession. So also as regards the vow of obedience, with this exception that the Coadjutors, when they make that vow, express specially their obligation to undertake the care of the instruction of children in Christian doctrine, as do the Professed. This expression, however, does not add any special obligation to the vow.

A third and principal difference is in the greater strictness of the obligation on the part of the Order. The vows of Coadjutors are not solemn for this reason only, that there is not a reciprocal obligation, and perpetuity so far as the Order is concerned. The Order, however, is not free from all obligation, but is only not bound by an absolute obligation, for it is bound not to dismiss a Coadjutor for every cause for which a Scholastic might be justly dismissed, but only for some much graver cause.

The vows of Spiritual Coadjutors therefore approach much more nearly to the perfection of solemn vows than do those of Scholastics. Hence it is far more difficult to expel a Coadjutor than it is to expel a Scholastic, since for many causes the latter may be expelled, sometimes against his will, and sometimes with his consent and that of the Order; while the causes which would justify the expulsion of a Coadjutor are fewer in number, and of a graver character, and in practice the expulsion of a Coadjutor is of more rare occurrence. It is reserved by the Constitutions to the General.

The cause must be not temporal, but spiritual, and positively and not merely negatively contrary to religion. In the case of Scholastics corporal infirmity often suffices, especially if they themselves should ask for their dismissal; but in that of Formed Coadjutors such a cause is not to be admitted, even if they themselves should ask for their dismissal. In Scholastics also it will be a sufficient cause for dismissal if they appear to be useless for the ministries of the Society, whereas in a Coadjutor this will not be sufficient unless he is at the same time pernicious to the Society. In a Scholastic it is not always necessary to wait until it appears that he is incorrigible, but it suffices if he shews himself to be of a difficult nature, while in a Coadjutor every means of cure is to be employed until he shews himself to be incorrigible. Further, since a Scholastic is as yet on probation, not to amend or improve will be a sufficient reason for dismissing him; but a Coadjutor has been admitted with his imperfections, which have not to be proved, but have been already proved, and so even if he should continue in them, he cannot be expelled.

There is a difference also with regard to the *external* solemnity of the vows of Coadjutors, or the more solemn way in which they are made, for they are to be made publicly in a church or chapel, before the household and externs, and in the hands of some one who admits them, which is not prescribed as regards the vows of Scholastics. This external solemnity is intended to signify the greater union of the Coadjutors with the Society, and the greater obligation of the Society towards them.

A longer trial and probation is also as a rule required in the case of Formed Coadjutors, and although no certain time is fixed for them by the Constitutions as it is for the Professed of Three Vows, yet in the Ordinances of the Generals in A.D. 1606 and 1616, which are common to the whole Society, a term of seven years is specified, beyond which the taking of the informations at any rate is not to be delayed. It is also required that they should have sufficient learning, and that they should be already priests.

Besides the solemnity of the Vows, there is a difference between Coadjutors and the Professed of Three Vows in this that the latter cannot, according to the Constitutions, be admitted before the lapse of seven years, whereas the term for the former is left to the judgment of the General. Again, although of ordinary law the Professed of Three Vows cannot be admitted before their promotion to the priesthood, yet for special reasons which may occur in their case, and which have no place in that of Spiritual Coadjutors, this may be done by way of dispensation. A third difference is that Formed Coadjutors do not make the other five simple vows, which are made by the Professed of Three Vows.

### The Temporal Coadjutors of the Society.

Besides those who are received for the performance of spiritual ministries in the Society, certain persons are admitted in order that they may be occupied in such actions as are necessary for the support of the body, and in other external and corporal exercises. These are called *Temporal Coadjutors*. They are called *Coadjutors*, in order that by this name may be signified a religious equality and modesty, for they are not to be reckoned as servants, but as brethren and associates and assistants, in a sense similar to that in which Martha said to Christ concerning her sister—"Speak to her, that she help me;"—and as we read in the Gospel that Simon and the others beckoned to their partners who were in the other ship, that they should come and help them. This name of *Coadjutor* is used also in order to signify that they are fellow-labourers in the same work which is done by the others, for by this name those are called in the Scriptures who co-operated with the Apostles in their preaching of the Gospel. These Coadjutors are called *Temporal* Coadjutors, to distinguish them from the *Spiritual* Coadjutors, whom they leave free for their spiritual occupations, and in this way they aid and share in their labours.

The necessity for such a grade in the Society is reduced simply to this, that by means of the assistance of the temporal Coadjutors, the priests of the Society, and those who are preparing for the priesthood may more freely and wholly occupy themselves in spiritual actions for the service of God and their own benefit, and in their studies and their ministries to their neighbours.

There are three things chiefly in which the labourers of the Society are aided by the Temporal Coadjutors. First, in those things which are necessary for the sustenance of the body, such as food, clothing, lodging and the management of temporal affairs. Although with these matters even priests and Spiritual Coadjutors are sometimes occupied, it is only in directing and ordering and presiding over such of them as are more important, and require greater authority in the minister; but the execution of them could not conveniently be accomplished without the aid of Temporal Coadjutors. Secondly, the Society is greatly assisted by those brothers in matters pertaining to the divine worship, in the chapels and churches, by their taking most diligent care of the sacred vestments and all that belongs to the adornment of the temples and the becoming guardianship of the Most Blessed Eucharist, and the offering of the Divine Sacrifice. Thirdly, they lend aid also in ministries to their neighbours, either in the House, by receiving them with charity and, as far as lies within their power, ministering to their necessities, or outside the House, by being the companions of the labourers, for the priests cannot accompany each other, since this would greatly hinder them in their ministries.

We find an example of a similar grade in the Acts of the Apostles, who said,—"It is not fit that we should leave the Word of God, and serve tables," and who therefore ordained seven Deacons to whom they entrusted this ministry. The likeness between the two grades is not of course complete, for the Deacons were ordained for the ministry of the altar, whereas our Coadjutors are not raised to any clerical grade. Deacons are not ordained primarily for temporal ministry, but for spiritual ministry, in solemnly and immediately ministering to the priest in the Sacrifice of the Mass, and in the Word of God, and in the administration of certain sacraments, in cases of necessity. It was only secondarily that there was committed to them the ministry of distributing the common alms amongst the poor and widows, whereas our Coadjutors are not assumed immediately to any spiritual ministry, and so they do not require ordination. The similarity therefore is simply in this that as the Apostles abstained from temporal ministries, even those of charity and mercy, in order that they might give themselves up to the Word of God, and assumed certain persons to aid them in those corporal works, so the Society exonerates her labourers and scholastics from temporal ministries for the sake of higher works, and assumes Coadjutors by whom they may be aided. As the Coadjutors of the Apostles were taken from among the clergy, so is it also most becoming that our Coadjutors should be religious, and taken from the same Order.

The number of Temporal Coadjutors to be received is therefore to be determined by the necessity for their services. No more are to be received than are needed for the purposes already mentioned; for otherwise the Society would be burdened with more persons than it could support, and so deprived of other labourers who are necessary to it for spiritual ministries. Moreover, a superabundant number of Temporal Coadjutors would be to them individually an occasion of sloth.

The qualities which are required in Temporal Coadjutors of the Society are determined and ascertained from the end of their state. There is required health and strength of body sufficient for their labours, and a disposition towards devotion and virtue, and a good and easy nature, and especially contentment with their lot of Martha. Hence although capacity of judgment, and knowledge of some art, or sufficient talent for acquiring it may be desired in them, yet no learning is demanded of them, nor is it permitted that they should learn in the Society more than they knew at their entrance, and even if they did not then know how to read or write, they are not to be taught without leave of the General.

The perfection of this grade in the Society, as it is a religious state, is apparent when we consider either the vows of Temporal Coadjutors, their end, or their actions.

In the bond of their vows they do not differ from Approved Scholastics or from Formed Spiritual Coadjutors, whom respectively they resemble according to the length of time during which they have lived in the Society. They twice make the vows of the Society, and are twice incorporated into it. They are admitted at the end of two years of noviceship, by means of simple vows which are of entirely the same character as those of Approved Scholastics. Hence they may at this stage be called *Approved Coadjutors*. After more lengthened trials (which, according to the custom of the Society, continue for at least ten years, although in rigour of law there is no fixed term, it being left to the prudent judgment of the superior, according to which in a Formula of Father Claudius Aquaviva, about ten years in the Society and thirty years of age is determined as the time), they are incorporated more intimately into the Society by means of the vows of *Formed Coadjutors*, which are of exactly the same character as those of Spiritual Coadjutors. They are not admitted to solemn profession, and that for the same reasons as in the case of Spiritual Coadjutors; and these reasons apply with even still greater force to Temporal Coadjutors. It suffices therefore that they should be consecrated to

God in holy humility, for, so far as concerns them, no diminution of merit before God follows from their not making solemn vows. If they live religiously, their union with the Order will be as indissoluble as if they had made solemn profession, and they are, as Gregory XIII. declared them to be, truly and substantially and perfectly religious; and therefore there is, on this head, nothing left for them to desire.

As regards the end and actions to which their state is ordained, theirs is without doubt a grade which is excellently adapted for the acquiring of great perfection, and which is at the same time most secure, and in this security it, in a manner, excels other grades. They share in the whole of that contemplative life which the Society professes in all its members. They ought to be devoted to spiritual and mental exercises, and to give themselves up, at the times appointed, to prayer, examination of conscience, spiritual reading and meditation. Although they do not say Mass or recite the Canonical Office, yet they ought daily to hear Mass, and to say the Rosary or the Office of the Blessed Virgin. This although not of rule is nevertheless of pious custom. Their actions being external and corporal, do not greatly distract their minds, or hinder them from frequently turning towards God, either by realizing His presence, or by referring to Him all that they do, and imploring the divine aid.

Their lot very much resembles that of the ancient monks who were not clerics, and who, after at stated times singing God's praises, laboured with their hands, for the support of themselves or others of the poor.

Our Temporal Coadjutors have also their times at which they sing with their hearts to God, and pray with their lips, and afterwards labour with their hands not for temporal gain for the support of themselves or others, but in order to aid and minister to the ministers of the Gospel. Hence it follows that they share the lot of Martha, not only corporally but spiritually. Although proximately they are occupied with corporal things, yet since these are means towards spiritually aiding their neighbours, and are embraced with that intention, they share in the fruit and merit of the spiritual actions of the Society. They ought besides in their own way to co-operate towards the salvation of their neighbours, by means of conversations and chiefly by their example, and especially by the patience and charity with which they receive all with cheerful readiness, and with the utmost diligence relieve their necessities, bearing if need be all burdens.

Thus they are made partakers of all the good works and merits of the Society, and enjoy its graces no less than do the Professed, as is declared by the Bulls of Paul III. Julius III. and Gregory XIII.

## How many grades of persons are there in the Society? And how are they distinguished?

A distinction of the members of the Society may be made in two ways; either as regards their bonds with the Society which have been entered into by means of vows which in some way differ; or as regards the ministries in order to which their states are proximately ordained. From either point of view there are only three orders of persons in the Society.

According to the first distinction there are in the Society—the Approved Scholastics, the Formed Coadjutors, and the Professed. All these differ in the manner of their vows, and consequently in the nature of their bond with the Society. In other words it may be said that there are in the Society some religious who are *Approved*, others who are *Formed*, and others who are *Professed*; or some who are religious *substantially*, but who are not yet established in their *final* grade ; others who are constituted in their final grade, but *without religious profession;* and others who are *professed*.

According to the second distinction, drawn from the different character of the ministries, there are—*Scholastics, Labourers* and *Temporal Coadjutors.*

Of those who enter the Society there are four classes of persons, but this distinction regards rather the disposition and intention of the persons who enter, than any grade.

Sometimes persons are received definitely for one or other of the three grades above mentioned, and sometimes they are received indefinitely for that grade which shall seem good to the superior. The latter form a fourth class, which is called that of *Indifferents*. This is a class of novices, for among novices only can there be a class of Indifferents, since at the end of the two years of probation, all are to be determined at least either to the state of Scholastics or to that of Temporal Coadjutors.

Those who are received for spiritual ministries are then admitted definitely to the grade of Scholastics, and indefinitely to the grades either of the Professed or of the Spiritual Coadjutors; for this distinction can rarely be made from the first, until the persons have been proved in their studies.

Sometimes however, when they are of advanced age or learning, they may be destined from the beginning when they are received, to the grades either of the Professed or of Coadjutors.

## CHAPTER XXIII.

*THE MEANS WHICH THE SOCIETY EMPLOYS FOR THE SPIRITUAL PROGRESS AND PERFECTION OF ITS MEMBERS.*

I.—OUGHT THE RELIGIOUS OF THE SOCIETY, IN VIRTUE OF THEIR INSTITUTE, TO GIVE THEMSELVES TO MENTAL EXERCISES? AND TO WHAT EXTENT?

MENTAL exercises, such as examination of conscience, meditation, contemplation, and generally, mental prayer do not fall under rigorous obligation, or obligation of precept, as it is distinguished from the obligation of religious Rule and perfection.

The religious of the Society are, in virtue of their Rule, bound to such acts at their stated times; and from this obligation none are excepted, neither the Professed, nor those who are occupied with other ministries.

When it is said in the Constitutions that no rule is prescribed to the Professed as regards those spiritual exercises, inasmuch as it is taken for granted that they will be spiritual men who have made such progress in the way of the Lord that they can run therein, this is to be understood in the sense that they are not prohibited by Rule from adding somewhat to the times defined for spiritual exercises for all; nay, they are tacitly admonished to do so, so far as a discreet charity shall dictate to each, and with the counsel of their confessors.

It is not to be understood as if they were not bound by the General Rule, but only that they are not limited by it, or forbidden to add to the prescribed times; and this it is desired and hoped that they will do. What is to be added is not prescribed by Rule, because there could not be uniformity, since the strength of all is not the same, nor are the occupations of all the same.

There is therefore this difference between the Professed and the Scholastics of the Society, that the spiritual exercises of the latter, and the times for them, are so defined that without leave of the superior nothing can be added to them, while the Professed have, on the contrary, a general leave for, nay, even an exhortation to more frequent exercises, because their ministries and state require it.

There are three kinds of spiritual exercises which are of Rule, viz. examination of conscience, spiritual reading and mental prayer, and under the latter are comprehended meditation and contemplation.

The examination of conscience is to be made twice a day, at noon and at night, and at both times for the space of a quarter of an hour.

Spiritual reading is in our state very necessary, both for the sake of meditation, for, as St. Bernard says, meditation without reading is exposed to error; and also for the sake of the spiritual fruit which the reading is itself wont to produce, it being very useful both for the enlightenment of the understanding, and for the enkindling of the affections; and finally, for the sake of others. Since Ours should stir up their neighbours to virtue, and instruct them, and sometimes also direct them in spiritual matters, it is necessary that they should peruse the writings of the sacred doctors, from which they may receive the necessary light. Spiritual reading is ordained sometimes for one's own profit, and sometimes for the profit of others, and both ends are necessary in our state. The first fruit, however, is that which is here principally aimed at, spiritual reading being commended as it is an exercise of the contemplative life; but it pertains also to perfection to ordain it towards both ends. This belongs to the more advanced, and especially to the Professed of the Society, by reason of their state, for they ought so to strive after their own perfection as to compass that of others also, and so to give themselves to the latter as to attain also to the former. Hence, if the same action can be useful for both ends, it will, all else being equal, be more perfect, if it is referred to both ends. The space of time assigned for Spiritual Reading is a quarter of an hour daily.

Frequent and assiduous mental prayer is also necessary in our state, since not only is it a necessary means towards the acquirement of our own perfection, and our labouring with fruit in the vineyard of the Lord, but it is also in part the *end* of our religious life, which is not only active, but contemplative. Hence since this exercise is most necessary for the whole Society, the more perfect the grade of the Professed is held to be, the more should it participate in the leisure of con-temptation, although not so as to hinder its ministries to its neighbours, but rather in such a way as to aid and promote them.

This obligation is not satisfied by one's not altogether breaking off interior consideration and intention, and recourse to God during one's works and spiritual ministries. Although this is not to be omitted, and although by means of it the precept or counsel of prayer is in great part fulfilled, yet no one should on this account neglect the prescribed times for prayer or meditation, since without the aid of these neither attention to God nor the fervour of devotion can be preserved during other employments.

The space of time assigned for this exercise is one hour daily, and eight or ten entire days annually.

## II.—ARE THE RELIGIOUS OF THE SOCIETY BOUND, IN VIRTUE OF THEIR INSTITUTE, TO ANY VOCAL PRAYERS?

Neither by rigorous obligation of precept, nor by obligation of Rule are the religious of the Society specially bound to vocal prayer.

The practice and custom of the Society has declared that the whole of the hour in the morning should be given to mental prayer, or meditation and contemplation. This is to be considered the ordinary law of the Society, from which it is not lawful to depart without leave of the superior or commutation of this duty made by him. Hence, by a pious and almost general custom it has been introduced that all, especially those who are not priests, should, outside this entire hour of mental prayer, recite the Office or the Rosary of the Blessed Virgin, taking their own time for this devotion. Should any one not observe this custom, he would act imperfectly, but he would not fail in an obligation which is properly of Rule.

Besides these private prayers and personal obligations, there is in the Society no obligation to public and common prayer at certain times. The Society, as we have seen, does not profess Choir. There is an ancient custom that the Litanies should be said daily by the whole community in our Houses and Colleges; but this exercise although pious and holy is not prescribed by any Constitution or Rule. It is not so received by custom as to induce the obligation of a precept, for no custom of the Society has this proper and special force. Nor can it be introduced under such an obligation, for that would be contrary to an express Constitution which declares—that no Constitution, Declaration or Order of living can induce an obligation under either mortal or venial sin. This custom, moreover, is not one which induces obligation, or which has been introduced by obligation, since it was begun by a special ordinance of the General, and has been continued by the same, nor is there in it any greater obligation than that of the ordinance in which it is founded, and that obligation is not of precept, but is one of simple obedience. So long as the will of superiors continues, the Society will be bound to recite the Litanies, in the same way as it is bound to fulfil other simple obediences, but not by any stricter obligation or for a longer time; and if that will were to cease all obligation would cease with it.

This exercise, inasmuch as it obliges the community, obliges also its individual members with the same kind of obligation, and no greater, to assist at it; for otherwise it could not, as public and common prayer, be fulfilled by the community. Nevertheless, if any one should be absent from it, he will not be obliged to say the Litanies privately. This is certain if he has been justly hindered, or if he was absent with leave of the superior, for in that case there remains no ground of obligation, since he was bound to say the Litanies not by himself but along with the community, and from this obligation he has been excused. Even if he should have absented himself in a way contrary to the obligation of obedience, although he will have acted imperfectly, he will nevertheless, since the occasion and matter of the obligation or obedience is already in the past, not be bound to substitute anything in its place which has in no way been prescribed; as, similarly, one who has omitted a fast prescribed on one day is not bound to observe another fast in its place on another day.

The case is not the same as that of one who has omitted his daily hour of meditation in the morning along with the others. The Rule simply ordains prayer for an entire hour daily; hence in virtue of the Rule this can be fulfilled at any hour of the day; and the hour in the morning has been assigned by common custom, not in order to extinguish the obligation if it is not then fulfilled, but in order to appoint a certain and very convenient time at which it is to be fulfilled, so that it should not be deferred; and therefore, if it is not then fulfilled, the Rule continues to urge so that as soon as possible it may be fulfilled.

The obligation of vocal prayers which are enjoined to be said for the Society, or for the dead, or for founders, or for other causes or necessities which may arise, does not exceed the obligation of simple Rule or obedience, and does not oblige with the force of precept; unless such vocal prayers should have been prescribed with some sign of an obligation of precept, such as—In virtue of Obedience, or, In the name of the Lord.

Besides the obligation of the Professed, who must be priests, to recite the Canonical Office, in virtue of their ordination, there is no second obligation in virtue of their profession; and if any one should be professed who was not in sacred orders, he would not be bound to say the Office. The obligation in other Orders exists in virtue not of profession only, but of profession with the addition of custom; and this seems to have arisen principally from the obligation to recite the office with the community in Choir. In the Society there is no such custom, nor is there any foundation of such custom. A religious is in virtue of his profession bound only to that which he has vowed, and especially to obedience according to the Rule; but a religious does not vow to say the Divine Office, and so if in the Rule this is not distinctly prescribed under sin, there is no obligation of common law, save by reason of custom. Hence only Choir religious can be so bound, and not lay brothers, although they also are truly professed and are religious men. Neither does any obligation arise from the religious living on alms, since this obligation is not annexed by any law to alms, and neither are they begged for on this ground, nor are they with this intention bestowed by the faithful. This is especially true of the religious of the Society, who are supported by the alms of the faithful for the sake of very different ministries.

Our privilege of anticipating, and of accumulating the Office, so that all the Hours and even Compline may be said in the morning of the same day, if it is to mean anything must be understood in the sense that in virtue of it this may be done without fault, even if no special cause should occur to excuse it. Such a dispensation cannot be argued against as without cause, for even if in a particular case there should be no special cause for changing the time, there remains the general cause of this dispensation or privilege, namely, the various and frequent occupations of the Society as a body, and the avoidance of scruples in individuals. There remains of course the natural obligation to observe due order and method in our actions, and so, although there is not always required a cause which should be of itself sufficient to excuse, there is required at least a reasonable cause of action, and the best cause of all will be that which is set forth by Pope Julius, when he says—"That you may more quietly and devoutly in humility of spirit render a service well pleasing to the Most High."

III.—Are the Religious of the Society specially bound to celebrate or communicate frequently?

With regard to frequency of celebration it is ordained that the Sacrifice of the Mass should be offered oftener than every eight days, and not more seldom without causes which are lawful in the judgment of the superior. The intention however was greatly to commend frequency, for in the third rule of priests it is said that they should strive so to live that they may rightly celebrate daily. The reason for the frequency not being determined and prescribed, is because it would not have been well to define it as less than daily, while at the same time, by reason of various causes and occasions of interruption which might occur, it was deemed more prudent not to ordain this by Rule, but only to indicate it generally as a counsel. The result has been that by received custom the observance in the Society is that only on rare occasions, and by reason of extraordinary causes, is the daily sacrifice omitted.

There is enjoined on Ours interior preparation by procuring cleanness of heart, and other fitting dispositions, in order to which it is said much to conduce that priests, who are already bound by the Constitutions to confess at least every eighth day, should confess oftener in the week. With regard to externals it is ordained that in saying Mass, Ours should have in addition to internal devotion, a becoming external manner, as regards pronunciation and otherwise; and with regard to the space of time occupied, that it should be such as to satisfy their own devotion and yet not be burdensome to others, but rather to their edification. The fourth rule of priests ordains that Ours are in saying Mass not much to exceed half-an-hour, and not to come short of it. In the ceremonies of the Mass, Ours are accurately to observe the rite which the Apostolic See has specially approved; along with uniformity, which is commended also as a means towards the union of charity, for as the Order is primarily one of priests, it should have a principal care and diligence with regard to the greatest of priestly functions.

All members of the Society who are not priests are bound to assist daily at Mass.

With regard to communion, it is common to all religious that, in virtue of their state, they should communicate frequently, and they are bound to do so once a month. But besides this common law, some Orders observe a greater frequency. St. Jerome in his Rule for nuns, ordained that they should communicate twice a month or more frequently; and in the Constitutions of the Friars Minor it is laid down that the brethren should communicate every fifteen days at the conventual mass.

The Constitutions of the Society prescribe communion every eight days, unless it shall seem otherwise to the confessor or superior, in which case the subject will not by his omission transgress the Rule. With regard to Scholastics it is ordained that they are not to be permitted to communicate more frequently, unless for special causes, and in giving permission regard is to be had rather to necessity than to devotion. This is because of their occupations or the distraction of their studies. Even Scholastics however may be dispensed to communicate on solemn feasts, such as those of the Apostles, and other greater feasts. With regard to others, coadjutors and novices, who are not engaged in study, there is not this limitation, and they are exhorted to approach the sacraments *at least* every eight days. This is fixed for them as the minimum, and it is insinuated that greater frequency is not denied, but permitted, and it will be far more easily allowed to them, than to Scholastics, to communicate within the week.

Communion every eighth day is received as an almost inviolable custom in the Society, so that the exception, "unless the confessor or superior should judge otherwise," is of most rare occurrence, except in case of sickness; and even then, it is if possible procured that the communion of the sick should not be deferred beyond eight days. This is laid down in the Rules for the Infirmarian.

This custom is in accordance with that of the ancient monks who, although they lived in separate cells, assembled at least on Sundays in the church, where they received the Eucharist at the hands of their president. Cassian censures those monks who on the plea of fear and reverence postponed their communions, thinking, he says, that only the just and spotless should presume, and not rather remembering that we are made holy and clean by means of our partaking. He adds that there is in these men greater presumption of arrogance than humiliation of themselves, for when they do receive they judge themselves worthy of reception, while it is much more just that, with the humility of heart with which we believe and profess that we can never merit these sacred mysteries, we should venture to approach them every Sunday as a remedy for our soul's sickness.

The custom is also received in the Cistercian Order, and it was counselled by St. Augustine.

Although of old there was greater frequency of communion on the part of the faithful, not only in the times of the Apostles, but afterwards for many years, yet in these frigid times this measure of frequency is judged sufficient, especially in fixing it for a community as a whole. St. Buonaventure says that there can scarcely be found any religious, not a priest, who is so holy that for him communion once a week is not sufficient, unless for some special cause, or on some solemnity, or by reason of extraordinary devotion. Not only to permit therefore, but also to prescribe of Rule this frequency for the whole of a religious community, is a sufficiently ample concession. It is very fitting for our Order, both for the general reason that this Sacrament is the fountain of all sanctity and perfection, and because of a special necessity of our state; for in order to greater security in treating with our neighbours, greater frequency of communion and greater union with Christ is required; and also since it is an institute of the Society to induce its neighbours to the frequentation of the sacraments, it is most fitting that it should lead them by its example; and finally it is an antidote to the heresies of these times with regard to this Sacrament and its frequentation.

## IV.—Frequency of Confession; and General Confessions.

Frequent confession is most useful in every state of life, but most of all in the religious state, in which greater purity of soul is demanded, and in that state frequency of confession is more easy. In the Society all who are not priests are bound, in virtue of the Institute, to confess every eight days, while priests are counselled to confess more often in the week. This, as a rule for the whole of a community, is sufficient, and it is, in accordance with prudence, necessary for our state of life.

A general confession of the whole life is required at entrance into the Society, and afterwards every six months, beginning from the last; and if any one should at a time confess to another than his ordinary confessor, he is on his return to confess all his sins to the latter, even if his confessions in the interval should have been made with lawful leave. These constitutions are not rigorous precepts, but are counsels of Rule, which concern a greater good. Such regulations are not prescribed as things necessary, but are counselled as useful; and the reason assigned for them is the manifold spiritual advantage which is derived from such confessions.

Although, absolutely speaking, no one can be extrinsically compelled to reiterate a confession of sins which has once been rightly made, yet supposing his previous consent by vow, promise or covenant, by which he voluntarily accepts the obligation of a Rule, and on that condition is received, he falls under this obligation, the force of which is that not of a precept but of a simple Constitution.

This ordinance is most expedient for religious not only in order to their greater repentance and satisfaction for sins committed in the past, but also in order to their better direction for the future, which greatly depends on a knowledge of the past. An ordinary confessor has, in virtue of his office, the care of the spiritual government of his penitents, and he does not "know their countenances" unless from their confessions, and therefore it is a most excellent counsel that they should lay themselves wholly open to him in order that they may be aided by him.

### V.—The Reservation of Sins in the Society.

The prelates of religious Orders hold within their Orders the place of bishops, and the more intimately they govern and exercise their office of spiritual fathers, and are bound to lead their subjects towards greater perfection, the more is the reservation of sins adapted to their state and, in a manner, due.

There are also special reasons which render it expedient in the Society. The first and principal reason is the peril which arises to Ours from their communication with their neighbours, and reservation is, as it were, a bridle which restrains a man. A second reason is the number of young men who are being trained in the Society, and whom it is most necessary to keep under religious discipline. Thirdly, since in the Society there are not so many corporal austerities prescribed of general rule, the spiritual discipline and vigilance should be more rigid, and it was in view of this that corporal rigour was tempered by St. Ignatius. Fourthly, it is also most necessary that the subjects should greatly confide in their superiors, lest they should be exposed by them to occasions of sin, and in order that in other ways they may be paternally assisted by them.

The second General Congregation, in which was first approved the reservation made by the second General, Father James Laynez, laid it down, that the declaration, and amplification or restriction of reserved cases belongs to the General. No inferior prelate therefore and not even Provincials can add or alter anything as regards either themselves or the Rectors. A General Congregation has of course this power, since it is superior to the General himself.

Only external sins which are manifestly mortal are reserved in the Society, and of these, not all, but only certain more grievous sins, which are as follows:— mortal sin against any of the three vows, or against the other vows which are made by the Professed; perjury, false witness, theft; sedition against a superior, or division from the head with grave damage to the Order; detraction, and sowing of discord among brethren; furtively receiving or sending letters which contain matter of mortal sin; silence with regard to an impediment which would exclude from the Society; lying in the examination before entrance, to the grave disadvantage of the Society; and finally every sin which has excommunication annexed to it in the Bulls or Decrees of the Society. All these cases are grave in a religious person, and may bring grievous scandal or dishonour on the Order, and they are not too many in number, considering Our state and its obligations.

Rigorously speaking, it is certain by law that a superior can oblige his subject to confess to him reserved sins, for this is the end of reservation; and whatever of this the superior remits, he does it of his own benignity or prudence, and not because he has not the right to persist in the rigour of the reservation.

The practice of the Society is contained in an instruction which declares that when a confessor, without mentioning the name of the penitent, asks leave from the superior to absolve from a reserved case, the superior ought in no way to be difficult, but rather easy and prompt in granting it. It adds that then only when there is a necessity of avoiding scandal, or other grave damage to the College or House, leave can be denied, until the penitent himself, or through his confessor, should communicate such knowledge to the superior as is necessary to prevent this. In such a case the penitent is bound to give this information, and hence he is not safe, or sufficiently disposed for absolution until he satisfies on this head the just will and necessity of the superior, and therefore the superior can rightly refuse leave. Even if the obligation of the penitent to give such information to the superior should, apart from the reservation, not be entirely clear and certain, yet if it should be a deed of greater virtue and charity to do so, that will be sufficient for the superior justly to refuse leave, until the penitent shall have manifested to him the whole matter, so far as is necessary for the application of a remedy. The superior has the right to hear the confession, and he is not bound to delegate his power, and, having regard to extrinsic causes, he is bound to look to the common good rather than to condescend to the unreasonable or imperfect will of the penitent. In moderation of this, however, it is added that if the confessor urges that in his judgment the severity of the superior will result in spiritual damage rather than in good, and that having tried all other means he has failed, and the penitent is hardened, the superior should at last not refuse leave, but condescend to the frailty of his subject, having regard always to charity, the end of which is to do good by means of correction or severity, and to temper severity when there is no hope of its success. In this case however, although the superior gives leave, the confessor ought to see that the penitent satisfies his obligation, in applying a remedy for the common evil, or scandal; for unless he does this he cannot be absolved, not from defect of jurisdiction, but because he is not sufficiently disposed. In order to this however the obligation of the penitent must be certain, and other remedies must be impossible or useless.

When leave is asked not by the confessor but by another priest, the practice of the Society is that it should not be so easily granted; and this is in accordance with reason and law. It is not always to be refused, but the circumstances of the matter and of the person are to be more attentively considered, and so either it may be given, or the affair may be entrusted to another person who is prudent, learned and religious, and to whom the penitent cannot reasonably object. Some difficulty and severity should be shewn, for otherwise the reservation would be almost of no value, but always with the prudent condition understood that if at length the superior sees that he himself can do no good, he should condescend, and commit the matter to a priest who is fit to be entrusted with it, and this for the avoidance of greater peril.

The Society, for the greater security and freedom of the penitent, and from reverence to the sacrament, abstains even from a lawful use of knowledge acquired through confession, as appears from an ordinance of Father Claudius Aquaviva, which is as follows—Although there are not wanting Doctors who hold that, preserving the seal of sacramental confession, it is sometimes lawful, for just causes, to the confessor, when it can be done without any suspicion of revelation of the confession, to use outside confession knowledge acquired through confession; yet since this doctrine both demands a circumspection in so great a matter which it is most difficult to observe, and might sometimes hinder that freedom of subjects, which the sanctity of this forum and the Institute of Our Society requires, in opening themselves and their affairs to their confessors; therefore it has seemed good to us to ordain in the Lord, as we do severely ordain, for the reverence with which our Society has always venerated the inviolable seal and freedom of this sacrament, that all superiors should diligently take care that neither they nor any of Ours should even introduce the foresaid doctrine, or teach it either publicly or privately, or practise it in any way (unless perhaps with leave of the penitent); but that in all cases our confessors should so conduct themselves as if they had heard absolutely nothing in confession, and persuade themselves that as the government of human affairs is very far removed from this sacrament, so it should in no way depend upon it.

### VI.—In what way does the Society aim at perfection of charity?

The end of religion is the perfection of charity, and consequently all the exercises of religion tend towards this. There are two duties of charity, namely, love of God, and love of our neighbours. The first operates in us and increases chiefly by acts of interior meditation and contemplation, and issues externally in acts of religion and divine worship. It greatly contributes to it if the acts of other virtues are done with an express and frequently repeated intention of the greater glory of God.

The love of our neighbours is chiefly exercised by external acts; and these may be divided into works of charity towards externs, and acts of fraternal charity towards Ours.

### VII.—The "negative" means by which fraternal charity and concord is preserved in the Society.

Of these means many are due under the obligation of justice, rather than under that of charity, such as, not to injure another by thought, word or deed. But since those specially offend against charity who sow dissensions among brethren, it is declared by the Constitutions that if any one is discerned to be an author of dissension and division between those who live together, or between them and their head, he is most diligently to be separated from that congregation as a pest, which might soon infect it, if an instant remedy were not applied; and this offence is moreover included among the reserved cases. The separation may be either by removal of the person from one place to another, or by his expulsion from the Society altogether, if it should be necessary for the common good, as might be the case when either the person is incorrigible, or the scandal which has been caused by him is so grievous that it cannot otherwise be allayed.

Another rule exhorts all to beware of that affection which leads men to feel and speak about other nations in a sinister manner; and the reason is because this greatly lessens charity, not only towards externs, but among the religious themselves. Much more is the vice of murmuring to be avoided, which is the fruitful parent of discord.

The spirit of obeying and serving all in all things is laudable, and greatly conciliates love, while the spirit of prescribing and all semblance of the same is, on the contrary, blameworthy and greatly alienates minds. Again, it is one thing charitably to admonish, and it is another to reprehend. The former may be a duty incumbent not only on equals, but on an inferior with regard to his superior; the latter is to usurp the office of a superior or judge. It supposes authority and the use of some harshness of words, as it were in punishment of the fault. In this sense the Rule declares that no one is to reprehend or order his equal.

Even superiors are admonished to observe paternal lenity and moderation in their reprehensions, so that if possible they shall not so much reprehend persons, as make manifest to them the reprehensible character of the matter.

Another rule forbids not only external contradiction or contention, but also internal dissension, not only in practical judgments, but also in doctrine and speculative science. Three things are to be avoided,—contrariety of opinions, external and verbal contention and contradiction with regard to them, and dissension in judgments with regard to action.

Diversity of opinions is not in itself contrary to charity, for, as St. Thomas quoting Aristotle says, concord in opinions does not belong to friendship. Nevertheless experience teaches that diversity of opinions and frequent contradiction are no small hindrances to the union of charity, and often beget discord, and at least lessen the fervour of charity, and diminish its perfection. Although opinions belong to the understanding, as St. Thomas says, yet they greatly depend on the affection of the will, and are so far not antecedent, but subsequent to the action of the will. Hence it may be feared that a variety of opinions proceeds from a want of union of wills. Either a contradiction of opinion is apprehended as a lessening of one's own esteem and fame, and so is an occasion of diminution of affection; or the contrariety often arises from a jealousy with regard to the estimation of one's doctrine. Human nature however is such that in matters which are not of faith or scientific demonstration, men of very diverse character cannot wholly agree, and by the Rule we are not forbidden to have any diversity of opinion, but it is prescribed that diverse doctrines should not be allowed. This is to be understood in the first place as regards solid doctrine, and that doctrine which is most approved in the Church, for with regard to it there ought not to be any diversity amongst Ours, since novel opinions at variance with such doctrine are not to be allowed. Secondly, with regard to the opinions in which catholic doctors differ, care is to be taken that as far as possible there should be uniformity in the Society. Thirdly, it is especially aimed at and necessary that there should not be any diversity affecting the whole body of doctrine, in such wise as that there should seem to be contrary schools amongst Ours.

Most of all is the rule directed against that diversity of doctrine which proceeds from the affection and will, and therefore one must not oppose the doctrine of another in an offensive manner in public lectures, sermons or books, for this would not only irritate the individual, but also beget great scandal.

Not only is unity of doctrine to be aimed at, but diversity of judgment with regard to action is also to be avoided. This is a still more frequent and fruitful occasion of dissension and disturbance, since it arises not only among the learned but among the unlearned, and between both great and small, and may occur with regard to nearly all matters. Such discords and bitterness of soul are greatly augmented by verbal contention. Diversity of judgment is only human, and if proposed with meekness and modesty and moderation of words, ought not to offend any prudent man, but contention, and rash contradiction and defence of one's own view does great damage, and is most carefully to be avoided. St. Augustine says that young men should be trained not to pertinaciously defend that which they have once affirmed.

Those therefore, who are too tenacious in their opinions and judgments, and who readily contradict others, should beware lest they decline and by degrees fall away from that bond of charity which the Society demands.

Another means for the promotion of charity is the avoidance of the contrary extreme of private affections, too great familiarities and particular friendships not only for others, but also for individuals of Ours. The general rule of the Society is that we should love no one save with that love which well-ordered charity demands, and all private friendships are forbidden which do not descend from divine charity, for, if they are founded in that, they are no longer private friendships.

The equality of charity does not exclude due order and just distribution, nay, its perfection and preservation proceeds not less from this difference than from that uniformity. As from private inordinate affections there arise suspicions, envyings, jealousies and other vices which injure charity, so by an undue equality order is disturbed, and virtue is deprived of its due honour and reward, and so men's efforts in pursuit of it are relaxed. Hence in the judgment of all the prudent, just distribution is no less necessary than is common benevolence, in order to foster charity. St. Paul wrote to Timothy—Let the priests who rule well be esteemed worthy of double honour, especially they who labour in the word and doctrine (1 Tim. v. 17); and Christ our Lord loved His disciple John with a special love. Not every love therefore, which is greater towards one than towards others, is blameworthy in religion, but only that love which exceeds due measure, and which is therefore, to distinguish it, called singular, or particular and private.

The signs of such a love are, first, if the ground of greater love is not the greater glory and honour of God, or greater usefulness to religion or to souls, or the greater virtue and sanctity which is discernible in the person loved; for whatever is not reduced to this motive, is alien to the order of religious charity. Secondly, if the affection towards one person in some way withdraws the soul from the love of others, so that one avoids or ill endures that intercourse and conversation with others which common charity demands, or does not so readily relieve their necessities. This is a clear sign that the excess of love towards that individual springs not from well-ordered charity, but from private affection. Thirdly, it is discovered also by means of other affections, for the love of charity is excellently ordered, and it is not manifested save at due time and place, and without offence of any one. If therefore the affection inclines towards the idle wasting of time, or towards anything else which is not in accordance with perfection and the Rule, it is a private affection, and is not the due love of charity.

Charity is most grievously wounded by superiors, when they are led astray by private affections in the distribution both of labours and honours, instead of determining these in accordance with the abilities and merits of individuals, and with regard to the common welfare.

## VIII.—The "positive" means by which fraternal charity is conciliated in the Society.

Of the means towards the end of charity which consist not in prohibition but in action, some are internal and some are external. The former are more general, and depend chiefly on internal spiritual progress. The principal bond of union of the members, one with another and with their head, is the love of God and of Our Lord Jesus Christ, with Whose divine and supreme goodness if superior and inferiors are closely united, they will very easily be united with each other. This bond is strengthened principally by prayer and meditation; and this is without doubt the most certain and solid way to obtain the unity desired. In order that it may be reduced to practice, the Constitutions exhort that all should mutually considering each other praise the Lord Whom they should strive to recognize in each other as in His image. This rule seems to be taken from one of St. Augustine's. Nothing so conciliates the love of true charity towards another as to behold in him singular adornments of virtue, and the gifts of the Holy Ghost, and to contemplate him as the image of God, embellished with the most excellent shades of the divine grace. If all therefore will strive to increase in these virtues and gifts, and frequently to consider and admire them in others, and in their hearts to regard others as superior to themselves, and to rejoice in their spiritual goods, and to give thanks to God for them, mutual charity will speedily increase, and that in a most marvellous manner.

There are certain external means which are ordained towards the end of charity which are also general, and which belong to other virtues, such as obedience, of which it is said in the Constitutions, that union is in great part effected by the bond of obedience, while poverty and humility and contempt of all temporal things are similarly spoken of.

There are other means which are more special, such as uniformity and conformity in external things, as, for instance, dress, food and manner of living; for similarity is a cause of love. The common table is in the Society so common that no one however grave and ancient, whether a superior or very learned, or of whatsoever condition he may be, is excepted from it, save by reason of sickness; with the sole exception of the General, to whom, on account of the heavy burden of his occupations and for other causes, this singular concession was granted by the Third General Congregation. The Seventh Congregation greatly commended the desire of the then General, which he had signified to it, to do away with his private table. He did not obtain his desire, but as matter of fact he deprived himself of his table. The table is common not only as regards place and time, but also as regards food; for the same kind of food is to be set before all without singularity, which is wont to offend the souls of the weak, and so to disturb charity. This ought not however to stand in the way of the relief of the necessities of all according to their needs. Such relief is not, says St. Benedict, acceptance of persons, but is consideration for infirmities, and he who needs less should give God thanks and not be distressed, while he who needs more should be humbled by reason of his infirmity, and so all will be in peace. St. Augustine also says that if those who are weak by reason of their previous manner of life are treated differently from the others as regards food, this should not annoy or seem unjust to those whom another manner of life has made stronger; nor should they regard those as more lucky who receive what they do not themselves receive, but they should rather congratulate themselves that they are able to do what these are unable to do.

A second principal external means towards mutual charity is that singular care of the sick and infirm which the Society professes; although this is not singular to it, since all religious Orders are conspicuous for the same, and it is greatly commended by all their Founders. Relief is not to be denied to any one because some from illusion or malice sometimes deceive and pretend sickness, but it is to be extended to all, lest perchance the good and those who are really in need should suffer.

Another means similar to this is hospitality towards all of Ours who sojourn at our Houses, with all tokens and deeds of benevolence and charity, without any distinction of nations or provinces, and without acceptance or limitation of persons, whether professed or novices, whether in health or sickness, whether known or unknown. The reception of them ought to be with external signs of the greatest friendship, such as according to the custom of the country pass between grave persons who are friends or kinsmen; and not with signs only but also and much more with all deeds of mercy and humility are they to be entertained, and no expense is to be spared, so far as religious poverty permits, and the necessity of a brother requires.

Another means towards charity is the custom of the Society that every day all should meet together in the same place, if possible, for familiar and friendly conversation, for an hour after dinner, and again for another hour or half an hour after supper. Although this custom was introduced for the sake of health, it is nevertheless retained principally for the fostering of charity, for, as Aristotle observes, friendship increases by converse, and it is loosened by taciturnity. Human nature will not bear the perpetual strain of study and spiritual exercises, and it requires some rest and relaxation, and the hours assigned for recreation are those which are least suited for mental labour. If this means is made use of with due moderation and prudence, not only will it not hinder, but it may greatly foster progress both in literary work and in spiritual exercises. It is also useful to the Society as a means towards its principal end of the conversion of souls, which the Society in great measure achieves by means of conversation.

Not content with this intercourse of those who live in the same place, the Society counsels also communication by letter with absent brethren, as a means towards the same end of fraternal charity.

Finally, the end and the ministries of the Society not only stand in great need of this union, but they also themselves in no small measure promote it. It is the end of the Society to procure the salvation of souls, and consequently it requires those ministries which are adapted to this end. Hence every one of its members ought first of all and more ardently to desire and procure the salvation of his brethren, than the salvation of externs, because charity should be well ordered. As charity inclines towards seeking one's own spiritual welfare before seeking that of another, so as regards others it aims at and strives after the spiritual welfare of spiritual brethren, and of the whole body of the Society, before the spiritual welfare of externs. Hence should spring that supreme care and diligence which the prelates of the Society ought to have for the spiritual progress of their sons. Hence also the rule of the Society,—that all should be prepared to be corrected by others, and with due charity to aid in the correction of others.

IX.—BY WHAT MEANS ARE THE RELIGIOUS OF THE SOCIETY AIDED TOWARDS THE ACQUISITION OF SOLID VIRTUES?

Besides charity and the other theological virtues and the virtue of religion, possession of all the moral virtues is necessary in order to exact perfection; and perfection will be more true and solid in proportion as these virtues are more solid. Hence St. Ignatius frequently admonishes Ours with regard to the acquisition of solid virtues.

Those he calls *true* virtues which are exercised not in outward appearance and in the opinion of men, but in the sight of God, and solely with the intention of His divine glory; and those are *solid* virtues which are founded in true humility of soul, and contempt of all temporal things, and pure love of God.

The acquisition of such virtues is most necessary in the Society by reason of the frequent perils which arise from our intercourse with our neighbours in stirring them up to the pursuit of virtue, and therefore we ought to be greatly on our guard lest we should be content with the appearance rather than with the reality of virtue, and to dread lest vain glory which, as St. Bernard says, is the virus of virtue, should attenuate or corrupt its reality. In our state, moreover, all the virtues must necessarily be proved by various occasions, and temptations and persecutions, and therefore unless they are solid, a great downfall may be feared. Again, in order to our end of the assistance and salvation of souls, a most efficacious means is the probity and virtue of the ministers who dispose them for being rightly governed by the Divine hand, whose work it principally is; and an example of virtue is a motive more cogent than any words. In our external manner of life there is nothing singular, to move our neighbours or attract their admiration as in the case of other religious Orders who with great praise and fruit profess a more austere manner of life; and therefore unless Ours are conspicuous for the reality and solidity of their virtue, and for the great prudence and moderation of their actions, they will not shine before men, nor be able to profit them; and unless along with true virtue, they have also *solidity*, their spirit will be extinguished, and they will easily be left with a mere semblance of virtue.

*Solidity* of virtue depends chiefly on two affections, namely, *contempt of honour*, to which true humility corresponds, and *self-denial of corporeal pleasures*, which demands perfect mortification of all the senses.

For the moderation of the desire of honour and for the fostering of humility there is ordained all that has been said with regard to dignities and those offices which have an appearance of honour, even if they should entail great burdens and labours, and which it is not lawful to procure within the Society, and much less outside the Society. Hence Ours are not allowed to obtain chairs in public universities through public competition or votes, or to receive the degrees of Master or Doctor, leave for which is not to be granted by superiors for the sake of the dignity, but only when necessity or the advantage of others demands it. Fixed places are also forbidden, and no right is recognised of precedence or pre-eminence by reason of seniority or office, or of privilege or exemption from common observance. It is only in the General and Provincial Congregations that the order of seniority is observed with regard to seats, and even then it is for the sake not of personal honour, but of order, and chiefly that the votes may be given first by the more advanced and experienced of the fathers. To superiors a place of honour is always due, for this the reverence due to their dignity demands; but in other matters which belong to personal comfort, they are on the level with the rest.

These and similar observances for the removal of every occasion of ambition and of every hindrance to humility would not suffice without a frequent exercise of humility, both internal and external; and opportunities for the exercise of both are found in the Society.

St. Benedict says that the first degree of humility is the abnegation of one's own will, and Cassian declares that no one can acquire true humility of heart who has not first learned to renounce his own will. This degree of humility is brought to an excellent perfection when not only the will, but the judgment also is submitted to the judgment of another. As the supreme excellence of man is in his understanding, so the supreme degree of humility is in the submission and subjection of the understanding. This exercise of internal humility, as commended and practised in the Society, we have already considered (see p. 118). Experience has shewn that no one can live at rest in the Society or remain long therein, who has not learned to moderate, to break in and frequently to renounce his own will and judgment.

Of the external actions of humility which are most necessary for acquiring, nourishing, increasing and preserving humility itself, a foundation is laid during the noviceship. Although such external actions are necessarily less frequent during the years of study, they are never wholly laid aside, and at the end of the studies their exercise is restored and renewed during the third year of probation, and it continues afterwards throughout the whole of our religious life. No works of mercy in hospitals, prisons and the like should be shunned, and the instruction of children in Christian doctrine is so commended in the Society as to be one of the principal obligations of the Professed, and it includes no slight exercise of humility, as it is also a work of great charity; two virtues of which the labourers of the Society stand most of all in need. Humility, says St. Bernard, is the foundation of the whole spiritual fabric, and *humiliation* is the way towards *humility*, as *patience* is the way towards *peace*, and *reading* is the way towards *learning*.

Mortification is without doubt the mother of all virtues, and it occupies a principal place in the Institute, which greatly commends mortification of the senses and desires, and in all matters of food, clothing, lodging and the like, having regard always but only to the end of the Society, and the necessities of human nature.

# CHAPTER XXIV.

*THE MEANS OR MINISTRIES WHICH THE SOCIETY EMPLOYS FOR THE SALVATION OF EXTERNS.*

1. — WHAT CAN AND OUGHT THE RELIGIOUS OF THE SOCIETY TO DO WITH REGARD TO THE MINISTRY OF PREACHING THE WORD OF GOD? AND WHAT HAS BEEN GRANTED TO THEM WITH REGARD TO THIS MINISTRY BY THE APOSTOLIC SEE?

Among the ministries of the Society for the salvation of its neighbours, the preaching of the Word of God holds the first place.

Among other things, says Innocent III., which belong to the salvation of the christian people, the food of the Word of God is acknowledged to be most of all necessary, for as the body is nourished with material food, so is the soul nourished with spiritual food. The Council of Trent says that the preaching of the Gospel is not less necessary to the christian commonwealth than is reading, and that preaching is a principal function of the bishops. In the Professed Society therefore, inasmuch as it was instituted chiefly to aid the bishops in the salvation of souls, the preaching of the Gospel is either its principal, or one of its principal ministries. Preaching is in its measure common to all the Mendicant Orders, and especially to the Order of St. Dominic, which has therefore its special name of—the Order of Preachers; but to the Society it belongs in virtue of its Institute to share this ministry with the prelates of the Church, and to exercise it in their place.

Faculty from a prelate of the Church is necessary for the religious of the Society, as for others, in order that they may lawfully exercise this function; for as St. Paul says,—"How can they preach, unless they be *sent?*" (Rom. x. 15). To *send* them belongs to the pastors of the Church, whose office it is to feed the flock of Christ, and justice demands that no one should without their authority usurp their office and jurisdiction. It is moreover, absolutely necessary for the preservation of due order in the Church, and the avoidance of schisms, and for preventing the sowing of the seeds of error. Hence all are excommunicated who without authority from the Apostolic See or from the local bishop, presume publicly or privately to usurp the office of preaching.

It is certain that faculty from the Apostolic See is sufficient, since the Supreme Pontiff is the Supreme and Universal Pastor, and he is independent of all inferiors.

The Society holds its faculty for preaching from the Apostolic See, by the Bull of Paul III. A.D. 1554 which declares,—We have taken the Society under Our protection, and that of the Apostolic See, and to every one of you who is found fit and has been deputed by the superior of your Society for the time being, We by these presents grant free faculty by Apostolic authority, and at Our good pleasure and that of the Apostolic See, to preach, propound and interpret to the clergy and people the Word of God everywhere and in all churches whatsoever, and common or public places and streets, and to teach them the way of truth, and of a good and holy life, so that in you by word as by example they may be edified, and to exhort and admonish them in the Lord.

Although this privilege is given absolutely and without restriction, it is nevertheless to be understood as limited by dependence on the consent of the bishops, and by absence of objection on the part of the parish priests, to whom it belongs in virtue of their office to preach and teach the people. This is in accordance with reason, for the avoidance of disputes and scandals. Although of the plenitude of his power the Pontiff could give faculty to preach everywhere without the leave of the bishops and even against their will and that of the parish priests, yet when this is not expressly declared, the grant is to be understood with reservation of their ordinary rights.

The Council of Trent says generally with regard to all regulars that, even although they may have been approved by their own prelates, they shall be bound, before they begin to preach in the churches even of their own Order, to present themselves to the bishop, and to ask his benediction; while in churches which do not belong to their own Order, they shall be bound to have, besides the leave of their superiors, the leave also of the bishop. It is also ordained that no one whether secular or regular shall presume to preach even in the churches of his own Order, if the *bishop should object.*

Gregory XIII. granted to the religious of the Society that, having been once approved by some ordinary and deputed by their own superiors, they might while on a journey freely preach everywhere, with two exceptions, first, not in towns or places in which the ordinary is living, save with his leave first obtained; and secondly, not in other places, from which the bishop is absent, if the curates of the parochial churches should object. These are, especially in the absence of the bishop, the *ordinary* pastors, and although they are not equally to be deferred to, by asking or waiting for their leave, yet for the sake of peace and to avoid scandals, the Pontiff did not will Ours to preach if they should object. This restriction does not apply to our own churches in towns where there is no bishop, but only parish priests; nor to preaching in streets or other places outside the proper parish churches.

It has been argued that this privilege of Paul III. confers nothing, for if the bishops give Ours leave to preach in their dioceses, there is no need of the Pontiff's faculty, because the bishop's faculty suffices, while on the other hand, if the bishop refuses leave, the Pontifical faculty is useless. But there is this difference created by the Pontifical faculty, that, apart from that Privilege, the bishop might solely by an act of his own will refuse leave to Ours to preach, however worthy they might be (because in that case the leave would be simply a grace on his part and, as it were, a delegation and liberal communication of jurisdiction;) whereas, in face of the Privilege, he cannot *justly* refuse leave, if the person is fit to preach, because this would be contrary to the Pontiff's will and intention. The faculty emanates from the Pontiff, and therefore an inferior cannot *without just cause* hinder it, although of the benignity of the Pontiff, the consent of the bishop is required *as a necessary condition*.

Although this faculty was granted primarily in favour of the Professed Society, it nevertheless extends to all other members of the Society who are clerics, that is, not only to those who are priests or deacons, but to all Scholastics and even novices of Ours who have received the tonsure.

The office of preacher requires fitness in the preacher, that is, sufficient learning and virtue. It requires sufficient learning, for " if the blind lead the blind, both will fall into the ditch," and learning without virtue is inefficacious, for " if the salt lose its savour with what shall it be salted?" (St. Matt. v. 13). The degree of learning and of virtue which is required is not however the same in all cases, and is to be determined according to circumstances of place, time and persons. Some are sent to preach to the common people, and to instruct and exhort them to an ordinary mode of reputable life; others are sent to enlighten the learned, to refute heretics, and to propound and illustrate in a higher style the mysteries of the faith; while others are sent to unfold with greater refinement the state of perfection and the spiritual life. In some therefore, greater learning is required than in others, and similarly greater perfection of sanctity and efficacy of spirit. In all, so far as doctrine is concerned, it is required that at least they should know the dogmas of the faith, and the sound moral doctrine with regard to virtues and vices, so as sufficiently to explain them in public without risk of error. As regards virtue, there is necessary at least the example of a reputable life.

The superior in the Society by whom its preachers are to be approved and destined to their office is, after the General, the Provincial. This power in the Provincials is not merely a delegated power, but is an *ordinary* power, since they share it in virtue of their office, and of law and privilege; and so there is nothing to prevent them delegating it to a Rector or other person, if they should judge this to be expedient. General delegation would not, however, be allowable, because it is not necessary, nor would it suffice to the Provincial's fulfilment of his office; but in a particular case by reason of a special necessity, and especially with respect to a determinate person, it would be both valid and lawful to entrust or delegate this power.

That the approbation of the superior should be by way of domestic examination is not of the essence of the act, nor is it of rigorous precept, but is an obligation of simple Rule, which it is very expedient to observe, although in some cases, where the fitness of the subject is well known and evident, it may be dispensed with. This rule is in accordance with the decree of the Lateran Council held under Leo X., which ordained that no one, whether a secular cleric, or a regular of any even a Mendicant Order, or any other whosoever to whom the faculty of preaching belongs, whether by law, or custom or privilege or otherwise, should be permitted to exercise that office, without having been first diligently examined by his superior (and with this the conscience of the superior is burdened), and found apt and fit for it by moral respectability, age, learning, probity, prudence and exemplary life. Prudence can scarcely be separated from learning and virtue, if these are found in union; but in a preacher as such, that prudence is required which is necessary in order to speak becomingly and with dignity of sacred things, and of those matters which belong to the good of souls.

The question of age is to be left to the prudence of the superior, since not in all persons or for all places and sermons is the same maturity of age required, and age may be in great measure supplied by other endowments, especially by those of judgment and solid virtue.

It has been objected to Ours preaching in streets and public places, that this is not a decent manner of treating the Word of God, and that it belongs to the reverence which is due to sacred things and actions that they should be done not in profane and common but in sacred places which have been specially set apart for them; that the Word of God is a very sacred thing, and so sacred as to be compared by St. Augustine in a manner to the Eucharist itself; and that the preaching of it is one end among others for which sacred temples are dedicated, and therefore that as it is not lawful outside these to perform other sacred functions, so neither is it lawful to preach sacred sermons; and that finally this mode of preaching is contrary to the custom of the

Church, and is moreover of no utility, because in streets and public places the Word of God cannot be either attentively or devoutly heard, and therefore that such a practice ought neither to be introduced nor to be permitted.

In answer to this, it is certain as of faith that it is neither evil in itself nor unbecoming to preach to the people in the streets and public places. This is evident from the authority of the Pontiffs, for it would be an intolerable error to grant a faculty for a thing which is in itself evil or unbecoming. It may be confirmed also by the example of Christ Himself, Who taught the multitudes on the mountain, on the sea-shore, from the ship, and everywhere as occasion offered. His Apostles did the same and, as it appears, not without a precept or counsel on the part of their Divine Master. In His parable of the Supper, the master of the house says to his servant,—"Go out quickly into the streets and lanes of the city. . . . Go out into the highways and hedges, and compel them to come in, that my house may be filled" (St. Luke xiv. 21, 23); and to His Apostles when He sent them forth to preach He said,— "That which I tell you in the dark, speak ye in the light, and that which you hear in the ear, preach ye upon the housetops" (St. Matt. x. 27), that is, in any convenient and public place whatsoever, adapted for public preaching. In those days the housetops were level and adapted for conversation, and those things were then done on them which are now wont to be done in the market-place. Hence "preach on the housetops" was the same as saying—preach in the market-place and everywhere. St. John the Baptist and before him many of the prophets, and in particular Esdras preached in public places; and since the times of the Apostles, many saints have preached on the highways and in the fields, such as St. Anthony of Padua, St. Vincent Ferrer, St. Peter Martyr and others. The custom is not forbidden by any positive law, divine or ecclesiastical, for where is the decree or canon which forbids it?

If it is objected that, given the lawfulness of the practice, there is no need for a Privilege, supposing faculty to preach, it is to be remembered that when a Privilege is granted it is not always in order to dispense from some law, but may be for other ends as well. In this particular case the Privilege produces two principal effects. One is that it is not only lawful to the Society, but that in virtue of the grant the Society has a certain *right* to preach in such places, so that it cannot be *justly* hindered by any one without reasonable cause. A second effect is to shut the mouths of gainsayers, and to compel them to confess that so to preach is not only not evil, but is also in itself very expedient, if it is done with due moderation and prudence. For the truth of this we have also, besides the authority of the Pontiffs, the examples of the Saints; and that not only in the beginning of the Church, when the plea of necessity might be urged, but also after the foundation and multiplication of temples, as in the times of St. Bernard, St. Dominic and St. Francis by whom it was done, as well as by many others in later times. Reason, moreover, shews that the states and conditions of men are very various, and great numbers of men do not come to the temples to hear the Word of God, many because they cannot conveniently do so, and others because from evil custom they will not, and so it is very useful that sometimes there should be sermons outside the churches in the streets or other public places; and this may result in the fulfilment of the words of Isaias, quoted by St. Paul,—"I was found by them that did not seek me, I appeared openly to them that asked not after me" (Rom. x. 20). Theophylact commenting on the words of St. Paul to Timothy— "Preach the Word, be instant in season, out of season" (2 Tim. iv. 2) refers opportunity of doctrine, or instancy *in season* to preaching *in the church*, and *importunity* of doctrine, or instancy *out of season* to the preaching which takes place *outside the church*. St. Thomas also expounds "in season" with reference to those who *will to hear*, and "out of season" with reference to those who *do not will to hear*, and this instancy should be such as that those who will not may be compelled to hear. Such preaching in public places may seem importunate to those who do not sufficiently consider the importance of the matter, and yet it is very opportune in order that the Word of God may be better shed abroad so as to reach all.

Again, preaching is not properly a sacred ministry, and ministers are not specially consecrated for it, nor is it ordained to any mystical signification, but only to the moral and spiritual advantage of the faithful, and therefore it does not demand a sacred place for its exercise, but only such a place as is adapted and suitable for the convenience and edification of the faithful. Although temples serve for the office of preaching, yet they are not in themselves primarily instituted for this end, but for the offering of sacrifice within them; and therefore they are blessed or consecrated, not properly for preaching, but specially by reason of the Divine Eucharist, and other sacraments. During the time of the Old Law sacrifice could be offered at one place only, namely, in the Temple at Jerusalem, while in the other cities and towns there were synagogues set apart for prayer and preaching. Churches are convenient for the ordinary sermons to which the faithful at stated times flock of their own accord, and they are set apart for prayer, and yet this does not hinder either preaching or prayer in other places, for the Apostle says—"I will that men pray in every place" (1 Tim. ii. 8).

It is, as we have seen, manifestly untrue that preaching in public places is contrary to the custom of the Church, and if it is less frequently the custom in later times it may be either because there is less necessity for it as regards the hearers, or because the fervour of charity has somewhat cooled in the preachers.

Simply to teach Christian doctrine for the instruction of children or the common people is not properly included under the name of preaching, since it is not in itself ordained for the teaching and exhorting of the whole Church, understood as comprehending clergy and people, learned and unlearned; and so this may be done by Ours, even if they have not received the tonsure, and that not so much in virtue of the Privilege, since for this a special privilege is not necessary, as in virtue of the general Approbation of the Society which was specially instituted, among other things, for the exercise of this office.

The Pontiff indicates in his Privilege the mode which the labourers of the Society should observe in their preaching, and sets forth two things, the end of preaching, and the actions or means to be employed in order to that end. The end ought to be to exhort and build up our neighbours to a good life; and the doctrine and the mode of preaching it should be such as is adapted for that end. It is most of all necessary in order to a due end that one should not seek his own praise or the popular applause, as St. Paul says of himself and his fellow-Apostles,—"We speak, not as pleasing men but God who proveth our hearts, for neither have we used at any time the speech of flattery, as you know, nor taken an occasion of covetousness, God is witness; neither sought we glory of men, neither of you nor of others" (1 Thess. ii. 4-6).

In accordance with this end the Society, supposing a pure intention of the Divine service, and a sincere zeal for souls to the glory of the Divine Majesty, and demanding also solid virtues, and especially charity and intimate intercourse with God in spiritual exercises, lays down two principal means. One is to set before the people those things which will be alike serviceable and suited to their comprehension, and to insist on those things which will avail for their instruction as Christians, and for the extirpation of vices and the sowing of the seeds of virtues, abstaining from all curious treatment of subtle matters. The other means is the use of prudence in correction, for although it is necessary to reprehend vice, yet in order that this may be done with profit, there is need of the greatest prudence and moderation, and especially that it should be done in a general way, without indication and consequent irritation of individuals. Especially is this true with regard to the faults of the pastors of the Church, of priests and men of position, as St. Ignatius observes, and the preachers of the Society are specially admonished that they should entirely abstain from the reprehension of such persons.

As regards the obligation of the Society in the matter of preaching, it is bound in virtue of its Rule frequently and assiduously to exercise this office; but this obligation does not rest on inferiors except when the superior imposes it upon them. To inferiors it belongs to be prepared and disposed, both as regards will and as regards ability so far as the latter lies within their power.

The obligation to preach, as regards inferiors, does not bind under sin, until the act has been prescribed in virtue of obedience; but is similar to other obligations of Rule, or of obedience to a simple ordinance. In a superior the obligation is more grave, not that he should himself exercise the office of preaching, for on the contrary he may be more easily excused, but that he should take care that the office is exercised in the place or places which are subject to him. There will rarely however be a grievous transgression, save in case of scandalous negligence or *quasi*-contempt of the obligation.

## II.—What can and ought Religious of the Society to do in the Administration of the Sacrament of Penance?

Another principal ministry which belongs to the Society in virtue of its Institute, is the administration of the sacraments, and especially of the sacraments of Penance and the Eucharist.

The administration of any sacrament cannot be lawfully undertaken by Ours without faculty or privilege from the Apostolic See, or from the local bishop. It was becoming and most expedient that the faculty for hearing confessions should emanate to the Society immediately from the Apostolic See itself, although with that subordination to the other prelates which right reason and the Sacred Canons demand.

It is certain that since the date of the Council of Trent it is not sufficient that a confessor should possess all that is required by divine or natural law in order to the exercise of this ministry, unless he has also the special approbation of the Church, as decreed by that Council. The Council lays down two ways in which a priest may be *approved*, or *declared fit* for the reception of jurisdiction in order to the hearing of confessions; and either of those two ways will suffice, but one or other of them is necessary, and no other approbation will suffice. The one is appointment to a parochial benefice, and the other is approbation by a bishop. The first was not introduced but was simply retained by the Council. Since to a parish priest there is committed the cure of souls, by the very fact of his appointment to his benefice there is sufficiently declared his fitness to hear confessions; and therefore, although he receives jurisdiction over only his own sheep, he is nevertheless reckoned as approved so that jurisdiction may be also delegated to him elsewhere and in any otherwise lawful manner. The second mode was introduced by the council. All priests who have not a parochial benefice, of whatsoever state, order or dignity they may be, require approbation by the bishop in order to hear the confessions of seculars, even if these are priests. A bishop may approve a priest as fit to hear confessions, and at the same time not delegate jurisdiction to him; for a *grant of jurisdiction* is a *grace*, which a bishop bestows of *liberality*, while *approbation* is an *act of justice*, or a *just judgment*, by which there is declared the *fitness* of a person to hear confessions. Approbation is simply a *public sentence*, or *authoritative declaration* of the sufficiency of a priest to hear confessions; and this the Council of Trent willed to be, as it were, a necessary disposition in order that a priest should be proximately capable of jurisdiction.

A bishop who has no jurisdiction cannot give approbation, since it is an act of jurisdiction. Hence a bishop who is consecrated, but has no bishopric, cannot give approbation to any one, and neither can a bishop who is only elected, because as yet he has no jurisdiction; but one who has been elected and confirmed, although he is not yet consecrated, can give approbation, because he is a true bishop, and can exercise acts of jurisdiction. The vicar of a bishop is reckoned as one with him, and exercises his jurisdiction; and the Chapter can also approve through its vicar, during a vacancy of the See; approbation not being an act of episcopal order, nor an act of jurisdiction specially delegated by the Pontiff, but an act of *ordinary* jurisdiction, and one moreover which is very necessary in order to the care and administration of the diocese, which is committed to the Chapter which succeeds, for the time being, to the late bishop.

By ordinary law it is necessary to have *obtained* approbation, and it is not sufficient to have applied for it, even if it should have been unjustly refused. If a bishop should approve unjustly and sin in so doing, the sacrament is nevertheless valid so far as approbation is concerned.

The moral reason why the Council willed to reserve the approbation of confessors to the bishops, was because they are ordinary pastors, and superior to parish priests, although these are also ordinary pastors; and because it was to be presumed that, as a rule at any rate, they would rightly exercise this power.

It does not suffice that a priest should be held and judged fit to hear confessions, even by the bishop himself, for this belongs to the *understanding;* unless he also obtains from him approbation, or leave to hear confessions, an act which depends on the *will.*

The bishops are *bound of justice* not to refuse approbation to mendicant religious *without just cause,* and they will *sin grievously* by doing otherwise.

The bishops can approve with limitation as regards persons and places; and this reasonably because they might judge a priest fit for hearing the confessions of certain classes of persons, or the inhabitants of certain towns or places, and not fit to hear the confessions of other persons, or fit to hear the confessions of men, but not those of women.

Approbation once given continues, so long as it is not recalled. It is not therefore extinguished by the death of him who grants it; since it is not a mere *grace*, but is a *juridical declaration* which is due *of justice*.

It can be recalled for a just cause, since the foundation or ground of it is not immutable; consisting as it does in learning, morals and other necessary conditions for the hearing of confessions, with regard to all of which the priest may change; and moreover, if it should turn out that the approbation had proceeded on notable error, it may be recalled.

A priest who has been approved by one bishop may be judged unworthy on the new examination which his *successor* has a right to institute; for he is a new pastor, and assumes his own obligations, and he is not compelled to ratify all the faculties granted by his predecessor. It is in his power, therefore, for the satisfaction of his own conscience, to call up all approved confessors for examination and to reject those whom he finds unworthy, and so to revoke the former approbations.

In rigour of law, and of his absolute power a bishop might recall to examination those of *his own subjects* whom he has already approved, although he ought not to do this to the injury of any one, or without reasonable cause. By a special privilege granted to Mendicants, they can be examined *once only* by the *same* bishop; but if they have been approved without previous examination, and it appears on examination that the approbation was not rightly granted, it can be recalled.

To regulars the bishop *does not give jurisdiction,* or *any grace or favour,* but *only* "approbation," or a *juridical declaration* of their *fitness to hear confessions.* This approbation is simply a *condition,* albeit a necessary condition, which renders them *capable* of receiving the jurisdiction which flows to them *from the Apostolic See,* by means of their Privileges.

The faculty in an approved priest of Ours to hear confessions is dependent on the prelates of the Society, not only so that, by reason of the subordination of obedience, it should not be lawful for him to exercise this function contrary to the will of his superior; but also because the, so to speak, substantial faculty to hear confessions, and the necessary jurisdiction is conferred by the superior. All faculty and jurisdiction for this ministry descends from the Supreme Pontiff to the priests of the Society, to whom it is communicated through the General, either immediately, or by means of the Provincials or other superiors to whom, either of ordinary right or by delegation, this power of creating confessors is granted. It follows that a prelate of the Society can withdraw from his subject all faculty and jurisdiction for hearing confessions. He can also grant the faculty in part and not in whole, for the hearing of certain classes of persons, such as, for instance, men only and not women.*

---

* If, besides *approbation,* the bishop should also *ex abundantiâ* grant *jurisdiction* to a regular, as he certainly can do, and as is very commonly done at the present day, the regular will have two distinct grants of jurisdiction, or jurisdiction through two distinct channels. It follows as a consequence that his absolutions of seculars will be valid, in virtue of the jurisdiction delegated to him by the bishop, even if he should have been

## III.—What can and ought Religious of the Society to do in the Administration of the Sacrament of the Eucharist?

No one can lawfully minister this sacrament to the faithful unless he has for so doing either *ordinary* or delegated jurisdiction, or the leave of an *ordinary* pastor, since it is one of the principal acts of feeding the faithful, and therefore belongs to their pastors, and cannot lawfully be usurped by any one on his own authority. The Pontiff can certainly grant this faculty independently of inferior prelates or pastors. This is most certain and of faith, and follows from his supreme power which is absolutely independent of all inferiors. It has been granted to Ours by Paul III. so that they can administer, and the faithful can freely and lawfully receive the Eucharist, at any time of the year, except at Easter and the hour of death, and that without the leave of the Rectors of the parochial churches being

forbidden to hear the confessions of seculars by his superior, that is to say, by that superior who had power to communicate to him the pontifical jurisdiction bestowed upon his Order. Besides sinning grievously against obedience, the regular is, however, deprived of all power to avail himself of the faculties which by Privilege of the Apostolic See belong to his Order, such as those for absolving from certain cases and censures. His absolutions, so far as these are concerned, will be absolutely invalid, since he enjoys those special faculties of his Order only as communicated, and in so far as they have been communicated to him through the superior who has power to do so in accordance with the Institute, or with the terms of the Privilege. These special faculties having been withdrawn by his superior's prohibition, and consequent withdrawal of the jurisdiction which he had previously communicated to him, the regular's faculties will be no greater than those which the bishop had it in his power to bestow. See Declaration of the Sacred Congregation of Bishops and Regulars, March 2, 1866; and Gury. Ed. Ballerini, 1866, vol. ii. p. 442.

required. Of course Ours cannot minister the Eucharist *in the church of another*, against the will of its Rector, since this would be to the prejudice of his rights.

It is to the *ordinary* pastors of souls that the care of the sheep belongs, especially as regards observance of the precepts; and therefore they are held to have special rights at the two times, namely at Easter and at the hour of death, when the precept of communion obliges, and it would be to their prejudice if without their leave or consent the Eucharist were then to be administered by others. This is not as if the Pontiff could not, if he so willed, grant this farther privilege to religious, since he could reserve this ministry to himself, and entrust it to whomsoever he pleased; but for the reason given he has not done this, and does not judge it expedient to be done. This limitation is always to be understood, even when it is not expressed, in general Privileges of this kind. By Easter is to be understood the eight days before and the eight days after Easter-day, because according to the more common custom of the Church, the ecclesiastical precept of communicating within the year can be fulfilled within that time. Where custom extends this time, the extension of time is also to be reckoned as Easter-tide. Those can be admitted to communion in our churches who have already fulfilled their parochial duties, and who desire again or more frequently to communicate during those fifteen days.[*]

---

[*] The existing law, while it binds all the faithful to receive paschal communion in the parish church, permits regulars to administer the Eucharist in their own churches to all the faithful on every day except Easter Sunday, and, in the city of Rome, Thursday in Holy Week. See Gury, Ed. Ballerini, 1866, vol. ii. p. 125.

It is not forbidden to Ours to communicate a sick person in his bed, when he communicates for the sake of devotion, and not because of his peril of death; and, even if he is in peril of death, so long as he does not communicate in order to fulfil the divine precept. That precept is fulfilled by one communion made within the period of peril, and since it is an affirmative precept it does not oblige on any particular day, but its determination may be arbitrary. So long therefore as the state of the sickness and peril is not such as to oblige the sick man to communicate at once and on the same day, it will be lawful to religious to administer to him the Eucharist if he desires to communicate from devotion, and without intention thereby to fulfil the precept, and with a purpose of asking viaticum on another day from the parish priest, if his peril should increase and his obligation appear to be more urgent. Similarly, if he has already communicated within the time of peril, so as to fulfil the divine precept, and with the intention of so fulfilling it, he can afterwards again and again during the same sickness receive the Eucharist from devotion at the hands of religious.

IV. — WHAT CAN THE RELIGIOUS OF THE SOCIETY DO AS REGARDS THE ADMINISTRATION OF THE OTHER SACRAMENTS?

It is not lawful for Ours to administer the other sacraments to the faithful, except in certain cases, and under certain circumstances. Power to do so is not necessary in order to our fulfilment of the end of the Society, and the possession and exercise of such power would not tend towards peace and union with the ordinary pastors, and would not be expedient for the well-ordered government of souls.

As regards Baptism, it is certain that it is not lawful for priests of Ours to minister it with solemnity to the faithful in those regions where they have ordinary pastors, to whom the administration of this sacrament belongs in virtue of their office. The same is true of the Sacrament of Extreme Unction, as regards its administration to seculars who are not inmates of our Houses. As regards Matrimony, Ours cannot, in virtue of privilege, except in missionary countries, minister this sacrament either by way of presence as witnesses approved by the Church in order to its validity, or by way of solemn benediction.

V.—THE SPIRITUAL EXERCISES WHICH THE SOCIETY EMPLOYS IN ORDER TO THE ASSISTANCE OF ITS NEIGHBOURS; WHAT ARE THEY? AND WHAT IS THEIR DOCTRINE?

The term *Spiritual Exercises* is not new, but is used by, among others, St. Buonaventure, St. Bernard, Blosius and St. Laurence Justinian, to signify not only interior acts of contemplation or meditation, but also other acts and exercises of various virtues, whereby the soul makes progress towards purity and union with God.

St. Ignatius left to the Society, amongst other instruments of virtue, a book which he compiled, not without great aid from God, and as the fruit of long experience, and which he called—The Spiritual Exercises.

In the beginning of this book he says—By the name of Spiritual Exercises is understood every mode of examining one's conscience, and of meditating, contemplating and praying with mind and voice, and of performing all other spiritual operations whatsoever. For, as to walk, to make a journey and to run are corporal exercises, so likewise to prepare and dispose the soul for the removal of all ill-ordered affections, and, these having been removed, for seeking and finding the will of God with regard to the arrangement of one's life, and the salvation of one's soul, are called *spiritual exercises*.

This book St. Ignatius wrote not only for the profit of his companions, but also in order that they, by means of the exercises and instructions which it contains, might strenuously labour for the spiritual welfare of all christian people. A most grave man of the saintly family of St. Bernard calls this book a "noviceship instituted for the whole human race."

To certain persons, however, at the outset it seemed to be a novelty, and it was regarded with suspicion, and calumniated, and so St. Francis Borgia, a singularly eminent disciple of St. Ignatius, and an illustrious model of the Society, besought Paul III. to have it examined in order that it might be approved by his authority. The examiners reported that the Exercises were full of piety and sanctity, and that they were and would be very useful and salutary for the edification and spiritual profit of the faithful. The Pontiff thereupon approved all and everything contained in them, and exhorted all the faithful to the use of them.

As regards the doctrine of the Exercises, no one can rightly call any point of it in question. It consists either of certain and dogmatic principles, or of statements of the received doctrine of theologians. The work is not in itself and directly intended for the teaching of theological doctrine, for it contains practical rather than speculative doctrine; and the doctrine is delivered by way of an art rather than by way of a science, and so has regard rather to practical truth or utility than to speculative truth. Since, however, meditation, to be useful, should suppose the truth of the matter meditated, there is supposed in the exercises or meditations the truth of the history, when they are founded on a history, as in the exercises on the Life of Christ, and on the sin of the Angels, and on the fall of the first man, and the like. In the other exercises, such as those on the reward of the good, and the punishments of the wicked, on God, on His benefits, and on the love due to Him, there is always laid a foundation of faith, and thereon they are almost altogether based. If anything is added, it is drawn either from certain experience, or from the teaching of the Fathers. This may be noted also in the spiritual instructions, for where it is necessary certain points are premised, which contain moral or dogmatic doctrine, as necessary foundations; and, also where it is necessary, a tacit objection is anticipated and met, lest a spiritual counsel should seem to be at variance with the teachings of theology. For instance, when a caution is given that one should not, while carried away by the fervour of the

Exercises, easily be induced to bind himself by any vow, it is straightway added—Although a work is of greater merit which is done under vow than if it were done without a vow, yet nevertheless account is to be taken of the peril or inconvenience which might occur in making this particular vow.

## VI.—THE ART, OR METHOD OF THE EXERCISES.

That the counsel of St. Ignatius with regard to the direction and, so to speak, art of this mental exercise, was most prudent and evidently divine, is proved most efficaciously from the result; for it appears from experience that many have hereby made progress in spiritual life, as Paul III. recognizes in his Bull. This is confirmed by the example of saints who have not only moved men to mental prayer and consideration, but have also endeavoured to teach them a method of praying and ascending towards God, such as St. Dionysius, St. Augustine, St. Prosper, St. Bernard, Richard of St. Victor, St. Buonaventure, St. Laurence Justinian, not to speak of Blosius, Tauler, Gerson, Dionysius the Carthusian and others. These however proceed by way rather of exhortation than of instruction, and therefore write at greater length of the praises and effects of meditation or contemplation, and do not so distinctly lay down a special method of praying. St. Ignatius in very brief rules and few words gives a wonderful instruction on this point, and he seems to have drawn it not so much from books, as from the unction of the Holy Ghost and from his own great experience and practice.

There were two reasons for the brevity of the Book of the Exercises; first, that the instructions might be more easily learned and practised, and that the exercises might be made with greater ease and relish; and secondly, because general principles alone can be common to all, while the particular application of them must be left to the prudence of the spiritual master or instructor, whose assistance is always supposed in the case of one who is only beginning to exercise himself in spiritual things.

The spiritual life requires two things chiefly, correction of morals, and union with God. To the first belongs purification from past sins, daily care of the conscience, and frequent confession of sins. The second is attained by frequent meditation and prayer, and by exercise of the various virtues. In order to both a right choice of a state of life is most necessary. But since a due esteem and right intention with regard to one's last end is the principle of all good actions, St. Ignatius presents this at the outset, and before the other exercises, as the foundation of the whole work of spiritual reformation.

He divides the Exercises into four parts, to which he gives the name of *weeks*, not as if it were necessary to spend seven days, neither more nor less, in each part, but because as a rule that length of time seems sufficient and convenient. The First Week contains the *Purgative Way*, and the matter of it is the grievousness of offending God, and all considerations which contribute towards the realization of this, and true repentance for sin. There is added an examination of conscience twice a day, morning and evening, both to preserve purity of conscience, and as most useful in order to confession. St. Ignatius advises that this examination should begin with thanksgiving for benefits received, either because that is no less due at the end of the day than is the remembrance and consideration of its sins, or certainly because it lends no small aid towards greater sorrow for having offended one's Benefactor.

There is also besides this general examination of conscience, a particular examination which is directed against some one special vice in order to its eradication.

The Second Week is ordained to this end that a man may rightly choose and constitute a state of life for himself in the future. Since the foundation of a right choice should in a christian man be the following and imitation of Christ, there are in the beginning of this week proposed certain considerations which should induce a man to a firm purpose of such imitation; especially those on the Incarnation and Life of Christ, which is set forth as the model on which our lives are to be moulded. There are then laid down the means for the making of a right election or choice, and all the instructions which are necessary for this purpose.

Henceforward the exercitant begins to be instructed in what is called the *Illuminative Way*, and he enters on the state of the *progressing*, as it is called, to distinguish it from the state of *beginners*, with which the Purgative Way is chiefly concerned.

But since perfection of christian life takes a long time to attain, and is arrived at chiefly by virtue of the passion and death of Christ, and through meditation thereon, these are proposed for meditation in the Third Week. This week also belongs to the state of *the progressing*, and consequently to the *Illuminative Way*.

In the Fourth Week the resurrection and glory of the Risen Christ is meditated on, and the *Unitive Way* is arrived at.

The matter of the meditations consists in that which is proposed for consideration; their form is the method and direction which is given in order to due and fruitful consideration. With this last St. Ignatius has taken greatest pains, and it was indeed a gift granted to him by a special grace, and obtained through great experience and practice along with the grace of God. Nearly all the instructions concern this, and they leave nothing to be desired.

The matter of the meditation should be sufficient, and adapted to the scope or end which is proximately aimed at, and to the way, or degree of the spiritual life which is being procured; but in the various weeks all the matter, or every meditation which might conceivably belong to it, is not given, since this would be a well-nigh infinite business, and every one can easily discover it for himself. Having received the points of the meditation briefly given, the exercitant can then reason on them with his own understanding or by aid of the divine enlightenment, and so with greater relish and fruit he will occupy himself in prayer and meditation.

At the end of the Fourth Week, which is ordained not directly towards amendment of morals or progress, but to excite hope and love of eternal things, and towards participation in a manner of eternal joys even in this life, there is added a contemplation for the purpose of begetting in our souls a spiritual love. St. Ignatius contents himself with putting the wise on the way, and since the rest belongs to the government of the Holy Ghost rather than to the operation of man, although the co-operation of man is not excluded, he says but little with regard to union with God, and the act of simple contemplation with simple intuition of truth.

Those who are raised by a special grace to such union with God should, on the cessation of that divine operation, immediately resume meditation lest, to borrow the words of Blosius, they should fall into the sleep of sloth.

Although the three ways—the purgative, the illuminative and the unitive, are distinct as regards their principal acts, yet they are not necessarily, nay, they ought not, as a rule, to be absolutely kept separate, but each of them should partake somewhat of the others. In the first week somewhat borrowed from the second and third weeks is necessary, in order that the exercises of that week may be made with greater relish and fruit; for fear, and sorrow, and detestation of sins are perfected and sweetened by the love of God and affections of virtue. In the third week it is frequently expedient to retain somewhat of the first and second weeks for the sake of greater security. The second week also, for both reasons, and as standing midway between the first and third weeks, should share somewhat of both.

## VII.—The Use of the Exercises, both by Ours and by Externs.

There is a twofold use of the Exercises in the Society; one, for the benefit of Ours, which may be called a *passive* use, and the other, which may be called an *active* use, for the aid of externs towards amendment of life or spiritual progress.

The first use begins, among Ours, at their first entrance into the Society, when in their first probation they begin to be purified from past sins; and this use is repeated again and again in the course of the noviceship, in order that they may be better proved, and principally in order that they may be more fully instructed and exercised. This use continues also throughout their lives, and in two ways; first, by daily meditation, prayer and examination of conscience, and secondly, by their once or twice a year leaving their studies and other external occupations, and exercising themselves in these and similar meditations, and giving themselves to the contemplative life alone.

This custom is useful not only for novices or for the progressing, but also for the perfect, for it cannot be that their interior devotion should not be somewhat relaxed by reason of their external actions and occupations, and moreover, the work is in itself very desirable and perfect.

If any one thinks that after making the Exercises for eight or fifteen days he has ascended to the summit of contemplation, or even that he is perfectly purified and enlightened, or that he has sufficiently perfected himself in the exercise of meditation, he most foully and childishly errs; for not only perfect union with God, but even mediocre perfection in prayer or meditation requires length of time and much practice, and it presupposes long-continued exercise of oneself in the extirpation of vices and the acquisition of virtues.

The Constitutions exhort all of Ours to train themselves so that they may have dexterity in the use of this spiritual weapon for the benefit of others. The results of the use of it supply abundant evidence of its excellence, and of its fitness for men in every state of life; for experience has shewn that many have by means of it been led to renounce the world, and others to amend their morals in their own state of life, either by doing penance for their sins, and entering on a good life, or if already living a good life, by making progress towards a better. This is only what we should reasonably expect, since the Exercises are ordained in the first place to obtain grace from God in order to such effects, and then to dispose the soul, and remove, as much as may be, all hindrances to the divine grace, and beget careful co-operation therewith.

The Exercises are not however to be given equally and indifferently to all; and to few of those from whom no ordinary fruit cannot be hoped for to the greater glory of God are they to be given in their fulness. Although they are of service to all, not all are by means of them made contemplatives or raised to the heights of prayer. Again, although one of the principal ends of the Exercises is the choice of a better state, yet they do not aim at all persons choosing the religious state, because, although that state is better in itself, it is nevertheless sometimes not expedient as regards a particular person; and every one ought to choose that which is best in his own particular case. Moreover, all have not the grace of vocation, and still the Exercises are of value in order to the choice either of some other state, or of a manner of life which is better suited for their spiritual welfare. A religious, although he may not any longer deliberate with regard to the choice of a state, does well to exercise himself so that in his own state he may choose the best method of progress; or, if he has already sufficiently deliberated and resolved on this, that he may renew his purpose and consider how he may more diligently remove any hindrance to its fulfilment. Seculars also who are to remain in the world are wise to avail themselves of this aid, in order that they may be better prepared for the perils by which they are surrounded, and that they may obtain greater grace from God. Finally, this remedy is to be supplied even to great sinners, not that they may at once become perfect, but rather because not only to be made perfect, but even to change their previous manner of life is very difficult for them, and they therefore stand in need of the most efficacious remedies.

VIII.—Ought the Religious of the Society to aid their Neighbours by Means of Familiar Conversation with them?

Familiar conversation with our neighbours is not in itself foreign to the state of perfection, and it is much in accordance with the special Institute of the Society. We have the example of Christ, Who conversed with men, and ate and drank with them, and yet not only did He observe perfection, but His was the most perfect of all states of life. In this He was imitated by His Apostles, who likewise embraced the religious state or the state of perfection, and who became "all things to all men," that they might gain all. St. Thomas says that it is lawful for religious to transact secular business for the relief of the necessity of their neighbours, because in that case it can no longer be called secular business, but a religious action, for as St. James says—"Pure religion and undefiled before God and the Father is this, to visit the fatherless and widows in their tribulation." If this is true of a corporal work of mercy, much more is it true of holy and religious conversation for the spiritual good of a neighbour.

The primary and adequate end of the Society comprehends labouring for the salvation and sanctification not only of its members but also of its neighbours, and it is evident as well as proved by experience that familiar conversation with them is a means which is well adapted, nay, morally necessary in order to this end. In order perfectly to fulfil the office of confessor, it is often necessary to treat familiarly with penitents, even outside confession, either for their better instruction, or for their spiritual consolation, or to keep them to the practice of frequent confession, and to the doing of the good works which are begotten thereof. Again, although general sermons or discourses are necessary for a congregation, yet unless they are fostered and, as it were, digested by the warmth of familiar conversation, they are easily forgotten; and besides this, it is often necessary to descend from generalities to mode and measure and particular circumstances, in accordance with the needs of individuals, and this can only for the most part be done in private conversations. Further, since secular men are generally animal rather than spiritual, it is necessary to condescend to them a little, and by blameless familiar conversation to attract and gain them so that by degrees they may be inclined to listen to spiritual discourse. Even if sometimes indifferent matters may enter into the conversation, yet if they are treated or rather if they are tolerated with this intention, our words will not be idle, but profitable and religious. For these reasons the Society makes use of this means as adapted for its work of the salvation of its neighbours.

In the use of it, however, two things are required namely, a right intention, which is that of its necessity alone, and great moderation and circumspection. This moderation again requires two things, of which one is that this means should not be used to the loss or damage of one's own personal perfection, and the other is that it should be to the spiritual fruit of one's neighbour; since, according to the order of charity, God is to be preferred to a neighbour, and one's own spiritual profit to that of another. All conversation with seculars is idle when no spiritual profit whatsoever can be in any way hoped for from it.

## IX.—Ought the Society to have a special care in the aid of those of its neighbours who are in danger of death?

Besides its general solicitude for the salvation of all its neighbours, the assistance of the sick and dying is one of the ministries which are most proper to the Society, and to which it is specially bound in virtue of its Institute, with that obligation wherewith it is bound to its other works.

# CHAPTER XXV.

## THE GOVERNMENT OF THE SOCIETY.

### I.—Is the Society fitly governed by way of Monarchy?

It is common to the Society with nearly all other religious Orders that its ordinary government should be monarchical, with some admixture of the aristocratic element. Monarchical government is in itself the best, but by reason of the frailty of men, and the danger of their erring either in judgment or in affection, it should be tempered with somewhat of an aristocracy. This is the received opinion both of moral philosophers and of theologians.

The monarchy of the Society is reduced to one General, beneath whose standard the whole Order is enrolled; and the Society in union with the General is ordinarily subject in spiritual matters to the Supreme Pontiff alone. Immediately under the General there are constituted the Provincials, and under each Provincial the local superiors. In this the Society resembles other Orders, for this manner of constitution is morally necessary in every Order which, as one body politic, is diffused throughout the whole world, and the members of which are distant from each other in different places.

They therefore require one head, to act on all the members, and to provide for the universal good of the whole body, and to make the best use of individual members for the general advantage.

By reason of the distance and extent and diversity of the various regions or nations in which the Society finds itself, there must necessarily be constituted, under the General, Provincials, each of whom proximately administers and rules his own province. Further, since in every province there are various places which possess Houses or Colleges of the Society, each of these must have some one to preside over it.

Hence also all these superiors possess *ordinary* and spiritual jurisdiction, each in the manner in which it is granted to him, and in accordance with his office. They are, in all propriety and rigour of speech, *ecclesiastical prelates*.

The government of the Society is *aristocratic* in several ways; and first, in this that it has its *General Congregations*. These, although they have certain fixed times for assembling, are also to be assembled on other fitting occasions. They have of necessity to be assembled on the death of a General, or when he is deprived or to be deprived of his office for any cause, for the election of his successor. To these Congregations aristocratic government belongs properly and in all rigour, for those who are assembled in them have a decisive suffrage; and so long as these Congregations continue the supreme power of the whole body of the Society resides in them, and they are superior even to the General himself.

A second way in which aristocratic government has place in the Society is through other Congregations which, although they are gathered from the whole body of the Society are nevertheless not General Congregations; since neither the Provincials nor many who have votes come from the various provinces, but only one from each province comes in the name of that province, and as its procurator. Such a Congregation is called—a *Congregation of Procurators*.

It belongs to a Congregation of Procurators primarily and principally to decree whether a General Congregation is to be called, or not; and in the decision of this question the members assembled have a *decisive* suffrage. With regard to other matters which may be treated in such a congregation, in virtue of the Institute and Constitutions, the members of it have *only a consultative* suffrage.

The aristocratic element appears in a third way in the *Provincial Congregations* which ought to be held in each province every three years. The purpose of these Congregations is to elect a person who shall go to the General in name of the whole province, and who shall have a vote in the Congregation of Procurators. A Provincial Congregation has to be assembled in every province whenever a General Congregation of the whole Society is to be called; for in the Provincial Congregation there are to be elected those who, along with the Provincial, shall have a vote in the General Congregation. In their election all have a proper active voice who may lawfully come to the Provincial Congregation. Besides these elections, no law or statute can be made in a Provincial Congregation; nor with regard to any proposed ordinance do those therein assembled have a decisive vote, but they can only consult and discuss matters with a view to its being decreed in a General Congregation, if that is to be called, or, if it is not to be called, to the matter being laid before the General.

In a fourth way the government of the Society is aristocratic from the number of prelates by whom it is governed under one Supreme General; namely, the Provincials and local superiors, who have the whole weight of government distributed among them.

The aristocratic idea is completed in the Councils, of whose advice and prudence the various prelates avail themselves. The General has his *Assistants*, chosen along with himself by the General Congregation; while to the Provincials *Consultors* are assigned, and also to the inferior local prelates. All these have only a consultative suffrage, while judgment remains with the respective prelates.

St. Ignatius willed that every superior of the Society should, according to the nature and measure of his office, possess entire power, and have provided for him *counsellors* only and *not co-judges*. This greatly contributes towards perfection in the religious state, since by this means a more pure and perfect obedience is exercised, and there is a greater dependence of the members on their head, and consequently a greater union, such as ought to exist between father and sons. There is also hereby removed an occasion of multiplying dignities in the persons of many judges, and as it were prelatures in the Order, and so the occasions of ambition are reduced in number. Finally, if ordinances, judgments and settlements of affairs were to depend on the opinions and wills of many, the peril of schisms and divisions would be multiplied.

The Society preserves in the character of its constitution its likeness to the Church, for although the Pontiff ordains the more grave matters with the counsel of the Cardinals, yet there always remains a perfect monarchy, because the *decision* of such matters depends on him alone. Although he very frequently, and in graver matters does not decree in opposition to the suffrages of a majority of the Cardinals, yet this is of his own prudence and free will, and not from any dependence on their suffrages. Bishops also have monarchical government in their dioceses, and they do not ordinarily require the suffrages of others. A religious Order may therefore very well share this mode of government, since in an Order the obedience of subjects ought to be more prompt, and the government of superiors more paternal.

The difference between the government of the Society and that of the Church is this, that the latter is reduced to one Supreme Prelate who is subject not only to no other man upon earth, but also to no community of men, and who is supreme over the whole Church, collectively as well as individually; whereas in the Society the General has not only a *personal* superior to whom he is subject, namely, the Pontiff (as follows necessarily from the general idea of the christian religion, and from the special idea of the religious state, and the yet more special idea of the Society), but he is also *subject to the Society itself,* by which he can be directed and corrected and, if need be, punished and deposed. The reason of this difference is clear, because the Pontiff holds his power not from the Church, but immediately from Christ, while the General holds his power from the Society. As the Pontiff in a singular and more excellent manner has his power from God, so he has also a special assistance of the Holy Ghost, which may supply the place of the direction or compulsion of a superior; but other inferior prelates, as they are chosen and constituted by men, so is it fitting that they should be subject at least to the community as a whole, or to a General Congregation of the same.

## II.—Is it expedient that the appointment of the General of the Society should be for life?

St. Ignatius, a man of singular prudence and sanctity, and who had a great knowledge and comprehension of the affairs of the Society, after much consideration and lengthened prayer, ordained that the General should be elected for life. This was also the unanimous judgment of the First General Congregation, and it has been confirmed by the authority of the Supreme Pontiffs. The Abbots of old were perpetual, and this is in accordance with the Canon Law, and with the Rule of St. Benedict. At the present day, the Generals of many religious Orders are perpetual, although the inferior prelates are removable, as is the case among the Carthusians, the Dominicans, the Carmelites and the Eremites of St. Augustine. This perpetuity is found moreover in the ecclesiastical monarchy, not only in the universal Pontificate, but also in the particular bishops. Hence it is evident that it is in itself better and, all things else being equal, to be preferred, that monarchy should be perpetual, or for life.

The government and influence of the General on the whole body of the Society, is with great power on his part, and with great dependence on the part of the body and of all its members; and therefore it requires a great knowledge of the whole Society, and of all the persons who belong to it, and this knowledge could not be acquired in a short space of time, and could be acquired only through that long experience which is most necessary in order to prudent government. It would not have been expedient that the General's term of office should end when he was just beginning to obtain this knowledge and experience; as would be the case if he were appointed for a short time, such as six or eight years, for within that time he could scarcely have twice obtained information with regard to the state of the Society throughout the world. No time shorter than life could be assigned, especially since as a rule it is only men of age and who have already borne the burden of labour who could be selected for this office.

Again, the only mode of creating the General is by election, and it is most expedient for the Society that General Congregations should not be frequently assembled. The Society is always sufficiently occupied with matters of great moment, and which concern the glory of God, and so it ought not, as far as possible, to be engaged and distracted with such Congregations; especially when there are taken into account the long journeys, and the labours and distractions of Provincials, prelates and other electors, who ought always to be among the chief men and principal labourers of the Society, as well as the many great inconveniences which commonly attend Congregations which are assembled for the election of Prelates.

A third advantage which is of great importance is that this perpetuity gives very little or no occasion to ambition; and finally, it cannot be doubted that perpetuity of office secures much authority for the General, both amongst externs and amongst Ours. A perpetual dignity is held in greater esteem by all than a temporary one, and a perpetual prelate has a firmer jurisdiction, is less dependent on his subjects, and consequently can have greater authority, and is more feared, while he himself is more free from human respects both of fear and love.

The danger of evils arising from the abuse of this authority, as regards either charity or justice, if compared with the advantages of perpetuity and the disadvantages and dangers of frequent elections and changes, is scarcely to be taken into account. It is moreover provided against by the diligence and prudence of the Society, to which the General is subjected in all matters pertaining to manner of life and mode of government, and cases are laid down in which the Society can depose him and, if need be, remove him from the Society itself.

Again, in the Society the occasions of this danger are

for the most part cut off, at least so far as it might issue in grave damage. They are chiefly two in number, namely excess by way of sumptuousness, or in food and bodily comforts and luxuries, or in expenditure, or in donations of temporal goods; and secondly, the desire of a higher dignity or greater honour. The first is in great measure cut off by the food, clothing and expenses of the General being regulated by ordinance of the Society, with which he must acquiesce; and one of the causes for deposition is his taking any part of the revenues of the Colleges for his own expenses, or giving it to any one outside the Society except by way of alms, or alienating the real property of the Houses or Colleges. The other occasion is obviated by the vow not to procure or accept any dignity save under obedience to the Apostolic See. There remain only the human defects of negligence and precipitation, and human affection by reason of which some are favoured more than others, and the like; and these are met by the counsel of the Assistants, and by the appointment of a *Monitor*, who is to be elected by the whole body of the Society. The Monitor, having first commended the matter to God in prayer, is bound with due modesty and humility to admonish the General of anything which he perceives to be required in him, to the greater service and glory of God.

III.—ARE THE OTHER PRELATES FITLY INSTITUTED IN THE SOCIETY?

According to the constitution of the Society, all inferior prelates under the General are created, not by election, or by the suffrages of subjects, but by the will or provision of the General.

It was not without a special providence of God and an inspiration of the Holy Ghost that St. Ignatius left this mode of government to the Society; and it is one of the things which are principally necessary for its preservation and progress, and especially for its peace and tranquillity. Besides the authority of the Founder and his companions, and the perpetual consent of the whole Order, we have in confirmation of this the authority of the Pontiffs Paul III. and Julius III. Long experience moreover has shewn that no inconveniences of any moment have hitherto followed from this mode of government; nay rather, that by reason of it the Society has been governed with great peace and tranquillity, and with observance of the due order of justice and charity. It is therefore well adapted for our Institute, in accordance with its special mode of life, whatever may be the case as regards other Orders or congregations, whose customs we in no way condemn.

The reasons for the preference of this mode of government are drawn chiefly from consideration of the greater evils which would follow to the Society from any other mode of creating its prelates, and which are avoided by this mode. In three ways may inferior prelates be created; first, by election made by the whole community; secondly, by some superior prelate with a definitive council or by a majority of suffrages; and thirdly, by one prelate with whom alone resides this power, although he ought in using it to have the prudent counsel of his ministers. The first mode is attended with great danger of begetting the spirit of ambition which, as the Constitutions often declare, is the pest of a religious Order. The more democratic an election is, the less perfect it is, and the more is it exposed to this vice. In every state of men the prudent and those who are free from private affections are in the minority, and so when the electors are a whole people or congregation or a great multitude, many of them will be either young, or not prudent, or with their affections not under sufficient control, and so it is easy to corrupt or deceive many, or to suborn them in other ways, and hence there arises a spirit of ambition in those who hope that by these means they may gain the prelature.

Such elections moreover are often fruitful in divisions and schisms, and there is also a danger of the prelate elected being offended with those who have not voted for him, and of his conniving and winking at faults in others which ought to be punished, and, what is far more serious, of his promoting to offices and dignities in the Order those who have not merited them, or who are unworthy of them.

By reason of the many disadvantages which have been discovered by experience to attach to this mode of election, and in order to avoid them, many religious Orders have abandoned it, while there are others who hold and desire that it should be abandoned; and in the Universal Church we find that the elections of bishops which were of old made by the people or by the clergy, have been put a stop to, while the election of the Pontiff is made by a few persons, and those select persons.

Against the second mode of election, namely, election

by a Council of Definitors, there militate all the reasons for which, as we have seen, the ordinary government of the Society, as regards all matters which are transacted outside a General Congregation, is carried on by its prelates alone, with the *consultative* but *not definitive* suffrages of others. If the Provincials were to be created by election, either the election would be made by the whole province in a Provincial Congregation, which would have the disadvantage of lending occasion to negotiations and pretensions, and in some provinces would be very difficult and inconvenient, as for instance in India, both by reason of the distances to be travelled, and the insufficient knowledge of the electors with regard to the fitness of persons residing in remote parts, and especially because it may often be expedient to have new Provincials from Europe; or on the other hand the election might be made by a few select persons of the same province, and in this latter case greater difficulties would arise than those which would be avoided. No less prudence and rectitude would be necessary in electing the electors than that which is required in electing the Provincial himself. Again, if this function were committed, as it were by law, say, to four of the most ancient of the Professed, or to persons holding certain offices, the consequences would be absurd. Seniority does not so ordinarily carry with it all the gifts which are so necessary in those who conduct so weighty a matter. Again, either the electors would have power to elect one of themselves, or they would not; in the former case, and when the number of electors is so small, it would be no slight inconvenience to be at once electors and eligible for election; while the latter case would be almost morally impossible, since if it is difficult, as St. Basil says, in a whole province to find a worthy ruler for one monastery, how could all the electors be excluded from election, since they themselves would be necessarily among the principal men of the whole province?

It was therefore morally necessary for the Society that the providing of Provincials should be entrusted to the General, since it was not expedient that it should be done by a Provincial Congregation.

The same reasons apply for the most part to the creation of local superiors or Rectors. If this is not done by election, it must be done by provision on the part of some superior prelate; and for many very good reasons it is committed of ordinary power not to the Provincials but to the General. It is easily to be believed, in the first place, that the General will be more free from private affections by reason of the greater responsibility of his office and his less dependence on others, as well as his less familiarity with the individual members of distant provinces. Secondly, perfect subordination and the union of the whole body with its head, which is so necessary in order to its welfare, is hereby better preserved. Thirdly, so great is the unity of the Society, that as concerns the mutual aid and affection of its members it is to be regarded as if it were *one province and nation*. Provinces are multiplied by reason only of the necessity which arises from the distance of places, while in all things else, so far as the idea of the Institute demands, there is to be observed the greatest unity and communication of all goods and mutual assistance, as far as possible. Hence the Rectors and superiors of one province are often provided from another province; while sometimes a father who in one province is a superior, is sent to another province to preach or teach. Fourthly, since the General is perpetual, he ought to have a comprehensive view of the whole Society and to observe from a higher standpoint what persons are necessary for particular places, and from what places or provinces he may provide Rectors for other places, if he should judge this to be more expedient. Although the principal power with regard to this matter resides in the General, he should nevertheless make use of the assistance of the Provincials in order that he may fitly and worthily provide superiors, and he can also often entrust this duty to them. Hence there is not excluded any advantage which might arise from committing the power of providing inferior superiors to the Provincials; while a greater advantage results from the General's thus watching over all, and being able either to confirm that which has been rightly proposed or done by the Provincials in accordance with the power granted to them, or certainly from his being able to correct that which he may judge to be inexpedient.

The perils which may accompany the informations with regard to individuals which are taken by the General, and which may arise from error, deception, ignorance, inordinate affections or other human passions on the part of his informants, to say nothing of false detractions, manifestations of hidden sins, and exaggerations of the smallest defects, or on the other hand false praises and commendations,—are common to every mode of election or provision which is made by means of men. It is evident by experience that neither the Supreme Pontiff, nor the bishops, nor kings or other princes can provide for offices and dignities otherwise than by taking the informations of persons whom they believe to be worthy of credit. Hence where there are many electors, every one of them must necessarily be led to form his judgment by means of informations, and there is less risk of error when one person only has to be informed, instead of many, and that one a person so grave that all owe to him the greatest reverence and fidelity, and so prudent and powerful that others cannot easily, or will not dare to deceive him. As regards those also from whom information is to be taken, there is less risk, since they are not only religious men with the fear of God before their eyes, but men who also specially profess that no kind of ambition or negotiation should be found amongst Ours.

No doubt there is a certain human advantage in this that a superior may be more acceptable to and better liked by his subjects if he has been spontaneously elected by their suffrages, instead of being imposed upon them from without, and in this also that he can, from his previous knowledge of them, begin from the outset to treat and love them as sons; but this advantage, in comparison with the disadvantages which follow from elections, is as nothing. If elections were always unanimous, and made with entire uprightness of intention, these advantages might be taken into account; but since elections are often made with contention and envy, the advantage to some is counterbalanced by the disturbance to others who have not voted for the superior who is ultimately elected; for these can hardly love or even patiently endure him, especially if they feel that he is not well affected towards them by reason of their not having voted for him. But in any case the advantage would be merely human, for those who profess perfection of obedience should be content, and St. Ignatius was most desirous to educate Ours in this spirit that withdrawing themselves from all human respects and affections, they should will to have that prelate who should be best adapted to govern them in the Lord. This is moreover necessary amongst Ours for a special reason, because Ours have no fixed domicile, but in virtue of the Institute should be prepared to travel, or to dwell in various provinces and regions, and they should therefore be accustomed to be governed by unknown as well as by known superiors. In the Society also there is less inconvenience in superiors being brought from one House to another, or from one Province to another; both because there are in the Society no filiations of Houses or Provinces, but all are, as regards love and every beneficence reckoned *as of the same House*, and the whole Society is regarded *as one Province;* and also by reason of the frequency of communication which takes place in the Society by means of letters and the various missions, from which it results that persons, especially those of most weight, and those who might be appointed to office, come to be sufficiently well known, and can themselves easily arrive at a knowledge of others in order to their government; and finally because the government itself is very uniform, and, as it were, of the same character in all the Houses and Provinces, and therefore is easily adapted for the exigences of all.

Nearly always, however, or, as a rule, superiors in the Society are selected from the same nation, and frequently from the same province; and if sometimes this is not the case, there is a cause, or an urgent necessity, or the person appointed has been educated and as it were naturalized in the province. The selection moreover is never made without much consultation of the principal persons of the province, or without the judgment and assent of many of its members. The affections and inclinations of subjects are also taken into account, and it is endeavoured that, as far as possible, they should be governed by persons who will be grateful and acceptable to them. The selection being made by one head does not exclude this kind of providence and prudence, nay, this can be the more easily exercised by one who has the greatest acquaintance with the whole Order.

The appointment of superiors other than the General is not in perpetuity; and rightly, because he alone is dependent on no one within the Order, while all others depend on him; and there is not the same necessity for perpetuity in their case as there is in his, his creation being by election, the frequency of which is to be avoided, as we have seen, while they, being created without election, can be easily changed and instituted by the General himself. Philosophy teaches that all things movable should be founded and rest on something which is immovable, so that by their changes they may mutually aid and preserve each other. The changing of inferior prelates in the Society is necessary for various causes and occasions which may occur, and because but few persons are fitted for perpetual government with profit to themselves and others.

There is no term of office fixed by the Constitutions for inferior prelates, but their continuance depends on the will of the General. The Constitutions however declare that Provincials are to be appointed for three years, although that space of time may be shortened or lengthened, as it may appear to be to the greater glory of God. This term is fixed only in order that at the end of it they might be more conveniently and without any note of censure removed from office; for if the time is to be lengthened that can be done without any difficulty, since it redounds to the commendation of the person. Greater inconvenience might be felt if one had to be removed before the expiry of that term, but this can rarely be necessary, and it can be done prudently so as to cause no loss of reputation. It can certainly be permitted sometimes for a greater common good, and it may also be inflicted as a punishment.

The Constitutions say nothing with regard to the term of administration of other inferior prelates, but only that the General can both constitute and remove them.

The Fifth General Congregation, however, enjoins that all, even local superiors (with the exception of the Rectors of the Houses of Probation and of the Seminaries, with regard to whom the former law remains in its entirety), should continue only for three years, within which time they may be removed or sent elsewhere by the General for just causes or for the common good; and that the term of three years cannot be lengthened, and that at the end of it such superiors should be free from office for at least a year, unless it should be necessary to promote any one of them to the post of Provincial.

With regard to Provincials also it is ordained that after their three years they should again be subjects for at least a year, and that they should not hold during that time even any other inferior prelature. This determination was made not in order that the dignity of prelate might be communicated to many, for the Society most vehemently desires to extirpate all affection for prelature, and as matter of fact the offices in the Society have in them much more of burden and solicitude than of dignity, honour or advantage; but in order that the burden of office might be more easily borne, and that those who are fitted for it, and therefore likely to be more frequently appointed to it, should not forget humility and subjection, and that they might learn from experience to sympathize with their subjects. By this means also there arise in the Society many men who are fitted for government, because the prudence which is necessary in order to good government is acquired chiefly by practice and experience. There is also left unhindered the principal institute of the Society as regards its ministries to souls, and the missions which are undertaken for this end, since the General can always send any one whomsoever, or apply him to another work or ministry notwithstanding the triennial law; for in reality and properly speaking, no right to their three years is acquired by persons who are appointed as prelates in the Society.

## IV.—The power of jurisdiction which exists in the Society.

There exists in the Society ecclesiastical jurisdiction, both in the forum of confession, and in the exterior or contentious forum, with regard to all its own members, and the causes pertaining to their persons, even if those causes are criminal, or of any other kind whatsoever.

This is evident both from common doctrine with regard to the exempt religious state, and from the many Pontifical Bulls, by which the Society has been exempted from the jurisdiction of all Ordinaries, and that from the outset at its confirmation. It is apparent from the first and fifth Bulls of Paul III. the first Bull of Julius III. the Constitution of Gregory XIII. *Ascendente Domino*, and his Bull *Satis superque*. From these Pontifical Letters it appears that the Society has *quasi*-episcopal jurisdiction over its subjects, such as exempt religious Orders have at common law; and that it has such jurisdiction to the full extent and with all the perfection with which it has been granted to other religious Orders, by means of its communication with them in their Privileges in virtue of the same Apostolic Indults, and especially with the Mendicants, in virtue of the Bull of Pius V. *Dum indefessæ*. From these, and from many special grants made directly and properly to the Society itself in various Pontifical Bulls, it also appears that this jurisdiction is in the Society *ordinary* as regards its subjects; since it is given to be exercised *in virtue of office*, and by the proper pastors, superiors and judges of such souls.

It is peculiar to the Society that *no community* in it possesses proper governing jurisdiction, with the single exception of a *General Congregation* of the whole body of the Society; for Provincial Congregations do not possess such jurisdiction. A General Congregation possesses it in the highest degree. In the first place, it has power to elect a General to whom it consequently communicates the whole of the jurisdiction which he holds. Secondly, after the General is elected, the General Congregation remains superior to him. Hence it can not only bind him by its laws and precepts, but it can also punish him, and even depose him for certain lawful causes. Thirdly, it has power to establish perpetual laws in the Society, and to change them. Fourthly, it has power to alienate or to dissolve Colleges or Houses already erected and accepted. These acts are proper to a General Congregation to this extent that jurisdiction for the exercise of them is not to be found in any single individual of the Society.

To a General Congregation it belongs also to elect the Assistants and the Admonitor of the General; although this may sometimes be done by the General himself, with the concurrence of the decisive suffrages of all the Provincials of Europe, or of the majority of them, when it is necessary to substitute another Assistant or Admonitor in the place of one deceased or sufficiently hindered from the exercise of his office.

Although the jurisdiction of a General Congregation is *ordinary*, as ordinary is distinguished from *delegated* jurisdiction, it may nevertheless be called *extraordinary*, as it is distinguished from that jurisdiction by which the Society is ordinarily ruled. It is undoubtedly not delegated jurisdiction, because it belongs to the Congregation by certain and established law confirmed by the Pontiffs, and it is exercised in virtue of office by the Congregation, and the Congregation can delegate and commit it, nay, can even confer it *as ordinary*. We call this jurisdiction *extraordinary*, because it does not belong to the ordinary government of the Society, or to its perfection and integrity, that a General Congregation should be always actually in existence; or that ordinarily jurisdiction should immediately flow from it to the Society, since it is to be assembled only in necessary cases, which may be called extraordinary. This jurisdiction moreover is not actual save for the time during which the General Congregation actually exists, and therefore again it may be called extraordinary.

The *supreme ordinary jurisdiction* of the Society exists *in the General alone*, both in virtue of his office, and in virtue of law; and the ordinary inflow of jurisdiction by which the Society is ruled springs either immediately from him, or with dependence upon him. Jurisdiction is committed by the Pontiff *immediately to the Society;* and *through the Society*, as existing in a General Congregation, it is *transferred to the General*.

The Pontiff did not confer this power on St. Ignatius, as Christ conferred ecclesiastical power on Peter, but he bestowed it *on the Society*.

## V.—The power of jurisdiction which exists in inferior Prelates of the Society.

The inferior prelates of the Society share its jurisdiction and power in greater or less measure in accordance with their respective offices, and with the distribution or communication of it which is made by the General.

Provincials, and local superiors or rectors of the Society possess *ordinary* and not merely delegated jurisdiction, for they are *ordinary pastors* and *true prelates*. To possess jurisdiction is *intrinsic to their offices*, and this suffices to its character as *ordinary*. Hence the General not only cannot absolutely take away his jurisdiction from a Provincial or Rector, for this would involve a contradiction, since to possess it is of the intrinsic idea of their offices; but he also cannot cause the Society to be governed without proper Provincials and local prelates, because for it to be governed by these belongs to its primary institution, and that the General cannot change. Only as regards the measure or extent of their jurisdiction do these prelates depend on the General, and this is not at variance with the idea of *ordinary* jurisdiction; for it is almost in the same way that the bishops and *a fortiori* the legates of the Pope depend on the Pope, and yet they have *ordinary* jurisdiction. Some measure of jurisdiction is, of the nature of the case, necessarily annexed to their offices, namely, that measure without which these offices could not morally and in due manner be fulfilled. Each of them has his own rules, and certain constitutions which affect him, and these declare the power which belongs to his office. That power is therefore to be regarded as *ordinary*, because it rests on certain prescribed law, and is possessed and exercised in virtue of office. Any farther powers which the General may be pleased to grant either to all, or to any inferior prelates, will be *not ordinary*, but *delegated only*.

In ascertaining the faculties of a prelate in the Society, the affirmative rather than the negative rule is to be followed; namely, that *each can do whatever has been granted to him*; and not—that he can do whatever has not been prohibited to him.

This power of jurisdiction of the prelates of the Society extends over all the religious thereof, and to all the acts or matter to which religious jurisdiction whether at common law or by privilege extends. It extends even over the Scholastics, because they are true religious, and true members incorporated into the Society; but with regard to novices there is a distinction. The Society has not over them proper *involuntary*, or *directive* jurisdiction, by which it may specially bind them in conscience, nor has it *coercive* jurisdiction by which it may compel them; and this because they have not vowed obedience, nor has the Society accepted any promise of obedience, or incorporated them into itself. But as regards *voluntary* jurisdiction they are in a manner subject to the Society, and are capable of the reception of those spiritual graces which the General has it in his power to bestow in accordance with the grant of the Apostolic See; and they are included in all Privileges which are granted to all who live under the obedience of the Society, and this novices do, although not under the obligation of a vow.

VI.— Do the Prelates of the Society rightly exact from their subjects a manifestation of their consciences, in order to their individual government?

It is a rule of the Society that all its members should from their entrance into it manifest the state of their consciences to their superior in order that he may have an intimate knowledge not only of their morals, but of their affections and inclinations; and this is to be regarded as among the substantials of the Institute.

This is in accordance with the spirit of the ancient Fathers, and of the Founders of religious Orders. St. Basil recommends it, and especially to those who have been on pilgrimage for some time outside the monastery. He says that they should, as soon as they return, give a perfect account to their prelate not only of their words and actions, but even of their thoughts. St. Benedict says that it is the fifth degree of humility. Cassian says that besides the great humility of this exercise, there is its utility for the instruction of the religious and for arming them against the snares of the devil, and he concludes that it is a general and evident sign of diabolical cogitation, if they are ashamed to manifest it to an elder. Although these Fathers are speaking chiefly of the younger religious, and it is true that a manifestation of their various temptations and the movements of their souls is more necessary in their case than it is in that of the more advanced, yet a faithful manifestation of conscience proportioned to the individual subject and to the will of the superior, has always been judged necessary by the Fathers for all by reason of their state; because it is ordained not only for instruction towards the overcoming of temptations, but in order to the whole spiritual government of the soul, with perfect obedience and humility, and in order to obtain greater grace from God, through the intervention of the superior. St. Buonaventure says that it pertains to a prelate to know the consciences of every one of his subjects, and he gives as reasons, that he may unravel their perplexities, foresee and guard against perils of sin, admonish the brethren to progress, correct those who are to be corrected, elucidate their doubts, inform each how he is fittingly to administer the offices entrusted to him so as to satisfy his brethren and not offend his own conscience. He says that this is of the substance of the pastoral office; and his doctrine confirms the declaration of the Society that manifestation of conscience is of the substance of its Institute. If it is of the substance of the office of a Rector to know the consciences of his subjects, it certainly must be of the substance of the duty of a subject to manifest his conscience to him.

Manifestation of conscience may be made under the seal of confession, or of a secret, or in any way the subject pleases, and which will be for his greater consolation. It may therefore be made in sacramental confession; for in no other way can it be made under the seal of confession. However much one may premise that he says a thing under the seal of confession, unless he truly confesses sacramentally, and speaks in order thereto, he will not bind under the seal the person to whom he speaks.

There is a great difference between the matter of manifestation of conscience and that of sacramental confession, for the latter consists only of sins actually committed, while the former includes much more, and not sins and defects only, but penances, mortifications, devotions and virtues; and among evils, not only actual sins, but also temptations, depraved habits and inclinations; and not only evil acts, but also imperfections, and occasions of evil, and transgressions of Rule, even when these are not in themselves sins. All these lie within the limits of manifestation of conscience, and a knowledge of them is necessary in order to the spiritual government of a religious person.

Manifestation of conscience differs also from sacramental confession both in itself and in its intrinsic end. Confession is in itself ordained solely towards obtaining remission of sins, and worthily satisfying God for them, and consequently towards amendment, inasmuch as a purpose of amendment is a part of the necessary satisfaction; while every other end besides this, although it may not be evil or at variance with the end and due circumstances of confession, is accidental to sacramental confession as such. Manifestation of conscience, on the other hand, is not in itself ordained for remission of sins, although it may serve towards this by way of consultation, and so may be made with a view to penance. Manifestation of conscience is ordained chiefly in order to *direction of life for the future*, and this requires manifestation of past acts *in so far as a knowledge of the past is necessary in order to provision for the future.* Since this direction is ordained not only for the avoidance of evil, but also towards progress in good, and not only in necessary good, but in that which is better and perfect, a manifestation not only of vices but also of virtues is necessary. It greatly contributes towards sound direction for the purpose both of progress and of preservation, if the superior has a knowledge of his subject's inclinations and temptations and also of the divine inspirations and aids with which he has been favoured, and therefore all these are rightly comprehended under the matter of this observance.

This direction moreover concerns not only the subject but his superior, for by means of his knowledge of his subject's conscience he should be greatly aided in his government of him, not only by counsels and admonitions, but also in his selection of ministries and occupations for him so that he should not place him in peril of falling, but in a state which will be advantageous for his spiritual welfare. This is most of all necessary in Orders which give themselves to ministries to their neighbours, for in these spiritual perils may more easily occur, unless the superior can foresee and guard against them, and, as St. Buonaventure says, he can scarcely foresee them unless he has a knowledge of the conscience of his subject.

Hence, in order to these ends it is necessary that this manifestation of such matters should be made outside confession, or that leave should be given by the subject to make use of the knowledge which has been acquired through sacramental confession. Such a knowledge as is not under the seal must therefore be given to the superior, for a superior ought not and cannot compel a subject to make sacramental confession to him. Hence a subject can either make manifestation in confession only, if that mode is more pleasing to him, and if there is no necessity for the other knowledge; or he can render an account of his conscience outside confession, and to exact this, at least as regards matters of which it is necessary that the superior should have knowledge, the superior has a right.

Without the subject's consent nothing can be revealed pertaining either to temptations which are not sins, or to natural inclination towards any vice, or to any similar matter revelation of which might be burdensome to the penitent. Hence if any use of such knowledge is necessary outside confession, the superior should exact from the penitent that he should give it to him outside confession, or that he should declare that he has given it concomitantly only in confession, and not so as properly to fall under the seal of confession; and this the subject will be bound to do in accordance with the Rule. This necessity of exacting leave from the penitent exists chiefly when the use to be made of the knowledge is merely external or *quasi*-political, or carries with it some suspicion of revelation; for if the use of it should be only in order to spiritual care and provision with regard to the penitent himself, without any fear or suspicion of revelation, and the matter did not directly and proximately belong to confession of sins, the use of such knowledge might more easily be allowed, without requiring the penitent's leave.\*

When the account of conscience is given outside confession there is and can be no secret of the seal, but there arises the greatest obligation of the natural secret, such as arises from a secret consultation with regard to a matter of conscience. This is morally necessary in order to render this burden or means endurable, and charity and justice demand it, and it is in view of this that the subject lays bare his conscience, not to defame himself, but to provide for his spiritual necessities, which he can and ought to do.

Hence in the Ordinances common to the whole Society and authorized by the Seventh General Congregation, this secret is commended in the strongest terms, and a superior who should violate it is to be severely punished and, if need be, with deposition from his office. Superiors are also strictly enjoined to observe the secret as regards defects of one subject which have been fraternally manifested to them by another, as well as regards those which the delinquent himself manifests as his own.

No doubt manifestation is a difficult matter for one who has not determined to profess the way of perfection,

\* See note on page 352.

or who does not faithfully persevere in his purpose of perfection and make progress towards it; but for one who is rightly affected and disposed in the desire of attaining to perfection, and of perfectly moderating all his passions, and of avoiding all occasions and occupations which might hinder his progress, as that man ought to do who professes the religious life, and of seeking in all things the greater service of God and of his Order, it will not be difficult for him to avail himself of this means. Love of the end renders easy a means which is necessary or conducive to the attaining of the end, even if otherwise that means should seem difficult; and in this sense Christ our Lord said that His yoke was sweet and His burden was light. Plutarch says that the first foundation of virtue is an immense love in the pursuit of it, and he places this very means among the principles of progress in virtue, and adds that, according to Diogenes, if any one desires to arrive at good fruit, he has need of a loving friend, or of a bitter and burning enemy, in order that he may avoid sin either through being corrected, or through being gently cured. If therefore this means did not appear to be so very difficult to a philosopher, in comparison with the attainment of ordinary virtue, why should it seem hard to a religious if it is regarded from the point of view of the perfection of charity, and the purity of heart to be obtained? The subject gains in the benevolence and esteem of his superior by reason of his fidelity and his signs of repentance and purpose of amendment, more than he can lose by reason of the sins which he has committed; for past sins, when blotted out by penance, do not defame a man even before God Himself, and hence they ought not to defame him in the eyes of a spiritual father who should steadfastly strive to imitate God. Superiors ought to be most cautious on this point lest they should come to be regarded by their subjects as judges rather than as fathers; while subjects, on the other hand, ought not to be too delicate so as to think that everything appointed for them that does not please them is done unjustly, or that if a particular prelate should happen at a time to be imprudent all the others are to be regarded as like him, or that, for this cause only, a necessary rule and holy custom should be changed.

As matter of fact it is ascertained by use and practice that there is less difficulty in this observance than might appear in speculation and apprehension, that is to say, in the case of persons who have an upright will to make progress in religion.*

## VII.— Is Fraternal Denunciation rightly made in accordance with the Rule, and particular government of the Society?

As spontaneous manifestation of conscience is necessary in order to the private and voluntary direction of

---

* Father-General John Paul Oliva in his Epistle on this subject of March 12, 1669, strictly prohibited superiors from acting otherwise with regard to manifestation of conscience, than as they are bound to act with regard to sacramental confession. Hence they cannot use knowledge gained through manifestation, for the external government of the subject, without his express and spontaneous leave; while all other knowledge so gained they cannot in any way reveal to any one, neither Rectors to the Provincial, nor Provincials or Visitors to the General himself.

the individual religious, so also denunciation by others is necessary in order to common correction of faults, and chiefly in the case of persons who hide and excuse their faults; and it ought to obtain in every well-ordered community.

This denunciation, which is called *fraternal*, is justly prescribed, and ordained by the Constitutions, since it is an act which is good in itself and necessary to the common good, so long as it is made to a lawful prelate, and with due circumstances. The rule of the Society is—that in order to greater progress in spirit, and principally in order to greater submission and humility, every one should be content that all his errors and defects, and all things whatsoever, which have been noted and observed in him, should be manifested to superiors by any one whomsoever who has come to a knowledge of them outside confession.

Hence all defects, even if they are grievous sins, and wholly hidden, are to be manifested to the superior by any one whomsoever who has certain knowledge of them, and this without previous admonition of the delinquent, and without regard had to amendment as the end, and with the view only of greater perfection, subjection and humility. The matter of fraternal denunciation is most universal, and, with the exception of the knowledge of confession and that knowledge which has been communicated under secret for the purpose of obtaining spiritual counsel, includes everything whatsoever, even the most hidden, certain knowledge of which has been arrived at in any way.

This rule supposes the renunciation which all who

enter the Society expressly make of all their rights to their own reputation; and since to him who wills and consents no injury is done, so no loss of reputation in the eyes of a superior, which may result from fraternal denunciation, can be an injustice.

Further, this renunciation of right to one's reputation is made in the Society in order to greater progress in spirit, as the Rule itself declares, and ordinarily there will be greater progress when correction is made by a superior than when it is made by a private person; and so the immediate manifestation to the superior of another's defect, without any previous admonition of him, cannot be contrary to charity. It seems, on the contrary, to make for charity, since what is aimed at by such denunciation, and results from it, as we suppose, is a greater good. Nowhere in the Gospel, which never bars the way of greater progress to any one, is there declared or conferred any right on the erring to be admonished by a brother before being admonished by a father.

The Rule only *declares it to be lawful* to manifest the defects of others, and that even without interrogation on the part of the superior. It does not *bind to manifestation* of the faults of others, and it certainly would not be expedient to impose this burden upon all, or even to permit it, because it would be most troublesome to superiors, as well as odious to the brethren, and might greatly lessen charity and fraternal union. It is in the power of superiors to commit this charge to certain persons, and these will be bound, according to the degree of obligation imposed on them; but this is less done in the Society than it is in some other religious Orders. In some Orders there are *zelatores* or *acclamators*, as they are called, who are bound under oath to proclaim what they may have observed; but in the Society there is no obligation imposed by ordinary law, but only a simple ordinance. Sometimes indeed the matter may induce a greater obligation of charity, and may even compel the superior to strictly prescribe vigilance. Hence the Sixth General Congregation ordains that in the case of faults which are to the detriment of the common good, or to the imminent damage of a third person, such as those which are infectious to others, or hurtful to the Order, every one not only can, but is also bound to manifest these to the superior, as to a father, in order that he may secretly and prudently provide for the good both of the subject and of the Order.

The Seventh General Congregation declares that those are to be severely punished who rashly and from inane suspicions, or any cause which cannot be proved, falsely impute crime to another, even if they do this only to the superior, since this is in reality an injury. It adds that superiors are to beware of lending an easy ear to denouncers, and that they should closely examine into all particulars until they shall have arrived at a knowledge of the matter denounced, so that they may either set free the innocent, or punish the noxious and false denouncer, in proportion to the magnitude of the case. Even if a real fault has been committed, the Society wills that it should be manifested with due charity.

A denouncer cannot use not only that knowledge which proceeds either immediately or mediately from sacramental confession, but also that which has been communicated to him by way of secret and for the sake of seeking counsel, direction and aid, for if that were allowed men would be deterred from this spiritual remedy. But apart from this, if the revelation has been made merely from motives of friendship, or from any other human motive, the Rule invalidates every promise whatsoever, even if it has been made under oath, not to reveal the matter to the superior.

## VIII.—The general doctrine of Denunciation, and its application to the practice of the Society.

Denunciation—as it is distinguished from Accusation, which in itself aims at, not the amendment of a brother, but the securing of one's own interests, or satisfaction, or the punishment of the offender,—is a lawful delation or manifestation made to a superior, in order that in the exercise of his office he may provide for the reparation or hindrance of some damage or loss.

The sin of a brother may be either already committed, or it may be in danger of being committed, or it may have been already committed, and there is also danger of its continuation or repetition. The proper matter of denunciation is sin which has been already committed, because correction concerns not a future act but an act already committed. A future sin, however, if it is already morally existing in a peril or occasion thereof, can be denounced to the superior, in order that he may prevent or hinder it. Even if in a particular case there should be no place for fraternal correction, there may be room for denunciation from the motive of fraternal charity; and so a rule of the Society ordains that if any one knows of the grave temptation of another, he should inform the superior, in order that he by his paternal care and provision may supply a fitting remedy.

Lesser faults are rightly manifested immediately to the superior, without any previous admonition of the offender. Grave faults are those which are either mortal sins, or which are such as to beget suspicion of such sins. All defects which are not of this nature may be reckoned among lesser faults. Even grave faults may be lawfully manifested to the superior without previous admonition of the offender, for the reasons already indicated, which apply to the religious state in general, and in a special manner to the Society, and which render such denunciation not only lawful, but expedient. Not only is paternal correction by the superior, to whom denunciation is made not as he is a judge but as he is a father, more likely, as in other Orders, to produce more fruit by way of amendment than may be hoped for from fraternal correction by the admonition of a fellow-subject, but in the Society the providence of a prelate is specially necessary, and chiefly by reason of its ministries towards its neighbours, and the various occasions in which on account of such ministries Ours may from time to time be placed by their prelates. There is also the greater dependence which Ours have on their prelates, not only in their offices and ministries, but also in their works of penance, mortification and prayer. There is further the special communion and fraternal union which is professed by the Society, a result of which is this, that the sin of one member might more easily infect the others, if this were not hindered by a special vigilance. Again, in accordance with the Institute of the Society, the religious are educated and trained in this observance from their youth, and the majority of them are young, and at an age when they stand in need of the providence and discipline of their prelates. Finally, the more the Society is concerned with its neighbours, the more does it stand in need of a good name and reputation, and the more necessary it is that this should not be fictitious and baseless, but founded in true and solid virtue; and this can scarcely be obtained and preserved unless superiors have knowledge of the defects of their subjects, so that they may appoint each to that which he can do without damage to himself and without scandal to his neighbours.

In particular cases it may have to be considered whether there is not an absence of all reason for immediate denunciation to the superior, for it may happen in a particular case that, on weighing all the circumstances, it is prudently judged that to acquaint the superior is neither necessary nor will be useful for the amendment of the delinquent, for the security of the Society or for the other good ends which are aimed at by denunciation (which, since it is a most rare case, is not provided for by law or rule); and in this case one is to abstain from denunciation, if the fall is hidden, and has given no scandal to others, and if there is no fear of future scandal. Although a lessening of reputation in the eyes of a prudent prelate, who loves his subject as a son, and who will keep his secret, may not seem to be a great loss, nevertheless, if it is done without reasonable cause, it cannot be excused from sin; for whenever the hidden sin of a brother is without just cause revealed to another, whoever he may be, there is by common doctrine the vice of detraction. Such sin is of its nature mortal, although it may easily become venial when the denunciation is made with a good intention, even if it is made imprudently.

When the fault of a subject has become known to a prelate by denunciation, he ought first of all secretly to admonish and correct him; and if he acknowledges his fault, and promises amendment, there is nothing further to be done, by way of either public punishment or disgrace, although the superior may impose a secret penance in proportion to the fault, either by way of satisfaction, or as a remedy. He can also remove occasions of sin, and he may with this end in view make some change in his subject's occupation or habitation, but in such wise as that no scandal or loss of reputation should result. If such a change however is not necessary in order to remove occasions of sin, he should not vex his subject, nor remove him from his office or treat him with less honour than before.

If the subject will not acknowledge his fault, or promise amendment, and the prelate is morally certain of his fault, on the testimony of at least one unexceptionable eye-witness, he may severely rebuke him, and this even in the presence of two or three grave persons, if he should judge this to be expedient in order to move him, or for his greater confusion. He may also threaten him that he will search into his life, that he has no confidence in him, and the like; and, according to the kind of person he is, he can enjoin or inflict some religious correction, penance or chastisement, if he considers it prudent in order to strike fear into him for the future. The proof and knowledge which he possesses is sufficient for all this, and to all this his paternal office apart from his power of jurisdiction, extends; for a father in the natural order can in a similar case chastise his son, if he is prudently persuaded that what has been said to him about his son is true, even if he has no juridical or full proof of the fault. Finally, he can prescribe to him with all rigour and, if need be, under pain of excommunication *ipso facto* to be incurred, that he should avoid a particular occasion, as for instance, that he should not go to such and such a place, or that he should avoid familiarity with such and such a person.

All these steps however depend on prudence, because by no human law are they either prohibited or prescribed, and they do not in themselves exceed the *dominative power* of a father,* nor do they result in notable disgrace to the subject.

If notwithstanding all this, the subject is pertinacious, and will not receive any admonition, and his fault is neither notorious nor capable of judicial proof, and it does not tend directly to the damage of the community, the prelate has nothing more that he can do with regard to his subject, save to pray for him, to watch over him, and

---

* With the exception of an excommunication which requires jurisdiction in the superior.

to remove from him all occasions of sin, so far as he can do so without disgrace to him, or scandal.

## IX.—THE THREE MODES OF PROCEDURE IN EXTERNAL JUDGMENT AGAINST THE OFFENCES OF SUBJECTS; AND FIRST, VISITATION, OR GENERAL ENQUIRY.

There are three modes in which prelates and judges can proceed in external judgment, in order to know and punish the sins of subjects, namely, by way of *Accusation*, by way of *Judicial denunciation*, and by way of *Enquiry*.

*General Enquiry* or *Visitation* differs from the other two modes in this that in it the judge himself takes the initiative, and no one else compels him by bringing the offence to his ears, and demanding his recognition of it. He himself makes enquiry, and so this mode is called the way of enquiry. It is made in two ways, namely, in general or in particular. A general enquiry is made in the visitations of religious Orders. The Council of Trent ordained that exempt regular prelates should visit the monasteries which are subject to them, and that the bishops should visit the monasteries which are not exempt. This is not only lawful, but is of official obligation. In the Society, the Provincials ordinarily, and Visitors delegated by the General extraordinarily visit in his name, since he himself cannot by reason of his innumerable other and most important occupations visit the Society in person. To the General however this function chiefly belongs, since he has supreme jurisdiction over all the members of the Society, although as a rule he does not exercise it in person, because as the Constitutions declare, it contributes greatly to the free communication of the head with its members, that he should for the most part reside at Rome, where he may more easily hold intercourse with all the places of the Society. By reason of the great dependence of the Society on its head, it is necessary that he should have a fixed abode, and by reason of his special dependence on the Apostolic See, he can have no more convenient abode than Rome.

When there is no special reason for visitation, besides the official obligation to make it, enquiry can be made only in general, so far as persons are concerned. A prelate can enquire in three ways with regard to faults. In the first place, in general as regards both faults and persons, as when the prelate in his visitation enquires whether there are any crimes in the community, or whether the laws and statutes are observed, or whether any one knows of another having committed any crime, or the like. This mode of enquiry is in itself just, and requires beforehand no other circumstance besides the right and act of visitation, because by this mode of interrogation no injury is done to any one, and it is morally necessary in order to begin the visitation, for such interrogation is not properly a judicial act, but is an act of general government, and it is as it were a preamble to judgment, should judgment be necessary.

Secondly, enquiry may be made by interrogation which is special as regards a particular fault, but is general as regards persons; as for instance, if a prelate were to enquire if one knows that any one in the house possesses anything as his own property, or has left the monastery at night, or the like. This again is without injury to any one, since the interrogation is made with regard to no one person in particular. It ought not however to be adopted, especially in religious Orders, unless the special sin which is enquired about has been committed, or unless there is a common rumour and suspicion of its having been committed, although there has been no disgrace or knowledge of the culprit. The reason is because, when there has been no previous rumour, some injury seems to be done to the community by this mode of interrogation, as appearing to beget suspicion that something of the sort has been done, especially when the sins enquired about are grievous and disgraceful to religious.

Besides these two modes of Enquiry, which are general, there is a third, which is *particular* with regard to such and such a person; and it may be made also in particular with regard to such and such a sin, as for instance, whether Peter has stolen? or whether he has committed some grievous sin? It is a common rule with regard to this particular enquiry, that it is not lawful to make it unless there has been a previous loss of that person's reputation in accordance with the character of the sin. When the enquiry is not made on occasion of some public sin, and in order to its punishment, or to take away the scandal, or to redress the injury resulting from it, but is made only on the ground of official visitation, or of customary government, there is then to be considered the person or the community with regard to whom the visitation is directly ordained and instituted. If it is directed to the whole community, it is not lawful to interrogate with regard to one more particularly than with regard to others, unless there has been a previous loss of personal reputation with regard to a particular vice, or with regard to the person's life in general, that it has not been moral or religious. But if the visitation is instituted with regard to a particular person by reason of his special office, then it will be lawful apart from any previous loss of reputation on his part, to enquire in particular how he conducts himself in his office, or whether anything has been noted in him, without descending to particulars. The reason is because, as in the visitation of a community general interrogation is necessary in order to commence the visitation, so when a visitation is instituted with regard, for instance, to the Provincial, it must necessarily be begun by an interrogation which is particular as regards him, and which is at the same time general as regards his life and office. No suspicion is thus begotten, because it is evident that the particular interrogation is made not because of any special suspicion, but because he is the proper and special object of the visitation. With regard to any particular vice of his there can be no interrogation, unless there has been by reason of that vice a previous loss of his reputation.

Hence it follows that in such visitations a subject, even when interrogated upon oath, is not bound to manifest a religious whom he knows to have sinned, when the sin is so hidden that no disgrace attaches to him.

The judge cannot juridically interrogate with regard to such a person, and therefore the subject is not bound to answer by manifesting the offender. If the judge interrogates absolutely, it is always understood that he is enquiring whether his subjects know of the sin of any one who is already defamed by reason of that sin.

There must be no confusion between the principles which apply to judicial denunciation and juridical visitation, and those which apply to paternal, secret and private denunciation made to a prelate alone, and to that prelate as he is a father and not a judge.

X. — THE MODE OF PROCEDURE BY WAY OF SPECIAL ENQUIRY; BY WAY OF JUDICIAL DENUNCIATION; AND BY WAY OF ACCUSATION.

Supposing sufficient loss of reputation or adequate suspicion of a crime, a prelate can proceed to a *special* enquiry concerning his subject; and this whether he has or has not hopes of his amendment, for now he aims principally not at the amendment but at the punishment of his subject, and to provide a remedy for the scandal which has arisen from his loss of reputation, or from the suspicion of crime which attaches to him.

Although the mode of procedure in a religious Order does not require all the niceties of law, it should nevertheless be sufficiently juridical so as to obtain public credit; and therefore the witnesses should be examined in presence of a notary, or a secretary appointed by the prelate from amongst the religious, who will faithfully commit to writing all the acts of the enquiry, and subscribe his record along with the prelate, so as to provide proof of the same.

The witnesses are to be interrogated distinctly and clearly, according to articles and heads which have been previously prepared by the prelate along with the notary.

Although when the suspicion of a crime has been noised abroad no proof of the fact of this is necessary, since previous evidence is supposed in order to justify entrance on the enquiry and to oblige the witnesses to answer, it is nevertheless best to examine some witnesses not only with regard to the crime, but also with regard to the suspicion or report of it, in order to the better conviction of the culprit.

The witnesses should be examined on oath, for otherwise their evidence does not afford sufficient judicial testimony.

Further procedure will be in accordance with the merits of the cause, as they emerge from the testimony of the witnesses. If no witness condemns the accused of the crime, so as at least to furnish a half-complete proof thereof, the accused cannot personally be lawfully interrogated; and so either further enquiry is to be made of other witnesses, or the case is no further to be proceeded with. Suspicion of the crime sufficiently proved amounts however to such a half-complete proof of the crime itself as to justify the accused person being cited and interrogated. He will be interrogated on oath, but in order that he should be obliged to answer, he must first be satisfied as to the lawfulness of the procedure against him, and the proof which has been already led is to be read to him.

Judicial denunciation may be commenced in two ways, either immediately, as when one begins a cause by assuming the office of denouncer before a prelate or judge; or secondly, by passing from evangelical denunciation to judicial denunciation.

It is not necessary that there should be previous suspicion of the crime in order that one may justly denounce it judicially. Previous suspicion is required when the procedure is by way of enquiry, in order that enquiry may take the place of an accuser; but when procedure is by way of denunciation the place of accuser is taken by the denouncer, although he does not entirely take the whole burden upon him, since he is not bound to prove his case in the same way as an accuser.

Judicial denunciation, which cannot be made without great and public loss of reputation, should be preceded by secret fraternal admonition, when there is hope of amendment therefrom. So necessary is this that, if the denouncer has not done it and should fail in his proof, he can scarcely be excused from calumny, and he will have to prove his innocence of calumnious intention in his denunciation. Religious are not exempt from this obligation, for they have no privilege of exemption; and this is much in accordance not only with perfection but also with the demands of charity. Hence even in the Society there is, in the matter of judicial denunciation, no renunciation of right to reputation.

Much less may denunciation be made after secret

admonition, if the latter has produced its effect; for in that case the end of judicial denunciation ceases, and it would be no longer denunciation, but grievous detraction.

When denunciation is from the outset made principally for the sake of the common good, or to prevent loss to a third party, previous secret admonition is not necessary, since the common good or that of an innocent party is to be preferred to the advantage and reputation of the guilty party; and the prelate may proceed at once according to rigour of law to the examination of witnesses, and to receiving the confession of the accused and the like, having regard not principally to his amendment, but to the indemnification of the common good or innocent third party. Since however the good of the subject, however guilty he may be, should never be separated from the common good, as far as the prelate is concerned, since both fall under his care and obligation, he is bound, if he has hope of being able to correct his subject, and sufficiently to meet the evil by means of charity and in the exercise of his pastoral office, to endeavour in the first place secretly to correct and amend him. If he succeeds, he can proceed no farther to public judgment or punishment. He must however be very certain with regard to the indemnification of third parties, and the crime must not be one of those grievous crimes which are at once to be brought to judgment.

Procedure by way of *Accusation* is not common in religious Orders, although it is not wholly excluded, for a religious who has suffered an injury can accuse the offender to his prelate. No previous suspicion, nor any attempt at fraternal correction is necessary, since the end of accusation is not the amendment of a brother, but the just avenging of a wrong. One can accuse without injustice and without lack of charity, if the accusation is made not from hatred, but either from affection towards the Order and desire that similar injuries should not be introduced into it, or from affection towards one's own advantage, such as for instance, one's due honour, good name or the like.

To accuse for the sake of avenging oneself, or in recompense for a wrong suffered, although not evil in itself, is nevertheless perilous and as a rule foreign to those who profess the religious state; and therefore this mode of procedure is not frequently resorted to and should, if possible, and when denunciation will serve all necessary purposes, be avoided in religious Orders.

### XI.—What form of judgment is observed in the Society?

No judicial denunciation is prescribed in the Constitutions or Pontifical Bulls, but whenever denunciation or the correction of defects is spoken of, it is always added that all things should be done *to the greater glory of God*, or *as charity demands;* or some equivalent phrase is used which relates properly to fraternal denunciation and paternal correction.

Similarly, when they speak of enquiry or interrogation, *paternal* enquiry or interrogation is understood, as the correlative to the denunciation which is made by a subject to the superior as to a father and not as to a judge.

There is no rule, however, in the Society which gives leave to a prelate to enquire even in this paternal manner into the life of a subject in particular, or with regard to any crime of his, when there has been no previous suspicion or rumour of such crime.

Much less is there any trace to be found in the Institute of procedure by way of accusation.

No mode of procedure which differs from the ordinary judicial forms of common law, is prescribed as peculiar to the Society by the Constitutions or Pontifical Bulls; but the Seventh General Congregation ordains that in particular cases, which may require judicial forms, recourse is to be had to the General.

It has been objected to the Society that it expels certain of its members without the observance of judicial forms, and on private information alone, and sometimes, as they say, without the party having been heard; and that, as expulsion from an Order is the most grievous of all the punishments which can be inflicted by the Order, judicial forms should then of all times be observed in the infliction of such a punishment; and that punishment is frequently imposed by the General who lives far distant from the accused, and so cannot himself examine into the case, or hear the excuses which might be made.

To meet this objection, it is to be remembered that there

are two ways in which the Society can expel one of its members, namely, either by way of punishment, or for other reasons which render the subject useless for its Institute, although they are not crimes, and cannot in rigour of justice be punished. Expulsion by way of punishment is involuntary as regards the person expelled, and it matters not whether he consents or objects, if he merits expulsion. Expulsion for other reasons may be sometimes effected against the will of the religious, but it may often be with his consent, and as it were, by covenant of the parties. When the expulsion is inflicted simply as a punishment, and apart from anything which would of itself suffice to justify expulsion, it can never be lawfully inflicted, unless after observance of regular order in the judgment of the crime so punished. In such a case expulsion is a judicial or legal punishment, and in the infliction of such punishments it is most of all necessary to observe at least substantial judicial order. The Constitutions of the Society do not ordain that such a punishment should be inflicted under any other circumstances, and the Society has in this matter no special privilege by means of Pontifical Indults; and therefore it ought to observe the common order which right reason requires before the infliction of such punishments, even if it were not bound to observe the rigour of common law.

This applies chiefly to the Professed, for as regards the other members of the Society, their expulsion is never so entirely penal or judicial that it may not be also conventional, or of consent on their part; and so in their case judicial forms are not so necessary.

When a member is expelled, not by way of punishment, or by reason of his incorrigibility, but for the sake of other advantages to the Order, and not against his will, but rather with his consent, no judicial order is necessary, but any information or knowledge will suffice which would in prudence be sufficient in the settlement of other grave affairs. Juridical proof or knowledge is not necessary in order to human contracts, and this is a sort of contract, since it is done of common consent of both parties, and all idea of injury or violence consequently ceases.

This mode of dismissal has no place as regards the Professed, since the Order has no power to dismiss them, unless for a cause which is absolutely necessary for the common good, or unless justice should demand it; and since they themselves cannot voluntarily depart, having made an absolute promise to persevere. Neither in the case of Formed Coadjutors is this mode of dismissal to be allowed, since they are no longer in any way on probation, but are already established in their final state; and therefore, although the Order has power to expel them, and that free from their vows, yet this is not by reason of any convention or covenant with them, but only for a cause so urgent that it could justly compel them even against their will to departure.

Two things are required in order to the dismissal of Scholastics of the Society; first, that the cause of dismissal should be just and sufficiently justified; and secondly, that the superior should have sufficient and morally certain knowledge of it.

It belongs to the first that the subject should have

been once and again admonished of his fault in order that he might amend, and that he should have shewn himself incorrigible, or have given no moral hope of amendment, and consequently of usefulness for the ministries of the Society; and in this way the cause is said to be justified. Sometimes, however, the crime may be so enormous as to suffice for immediate expulsion, either in order to avert dishonour from the Society, or because no hope can be entertained with regard to the reliability of such a person, or his fitness for the Institute.

It belongs to the second requisite that denunciation by one or two persons should not easily be credited. If the fault is denounced to the superior as to a father, even if it should be proved with the utmost certainty, he is to proceed, not to expulsion, but to the amendment of the subject, which is the end of such denunciation, and because the knowledge has been given to him, as it were, under this law or condition.

If however, some great and urgent reason for the common good demands expulsion, any certain knowledge whatsoever of the cause (excepting always of course knowledge derived through sacramental confession) suffices; because the denouncer himself is in such a case bound to manifest the matter in that way which may be necessary and sufficient in order to the relief of the common good. When, after paternal denunciation all diligence has been used in order to the amendment of the subject, and has failed, one may lawfully pass to judicial denunciation, since this is merited by the contumacy of the subject; and therefore if the fault and contumacy are morally certain, this will suffice. Even when there has been no previous paternal denunciation, but the superior himself, watching and observing the morals of individuals, has noted in any one manifest signs of certain defects, or these have been brought before him, as he is a judge, by others, or the culprit himself has confessed his fault outside sacramental confession, and outside secret and paternal consultation, any one of these means of information suffices so long as the superior arrives at morally certain knowledge.

It is not only permitted to, but enjoined on the superior that, before decreeing the expulsion of any one, he should treat the matter with mature counsel of some prudent men; and he is also admonished to hear the accused, and if he has any excuse or purgation of himself to make to give him the opportunity; and thus all natural equity will be observed.

Common and ordinary affairs are in the Society settled by the immediate superiors, and those of a graver character are settled by the Provincials, but the final settlement of an affair which is so grave as the dismissal of one who has already made his vows is reserved to the General. This, far from its being a grievance, is in favour of the subject, since thus the punishment or remedy, as the case may be, is resolved on with more mature counsel and therefore with greater difficulty. Neither are subjects hereby deprived of all aid in order to their defence, not only through recourse to the General by means of letters, but also by answering for themselves before their more immediate prelates, and by alleging all causes of excuse, or, what is wont to be more efficacious, by promising amendment. If the Provincial were himself to settle the affair, that would be sufficient to satisfy the rights of the subject; and therefore when the whole affair with its final determination is carried to the Supreme Prelate, the subject has an additional opportunity afforded to him.

XII. — IS THE RULE OF THE SOCIETY WELL ADAPTED AND SUFFICIENT IN ORDER TO ITS ADEQUATE GOVERNMENT, AND RELIGIOUS DIRECTION?

Every well instituted human government requires, in addition to natural and divine law, some Rule or norm which is proper to, and adapted for itself.

Besides the Constitutions, there are many other ordinances in the Society which are comprehended under the general name of Rules. If therefore we wish to apply the distinction between a Rule and Constitutions to the case of the Society, we may say that the Rule of the Society is that compendious idea and sum of the whole Institute which is contained in the Bulls of Paul III. and Julius III. since they embrace the end and substantial means employed by the Society; while all other laws are comprehended under the name of Statutes or Constitutions.

The Rule of the Society, so understood, and as gathered from these Pontifical Indults, contains fifteen heads:—

1. That the end of the Society is to give itself to its own perfection, and to the salvation of its neighbours.

2. That there ought to be in the Society various grades of persons, so that every one may, according to the grace ministered to him by the Holy Ghost, co-operate towards the said end.
3. That there should be one General in the Society, to whom it belongs to distribute those grades, and all offices and ministries, and to govern the whole Society.
4. That the whole Order is enrolled in a special and proper manner under the obedience of the Pontiff, and is therefore consecrated and bound to him by a special vow of obedience.
5. That the Professed of the Society make a solemn vow of poverty, chastity and obedience.
6. That the Society has commended to it in so many words the instruction of children and the unlearned in christian doctrine.
7. That the Professed Society should not only individually but also in its various communities profess and observe poverty.
8. That the Society can have Colleges which possess their own revenues for the support of its Scholastics; and that the government of those Colleges and students, and the administration of the goods of the Colleges belongs to the Professed Society, in such wise however that it cannot convert those goods to its own emolument.
9. That the Scholastics of the Society should, after sufficient probation therein, be admitted into the Society by means of the substantial vows of religion made in accordance with its Constitutions;

that is, not by solemn but by simple vows, so that it should remain in the power of the Society to dismiss them free from their vows, should their dismissal be expedient.

10. That the Society may admit Spiritual and Temporal Coadjutors by means of vows which are also simple, and which are to be made in accordance with its Constitutions.

11. That in the Society there should be General Congregations, to which it will belong to make, and to explain and alter perpetual Constitutions, and to transact its graver affairs.

12. That the General should be created by election of a General Congregation; and that as regards all things else, and the providing of all inferior prelates, the power should be with the General.

13. That even the Professed should not be bound to sing or recite the Canonical Office in common or in Choir, but only privately; and that those only are so bound who are in sacred orders.

14. That in their external manner of life, in dress, living and the like, Ours should follow the custom of poor but respectable priests.

15. That Ours should not be received to solemn profession until after lengthened and most diligent probations by which their life and doctrine may be discerned.

This is the sum of the Institute and, as it were, the Rule of the Society, which was expressly set forth as regards all these heads by the Supreme Pontiffs in the foresaid Indults, and confirmed by them, and afterwards most exactly explained, approved and defended by Gregory XIII. Gregory XIV. and Paul V. in their Constitutions.

After this Rule, the first place among the Laws or Statutes of the Society is held by the Constitutions which, with the very best counsel and not without great light from God obtained by lengthened prayers, were composed by St. Ignatius. Ribadaneira relates that such was the modesty of the saint that he would not hold the Constitutions composed by him as ratified and confirmed until they had been approved by the judgment of the whole body of the Society. This was done after his death in the First General Congregation.

The Declarations of the Constitutions are of the same authority with the Constitutions themselves; and both together with the Examen, have the same author, namely, St. Ignatius.

In every religious Order the utmost care and diligence is necessary in the choice of persons to be received, for unless their talents and condition are suited to the particular Order which they enter, the multitude of religious will increase, but the splendour and perfection of the Order will be greatly diminished. This care is greatly commended by the Fathers, and St. Ignatius imitated them in this by making the preamble of the Constitutions to be—an Examination of persons to be received.

2. Since great caution and prudence is necessary not only in receiving, but also in retaining the members of

an Order, he has in the Constitutions ordained at length all things that are to be observed in the dismissal of those subjects of whom there cannot be entertained a hope that they will be useful to the Society.

3. He teaches the manner of governing and of promoting those who are on probation, that is, both the Novices and the Scholastics; and since the religious life is nearly in the same way common to, and of the same nature as regards all, he here sets forth generally what belongs to the government of individual members of the Society as regards both body and soul.

4. The fourth part contains what is necessary to progress in learning, and generally what relates to the studies of the Society.

5, 6. In the fifth and sixth parts the various modes in which the religious are united to the body of the Society by means of their religious vows or profession, are treated of, and what every one who is already established in a special grade should observe. In the sixth part especially, the perfection of the vows of the Society, and the regular observance which is demanded of its religious while they live, and the piety which is to be exercised towards them when they are dead, is accurately set forth.

7. The seventh part treats of the Society's ministries to its neighbours.

8. Since by reason of these ministries the Society must necessarily be dispersed through the various quarters of the globe, St. Ignatius has with exceeding providence prescribed in the eighth part the way in which the members are to preserve their union, both one with another and with their head.

9. The ninth part relates entirely to the Head, or General of the Society.

10. The tenth contains general counsels which may greatly contribute towards the preservation and increase of the Society.

Thus nothing seems to be omitted which could be of service for the government of the Order, in accordance with its own special end and institute.

Since, however, the observance, practice and comprehension of all the Constitutions does not belong to all individuals of the Society, but to those to whom the government of it has been committed, it is to these that it chiefly belongs diligently to peruse *the entire volume* of the Constitutions, and to have it at hand, so that they may be prepared, when need arises, for the execution of the Constitutions, or to give an account of them; while for the use of the others who are simple religious a brief *Summary of the Constitutions* has been extracted. This Summary is also known by the name of the *General Rules*, because in it the general heads of perfection, which are to be observed by all who profess this Institute, are set forth.

A religious Rule commonly declares first the end of the particular state, and then the means towards that end, which, according to St. Thomas, may be divided into three parts, namely, those means which are purely of counsel, simple ordinances, and proper precepts.

Besides these there are in the Society other rules which are called the *Common Rules*, not so much from their object, like the preceding, as from their subject, or the persons for whom they are made. They, like the General Rules, are laid down for all the religious of the Society, and in this they differ from the Rules for special offices. No superior under the General can be the author of either, as was decreed by the First General Congregation. The Constitutions give certain general principles of perfection, and such counsels as belong to what we may call the substance of interior and exterior perfection; while the Common Rules descend to particulars of external observance and of what belongs to the order and fitting disposition of common life.

Besides the General and Common Rules, there are in the Society special rules for its different ministries and offices. This should not be regarded as grievous or burdensome, but as most useful in order that every one may proceed with great clearness and light, and may know in what way he should satisfy his obligation in the fulfilment of his function.

The Rules of the General are the Constitutions themselves, together with the whole of the Institute, and so for him no special Rules are provided.

There are Rules for Provincials, and for all inferior prelates; and since these need counsel and aid and admonition, there are Rules also for their Consultors, Ministers, and Admonitors respectively. So also there are special Rules for the Masters of Novices and Spiritual Prefects, and generally for all who are in any office or ministry, whether temporal, or literary, as in the case of Scholastics, or spiritual as in the case of priests and preachers.

Besides these, there are the Decrees or Canons of General Congregations. Although these Councils are more rarely assembled in the Society than they are in other religious Orders, since the Society has a perpetual General, and since all things pertaining to its Institute have been most fully arranged and digested, yet their existence is sometimes necessary. When a General Congregation is assembled, it has authority to make Decrees and perpetual laws, and to explain, and even, if need be, to alter the Constitutions, in virtue of the first Bull of Paul III. and another of Julius III. Ordinarily, however, the Decrees of a General Congregation are for the purpose of solving doubts which have emerged, or of adding something which is necessary or fitting in accordance with the change of times, or with the results of observation or experience.

The Generals can also issue their own Ordinances; and these do not expire at the death of the General, or until they are recalled. They differ from the Decrees of General Congregations in this that a General can revoke an Ordinance of his predecessors, while no General can abrogate the Decrees or Canons of General Congregations, since such a Congregation is superior to him; and in this sense the Bull of Julius III. says that it belongs to a General Congregation to make or alter Constitutions.

In the same sense is to be understood what was declared by the Fourth General Congregation that the General can by his own ordinary authority explain the

Constitutions, although his explanation has not the force of a universal law, but avails only for the practice of good government, because as it belongs to a General Congregation to make laws, so does it also belong to the same to explain them in the sense that the explanation should have the force of a universal law. The General can however ordain that his explanation should be observed in practice and government, so long as a General Congregation has not explained the matter otherwise; and this ordinance does not cease at his death.

It must therefore be evident that the Society has been instituted and furnished with most excellent and sufficient rules, and that so far nothing is left to be desired in order to its government, and that all that is required is vigilance and charity on the part of prelates, and humility and obedience on the part of subjects, in order that it may, with the aid of the divine grace, attain the end at which it aims.

All those therefore should be suspected by us who desire to introduce any alteration in the principal matters of this Institute, for they are not moved by that spirit wherewith the Society was founded, but by I know not what alien spirit, if it be not the spirit of ambition which is always endeavouring to disturb all things. Things which have been established by such authority and with so much consideration, and confirmed by long experience, and which carry the weight of such names as, in addition to that of St. Ignatius, those of James Laynez, Francis Borgia, Everard Mercurian and Claudius Aquaviva, all of whom were men illustrious for their life and doctrine and gifts, and for their prudence and uprightness in government, and who also availed themselves of the counsel of great men, are not easily to be altered, and not except at the dictation of experience, and by reason of enormous evils which have resulted from them, and there is no grave evil which can with the least appearance of truth be shewn to have arisen from any principal Constitution of this Institute. Any such unquiet spirit is with every endeavour to be resisted, and should any graceless sons of the Society desire any alteration, they are either to be admonished to a change of affection, and to clothe themselves, by the aid of the divine grace, with the spirit of humility and obedience, and then their inordinate affection will vanish on the instant, or, if they will not accommodate themselves to the Institute, or cannot be caused to do so, it is better that they should be severed from the Society.

# CHAPTER XXVI.

## SEVERANCE FROM THE SOCIETY.

### I.—Can a Professed Father be expelled from the Society? And for what causes?

It is certain that there are cases in which the Professed of Four Vows can be expelled from the Society; and this extends even to the General. Since the Profession and Vows are made in the Society in accordance with its Constitutions, there can be nothing contrary to justice, or to any covenant included in the Profession, in the expulsion of a Professed Father for just causes in accordance with the Constitutions.

The Society can expel its Professed Fathers not only for excessive contumacy or incorrigibility, but also for a grievous crime which might redound in scandal or dishonour to the Society. It has, as regards this last point, greater freedom and more ample power than that which, as a rule, is possessed by other religious Orders.

### II.—Can a Professed Father of the Society be transferred to another Order? And in what way?

The General can give leave to a Professed Father of the Society for a just cause to pass from it to any other religious Order, even if the cause should not include such guilt or incorrigibility as would justify his expulsion.

It may often happen that although a subject has not committed sins worthy of expulsion, he may hope for greater spiritual profit by his departure to another Order which, although in itself less strict, is nevertheless better suited for him, as being less at variance with his nature, or as requiring less external activity, or for other reasons.

If departure from the Society is by way of expulsion which is punitive and involuntary on the part of the subject, it requires a proportionate cause, in accordance with the demands of the Constitutions, to justify it; and in that case it is not necessary that expulsion should be accompanied with leave to pass to another Order, for no one can be *compelled* to pass to another Order, nor would another Order receive such a person against his will. But if the subject himself should accept departure to another and less strict Order, the Society has power to permit him. This is a special privilege belonging to the Society, participation in which by other religious Orders by way of general communication of privileges, is expressly prohibited by the Pontiff.

The Society can, without expelling a guilty Professed Father, punish him within the Society, and consequently it can give him his option either to remain under certain penance in the Society, or to pass to another and even more austere or solitary Order; for in this there is no injury or unjust compulsion, and in so doing the Society acts benignly rather than with severity.

When there are no causes for expelling a Professed Father against his will, the Society can in no way expel him so that he should remain in the world, even if he himself should give his consent. It can only give leave to him who desires to pass to another Order. This as regards a stricter Order is easy, but the only Order which is to be accounted as, with reference to this, more strict, is that of the Carthusians. For leave to pass to any other Order a great cause is necessary, and it should be the greater in proportion as that Order is less perfect or strict. There is to be considered in the first place the Society, which suffers loss by deprivation of a full-grown member after all the labour and expense which has been bestowed upon him; and then also the good of the religious himself, lest occasion should be given to him of living in a worse manner, or less perfectly. The best, and almost only cause will be when he is judged to be useless for the ministries of the Society, because he is incapable of them, or because he cannot be employed in them without great damage to himself.

In such a case, by consent of both parties a divorce may be effected by his departure to another Order; and for this sufficient authority has been granted to the Society by Gregory XIII.

III.—To what is a Professed Father of the Society bound, who has been expelled from it, or who has left it in any other way?

A Professed Father can be expelled from the Society in two ways, either under the burden of entering another

Order, or, if he does not make profession therein, of returning to the Society; or secondly, without hope of reception into the Society again, and without any special obligation besides that which of the nature of the case arises from profession.

The first case has no difficulty, for the sentence was just, and it was accepted by the religious, and he specially promised to fulfil it. If he does so and makes profession in another Order, every higher obligation of his previous profession ceases and he will be bound only to observe that which he has last professed, and this whether his new Order is stricter or less strict, because the commutation was lawfully made. If however, he does not fulfil the condition, either by not entering another Order or by leaving it after entrance and before profession, he will be bound to return to the Society. If he does not return, he is to be regarded not as expelled, but as an apostate and fugitive, and consequently as bound by all the obligations of his Order, and as lying under the censures inflicted on apostates.

In the second case of a Professed Father who has been not conditionally but absolutely expelled from the Society, his obligations with regard to poverty, chastity and obedience are the same as those of a professed religious who has been expelled from any other Order; but his obligations otherwise differ from those of an apostate from the Society, who not only remains bound by all his vows, but is in law actually subject to the Society, to which he is bound to return. Every apostate is bound also to observance of the Rule, and consequently to observance of the special vows which he had made in accordance with the Rule.

We may fittingly conclude this digest of the great work of Father Suarez—*On the Religious State*, with the pious hope of the holy author that, although it may not be what the dignity and excellence of the subject demands, it may yet be to the praise and glory of Jesus, Who with the Father and the Holy Ghost liveth and reigneth for ever and ever. Amen.

FINIS.

www.ingramcontent.com/pod-product-compliance
Lightning Source LLC
Chambersburg PA
CBHW051248300426
44114CB00011B/945

The theology of Croatian thinker Miroslav Volf is reaching a high level of recognition and acceptance among Christian theologians in different parts of the world. Volf's theology is in a way biblical reflection on practice by a Christian who has experienced the conflicts of the break of a nation followed by a cruel war. This book by Palestinian evangelical Rula Khoury Mansour is a valuable effort of an insider researcher to use Volf's theology as a frame of reference in order to understand church conflicts in her country and respond to them from a pastoral and contextual perspective. Here we have a helpful analysis of internal church conflicts within an ethnically and socially conflictive situation and also a pastoral response based on a relevant theological proposal. I hope that Dr Khoury Mansour's methodology and conclusions will inspire similar efforts to understand conflicts and respond pastorally to them in other conflictive areas of the world today.

**Samuel Escobar**
Emeritus Professor of Missiology,
Palmer Theological Seminary, Pennsylvania, USA

In 1996 Miroslav Volf in his book *Exclusion and Embrace: A Theological Exploration of Identity, Otherness, and Reconciliation* offered the church a good service by calling it to understand the metaphor of salvation as reconciliation. In reality, it is God's call to the church to realize its task to be an agent of peace and reconciliation as it serves in the midst of fragmented societies. Dr Khoury Mansour has taken that call forward to apply it to a complicated Middle Eastern context where splits and strife are, unfortunately, part of our daily life. She approaches the topic not just with deep sociological and theological interaction but also with much compassion and sensitivity. Her arguments and conclusions will prove to be helpful and applicable beyond the Middle Eastern context. This monograph is a must-read to all who are interested in effectively contributing to human flourishing in which peace and reconciliation play such a pivotal role. I am also delighted that Dr Khoury Mansour is the first female Langham Graduate from the MENA region, and I am hoping that she will be the first among many female scholars to follow her steps in the near future.

**Riad Kassis, PhD**
Director, Langham Scholars

In this work, Dr Khoury Mansour joins a plethora of gifted women theologians whose impact is glocal. She honors the Prince of Peace in his homeland as she addresses church conflicts among Palestinian Baptist churches in the Holy Land. In the footsteps of Jesus of Nazareth she masterfully provides an inspiring and challenging theology of reconciliation engaging both Palestinian culture as well as the theology of Miroslav Volf. Her theoretical and practical insights combine western and eastern discussions into an informative, inspiring, and challenging discourse that calls us to be a community of forgivers and agents of reconciliation. I strongly recommend this book for pastors and theologians, as well as readers interested in reconciliation.

**Rev Yohanna Katanacho, PhD**
Academic Dean,
Nazareth Evangelical College, Israel

In this original book, Dr Khoury Mansour presents a composite, culturally sensitive model of conflict transformation. She gives an extensive ethnographic documentation of one case study – the Palestinian Baptist churches, who suffer from recurring splits – alongside close examination of three models of conflict resolution that have direct bearing to it – theological, cultural, and legal-secular. She then turns to do a cultural translation of Volf's theological model by using core elements from the other two, to make it relevant to the context at hand. Beyond the thick, multi-layered analysis of one particular intra-church conflict, this book provides an important inspiration to those seeking to promote peace and reconciliation within and across communities.

**Amalia Sa'ar, PhD**
Associate Professor of Anthropology,
University of Haifa, Israel

This is an innovative and compelling book on conflict and reconciliation in church. It is based on close ethnographic research and careful theological analysis, and its author has extensive experience both as a public prosecutor and an active church member. A unique and exemplary book.

**Miroslav Volf, Dr Theol Habil**
Henry B. Wright Professor of Theology,
Yale Divinity School, Connecticut, USA
Founder and Director, Yale Center for Faith and Culture